Praise for

I Let Him Go

'Heartbreaking'
Guardian

'Thoughtful and dignified… honest and affecting.
This book will leave you thinking long and hard'
Sunday Express

'*I Let Him Go* is a heart-rending read'
Good Housekeeping

'Heartbreaking… stirs harrowing emotions
and memories'
Mirror

'Harrowing but profoundly moving'
Mail On Sunday

From the Mother of
James Bulger

DENISE FERGUS

I Let Him Go

A mother's heartbreaking story of
the murder that shook the world

30TH ANNIVERSARY EDITION
IN MEMORY OF JAMES

First published in the UK by John Blake Publishing
an imprint of Bonnier Books UK
4th Floor, Victoria House
Bloomsbury Square,
London, WC1B 4DA
England

Owned by Bonnier Books
Sveavägen 56, Stockholm, Sweden

www.facebook.com/johnblakebooks ⚫
twitter.com/jblakebooks ⚫

First published by Blink Publishing in 2018
First published in paperback by Blink Publishing in 2018
This edition published in 2022

Hardback – 978-1-911-600-12-1
Trade paperback – 978-1-911-600-13-8
Paperback – 978-1-78946-682-9
Ebook – 978-1-911-600-14-5

British Library Cataloguing-in-Publication Data:

A CIP catalogue record for this book is available from the British Library.

Design by www.envydesign.co.uk

Printed and bound in Great Britain by Clays Ltd, Elcograf S.p.A.

1 3 5 7 9 10 8 6 4 2

A portion of the proceeds from the sale of this book will be donated
to the James Bulger Memorial Trust.

John Blake Publishing is an imprint of Bonnier Books UK
www.bonnierbooks.co.uk

In memory of James and for all my beautiful children:
Kirsty, James, Michael, Thomas and Leon x x x

Contents

Prologue

When I gave birth to my baby boy, I was full of hopes and dreams for him. But the one thing I didn't ever imagine was burying my son's tiny body after his murder. No parent wants to outlive their child or say goodbye – it's impossible to imagine – but my final hours and minutes with my beautiful James will be etched on my mind until my dying day.

Getting my purse out to buy two pork chops for tea was the last thing I did before my world imploded forever. I went into the butcher's holding my little boy's hand, making one final stop before heading home, and I left without James' hand in mine.

That was how our last moments together went: no long goodbye, no last cuddles and snuggles with the baby who meant more to me than life itself, just me letting go of James' hand for a split second, rummaging around in my purse for the right change, and my two-year-old son being led away to his death by the ten-year-old boys who murdered him.

I remember clearly going to The Strand shopping centre in Bootle and parking up. We had a list of what needed doing and we were very efficient. Nicola – my brother Paul's fiancée – had my other brother John's little girl, Vanessa, with her. We're a close family, and Nicola was looking after Vanessa for the day. As all mums know, you dash around like a mad thing trying to get everything finished while the kids are in a good mood and playing ball. Once they hit that wall of boredom, you have no chance of getting anything done. We got all we needed and decided to buy something nice for tea for the blokes after their hard day of DIY.

We went into A.R. Tyms, the butcher's, happy this was the last port of call. James was restless and running around a bit. He had been so good but was reaching the end of his patience. It was time to get him home so he could play with his toys and have his tea. Then it would be bath, stories, pyjamas and bed – the same routine we had every night. There was nothing I loved more than tucking him up at bedtime and knowing he was safe and cosy. Because we only had one bedroom, James had a little bed at the side of ours, which was fine by me as I liked him close.

I went into the butcher's and straight to the counter, looking at what there was on offer. I said hello before pointing out the chops I wanted, all the time telling James to stand still.

The butcher's shop was small so there wasn't much space for James to get up to lots of mischief, but he was playing and dancing around a bit – it was definitely home time. I remember clearly that I was by the counter, he was running around in circles and Nicola was in the corner by the fridge with Vanessa.

James was laughing and I beckoned him over to stand by me. I held on to his hand as the man wrapped up the meat and chatted to me. He was very friendly and said hello to James before telling me what I owed him. And this is the last thing I remember: I let go of James' hand and looked at him saying, 'Just stand right there by me, don't move, okay?'

He was there right by my left thigh. I smiled at him and pulled my bag from my shoulder, took out my purse and went to open it to get my money. As I snapped open the clasp, I glanced down and James wasn't there. Immediately I looked over to the fridge cabinet and expected him to be playing with Nicola and Vanessa. He wasn't there. I shouted, 'Where is James?'

Nicola told me not to worry, that he would be playing just outside the shop and that he couldn't have gone far. I got to the doorway and stopped to look left, right and left again. The place was packed and there were so many people I couldn't see a thing – which way would he have gone? My heart was thumping and even then I was full of icy dread. It is like fingers of fear grip your heart and crush it so you can't breathe. I knew right then it was bad, I just knew. It was one of those moments where the world feels like it is turning in slow motion, and you struggle to take in what has happened. I remember this voice in my head, *Not James. Not my beautiful boy.* This couldn't be happening to me, I didn't ever let him out of my sight.

Which way, which way would he have gone? I kept asking myself – left out of the shopping centre doors or right into the crowds. In a way it was a silly question, as he didn't even know his left from his right, he wouldn't have understood what he was doing. I stood there feeling sick to the pit of my stomach and I turned left to start the frantic search.

People often ask me if I blame myself for what happened that day – for taking my eyes off him for that split second. For letting go of his hand as I looked for my purse. They ask if I blame myself for not seeing what the CCTV footage later showed: Venables and Thompson beckoning James away from my side and out of the shop at 3:39pm?

The answer is: of course I do. There aren't the words to describe how I still feel now, every day. I was the one who let go of his hand; I was the one there meant to protect him. But do you know what my biggest regret is? That I didn't turn right instead of left – if I had taken the right turn and gone around the corner, I would have seen James being led away, just four short minutes after he had left my side, trustingly holding hands with the boys who were about to murder him.

Chapter 1

A Liverpool Girl

When I tell it like that it almost sounds like it happened to someone else, in fact for a long time afterwards I felt as if it had, as the shock and grief were like a heavy veil that blocked out the world. When people say that life can change in an instant, that fate can collide in the most destructive way, I am living proof it does. Once it does, there is very little that matters.

For over 30 years I have been known as 'Denise Bulger (later Denise Fergus), the mum of murdered James', but before he was abducted on 12th February 1993, I was Denise Matthews from Kirkby and all I wanted was my own family. I had a happy and simple childhood with loving parents who gave us the very best they could, like all good parents do I suppose. We didn't have much to go round but we didn't ever go without and all I remember are happy times. There were 13 of us altogether (12 now that my older brother, John, sadly died a few years ago). It is funny – I can never remember the age order when I am reciting the names of my brothers and sisters, so I have to list them as boys versus girls: the boys are John, Joe, Ronnie, Ray, Paul and Gary; the girls are Joan, Barbara, Rita, Sheila, Eileen, Pat and me. When I think back to my childhood now, it must have been chaos – but mostly I imagine all the washing! Although there weren't 13 of us all living there at any one time, the ironing pile is bad enough in my house with three lads, never mind any more than that. Mum had a twin-tub and I remember starting to wash and rinse my own clothes from a really young age in order to help – I don't know how my mum did it, but she never made it feel like hard work.

They were amazing parents, Eileen and Hugh, and although my dad was my mum's second husband (she married him after her first died) and some of my brothers and sisters (John, Joan and Joe) came from that marriage, we were a tight-knit clan. We never questioned or referred to it, instead it was just one of those family facts that didn't make a difference.

I was born second to last, almost the baby of the family until my little sister, Sheila, arrived. Mum seemed to give birth like clockwork and there was a neat two-to-three-year gap between all of us. When I think about the fact that I am 50 years old at the time of writing this book and my youngest son is 18 years old, I realise that's a lot of pregnancies!

Dad worked hard and very long hours to give us all he could and support us. I only knew one home growing up and that was Scoter Road, in Northwood, Kirkby, where I stayed until I met and moved in with Ralph. Historically, Kirkby was developed in the 1950s as a housing overspill of Liverpool. Because of the damage caused by the Blitz, much of the housing that survived in the inner city of Liverpool was considered substandard and they were more like slums. So people were moved out to newly developed estates like Kirkby, which became one of the largest and fastest growing communities in Liverpool. I don't know if that's why there is such a fiercely loyal feel to it, but all I do know is that when the chips are down, there is truly no better place to live. The love and support I received, and still get to this day, has made all the dark days after James' murder far more bearable and for that I will always be grateful.

At the time my parents moved into their house, Kirkby was still a bit of a mud ground – there was no road or anything really and Mum and Dad were some of the first to move in. People often raise their eyebrows at the fact there were 13 of us and we only had four bedrooms, but by the time I came along the older few were marrying and moving out – there was over 25 years between me and the eldest – so it freed up some space. It was a bit like a relay race! In my bedroom were Sheila, Rita and me, then Gary and Paul shared a room, and there was one for whoever else was in and out of the house, and Mum and Dad had their room.

That all sounds fine, but queuing for the bathroom was a bit tricky at times and probably caused the most fights!

It was a free and easy childhood, very typical of the times, but one I look back on now and can't imagine given what I am like with my children. Mum used to feed us and then send us younger ones out to play with our older brothers and sisters before being sent to bed. If I try and explain that to my boys now, they look at me like I am a mad woman, given they were never out of my sight. It was a simple way of life and I feel lucky that it was so pure – we didn't have a spare penny for any kind of expensive activities like the cinema or youth clubs, so we had to make our own fun. We were allowed to roam free and learn about life on the streets – the irony is not lost on me that I enjoyed the most relaxed childhood imaginable and my son's murder ended up making parents all over the world too scared to let their children out the front door. We played rounders, kerb ball and cricket in the street and had bikes and endless races – all cheap entertainment. Every front door was left open and anyone could wander in and out and get fed and watered – I suppose it's the way kids should be allowed to live in an ideal world.

When it came to school, Sheila, Paul and I were in the same building at the same time. We were split up due to age but the school was so small that we would mix anyway and I would often slip into the older playground to embarrass Paul – he would bribe me with his biscuits to get rid of me, which was great as that was all I wanted really. I drove him mad because I could see how much it wound him up to have me following him around. At lunchtime we all went home to eat as Mum loved cooking and we much preferred her food to the stuff we got at school. Paul used to have to walk me home and he hated that too – he would meet his mates halfway and then be stuck with me making a show of him and winding him up, playing for laughs. I was a nightmare! They were carefree days when there was nothing to really think or worry about.

I didn't really like school much and, as a result, I didn't try very hard – I was there for the laughs and my mates. I wasn't remotely academic and spent most of my time being distracted. It was always affectionate and I never wanted to be a menace, but mucking about was a way to pass the time. I suppose I was cheeky and that was a gene James definitely inherited. I didn't have a favourite subject although, if pushed, I would say that I didn't mind a bit of typing, but that was probably the extent of my curriculum interest. I couldn't wait to leave and, when I got to 16, I had a few days off to look after my mum. She'd had an eye operation and needed someone to care for her – the older ones were at work and I certainly didn't mind leaving the classroom to help out.

A few days as a nursemaid turned into a few weeks, and before I knew it I'd missed a lot of the year – I decided I wasn't that fussed about taking my exams or leaving with any qualifications, so I didn't bother. There wasn't any real pressure from home and, although the teachers were encouraging, there wasn't much to hang around for.

I made some great friends but, as with anything, your life changes and you pick up and lose people along the way depending on your circumstances. I'm not in touch with lots of the people I knew back then and I suppose it is harder for me to trust and make friends after what happened – people's intentions aren't always as they seem, and losing James and fighting in his name has made me wary of hidden agendas.

After I left school I got seasonal work in an ice cream factory, I loved it there and formed a great circle of friends. I still lived at home as I couldn't afford to move out as a single woman, especially once the ice cream factory closed down and workers were laid off because the machines were doing all the work. One day I went in and the boss tried to get me to clean up the floors – I told him that wasn't my job and as far as I was concerned I was there to work on the machines. That, as they say, was that!

I was at a crossroads in my life – I had lost my job and was still living with my mum and dad. I was a bit lost. Though I was a hard worker, I am not embarrassed to say that my life plan didn't ever involve having some high-powered career. I knew I didn't have the qualifications for that. I had always thought motherhood would be my biggest role – children were always on the agenda for me and I couldn't imagine a better purpose in life.

With all my older siblings having families of their own,

it meant that growing up I was never far away from a baby. As a result, I felt really relaxed around young kids and knew how to handle a baby with confidence. I often think it's a good job we don't know what's in store for us because, despite always knowing that I wanted to have lots of babies, I didn't ever imagine that would involve giving birth five times and only having three children to bring up.

With the arrival of my little nieces and nephews I was never far away from a cuddle – in fact I became known as the 'baby hogger' and used to dream up lots of clever ways to wake up a baby so that they needed comforting by me. Once I was caught red-handed knocking into the pram deliberately so that my nephew would wake and I could pick him up without being scolded and told to 'let the baby sleep'. 'Don't worry, I'll see to him,' I would shout as I seized the chance to comfort, cuddle and rock the baby. I was so bad that I got the blame when the baby woke up, even if it wasn't my fault! I used to imagine what it would be like to hold my own baby whenever I wanted to and, once I had James, my favourite thing was to hold him as he slept and feel his little chest going up and down.

All this coincided with the night I met Ralph Bulger in Kirkby Town, a night club not far from where I lived. I was on a night out with my sister and a couple of other mates when we bumped into a group of lads at the bar. I got chatting to Ralph and he bought me a drink, before asking me out on a date the following week. We hit it off and quickly became serious. I was so young at 18 and Ralph was my first serious boyfriend, and I suppose I quickly got caught up in the excitement of making a life together without giving too much thought to how compatible we really were. At that age we think we know it all, don't we? There is little thought of what the future might hold. All I had ever wanted was a home and family of my own, and here was a man who could give it to me. We loved each other and seemed to want the same things so it all seemed very straightforward, and for a while it was.

We moved into a little bedsit in Springfields Heights, a high-rise tower block in Southdene, still in Kirkby and near to our families. It was surrounded by houses and had a few shops over the road on Broad Lane. We didn't own much but I appreciated what we did have. Our families were extremely generous and we were given furniture, bedding and pots and pans – lots of bits to help us make a home and get settled. In reality it was so small that there wasn't room for much, but that didn't stop me making it as cosy as possible. When you came in through the front door there was a long hallway. If you turned right there was a bathroom with bath, sink and loo – no shower, it was all very basic. The living room was right outside the bathroom and also contained our bed, a fireplace and then a couch right underneath the window. Just off the main room was a small and separate kitchen, and that was it – nothing grand but it was our home. I didn't know my neighbours at all the whole time I lived there, as I have always been one to keep myself to myself, but we quickly fell into the routine of being a couple. Ralph worked in security and was in and out of work and I fell pregnant almost immediately. Finally it felt like I was living the life I'd always imagined I would; all the pieces slotted into place and I was so happy.

I had been with Ralph under two years when I got pregnant with our first baby; I was 20 and actually gave birth just after I turned 21. Our news wasn't altogether celebrated by our families – their joy was tempered by the fact that we weren't married. But I didn't care about our circumstances and what was 'proper' – all I cared about was the baby growing inside me, and I vowed to love and protect him or her with everything I had. Our families got over the shock and then became as excited as we were – everyone loves a new baby to fuss over and they all knew how much I wanted to be a mum.

The pregnancy passed really calmly and I felt great. I was active, healthy and, apart from the odd bit of morning sickness and an achy back, I had nothing to complain about. I approached pregnancy straightforwardly – I wasn't ill, I was just having a baby, and so I carried on as normal. I looked and felt fine and so had no reason to change anything or worry – I certainly had no clue that things would end the way they did. The baby was active and moving right up until the morning I went into labour. Obviously I was apprehensive, like all first-time mums, but the pregnancy had gone like clockwork and we had all the baby things in our little bedsit ready. As we set off for the Fazakerley Hospital's maternity unit, on the morning I went into labour, I was excited at the thought we would be returning as a family of three.

As soon as we arrived they broke my waters and I quickly progressed to full labour. The contractions were coming regularly and the nurse wanted to take a quick look at me before I went to the labour ward. I was taken to a side room and left to get comfortable and a nurse returned a few minutes later wheeling in a great big machine. She brought it over to the side of the bed and started strapping two thick belts around my contracting stomach. As she fastened the final one and flicked on a switch, I watched the green light start flashing as usual. This was all routine, to check the baby's heartbeat and I felt really calm – if anything I was keen for the nurse to finish so that I could get on with business of having the baby. Despite the pain, I was impatient to meet my little one.

The nurse then started filling in charts and busied herself as the monitor did its job, she told me she would be back in a few minutes. Ralph was there as I lay on the bed breathing through the contractions, holding my tummy. After quite a long time the nurse came back in, smiling warmly, and made her way over to the screen. 'How are we both getting on there?'

She glanced at the screen, pressed a few buttons and, immediately, the atmosphere changed.

'Right, okay, you wait there – I'm just going to get the doctor to take a look at you.' She kept her voice light but I could see the panic in her eyes and I knew something was terribly wrong but I still didn't imagine what was coming. I was 38 weeks' pregnant, technically full term and ready to give birth.

What happened next was like something out of a film – the doctor swept into the room without even saying hello, looked at the screen and fiddled around with a few buttons. Finally he turned to me and said, 'I am really sorry but your baby seems to be dead.'

It sounds really dramatic, but I was actually very silent, though my heart was racing. I just remember thinking, *What is he talking about – the baby can't be dead – I'm pregnant! I just felt my baby move, he doesn't know what he is talking about.*

It was like he had the wrong woman. He then slightly backtracked and said that they weren't 100 per cent sure my baby was dead, that there was a chance of survival. The exact words were that it was 'likely but not definite' that I would be giving birth to a dead baby. I can't really remember anything except for an overwhelming sense of worry and guilt – had I done something wrong? How had this happened to the baby I was supposed to protect?

I don't know how I got through the birth – except by clinging on to the possibility that it would all be okay. I remember feeling hopeful despite everyone's worried expressions and convinced that my baby would come into the world crying indignantly to prove she or he had outwitted the doctors. The labour actually wasn't as long as it can be for a first baby and I did the whole thing with just gas and air to take the edge off. Eventually the midwife told me that I was ready to push and, with Ralph by my side, I gave birth to our daughter. As soon as she arrived, I felt the normal sense of elation that the labour was over and my baby was here, before everything came crashing down again.

Kirsty Bulger was born on the morning of 22nd Feb 1989, and weighed 3lbs 3.5oz.

The nurse wrapped up my baby and gasped, 'It's a girl. She's perfect.'

My heart leapt and I thanked God a million times over that my little girl was alive after all. I said to the nurse, 'So she's okay then?'

She looked at me, her face clouding over, and said, 'Oh no, I didn't mean she was alive, I'm so sorry.'

Thinking back now that moment of hope was all consuming, a flash of pure adrenalin where I felt that it would all be fine, that this nightmare wasn't real and I would wake up and everything would go back to normal. It is impossible to describe how easy it is to tell yourself that there is a chance – however slim – that it will be okay. It was similar to how I felt when I was shown CCTV footage of James being led away by two small children rather than a menacing adult. The human brain has an amazing ability to let us hold out hope until there really isn't a single scrap to speak of.

Chapter 2

Loss and Life

Everything fell apart into tiny pieces, right there. I don't remember much except feeling in a total daze after the birth. This wasn't how it was supposed to be: a long labour and no baby. Ralph was trying his best to be strong but didn't really know what to do, and so he was in and out of the room a lot as the nurses cleaned me up and took the baby away.

Once I was comfortable the doctor came in and explained that I would be going home empty-handed, like I had failed to scoop first prize in a pointless competition. I was then asked if I would like to hold my little girl and have some photos taken as a memento. I wasn't sure at first but decided I couldn't leave without having her in my arms – I had made her, grown her inside me and, now she was out, I was desperate to cuddle her. That maternal urge kicked in regardless of the sad outcome – my hormones didn't understand that my baby wouldn't be coming home with me.

I will never forget her little face, it was so tiny, like a round button really, but completely and utterly perfect. I don't know what I expected but it felt even more heartbreaking and difficult to understand because, physically, she looked just like she should – so why wasn't she breathing when she looked so normal? The thought of holding a baby that isn't full of life, pink and crying, is not what you imagine. I thought it would be a scary experience, but she was my baby and it all felt so natural, even though she was dead.

She was beautiful, with a wonderful complexion, dark hair, fine eyelashes and perfect little fingers and toes. I studied her face, desperate to take in every little detail – I will always remember that her mouth was turned down, like she had been crying and her bottom lip was out in protest. I held her for a short while, kissed and rocked her and I didn't want to let her go. Ralph decided that he didn't want to hold Kirsty, but he stayed with me as I did. He tried his best to keep everything together but we both sat there in a trance for a long time. The nurses took photographs for me and eventually they carried her away so they could move me. Later on they offered to bring her back for another cuddle but Ralph said no, as he felt it would be too hard for me to say goodbye again – he could see how broken I was at the thought of letting her go.

A few hours after Kirsty was taken away, Ralph asked me

to marry him. I was still in total shock, lying on my bed and staring up at the ceiling, when suddenly Ralph asked me to be his wife. I said yes and we hugged, both still unable to process what had happened but grateful to have each other.

* * *

Losing Kirsty was a pain so deep inside me that I don't have the words to describe it – I would happily have traded places with my baby so that she could have lived the life she was due. You feel so useless as a mother – your one job above all else is to grow your baby and then protect your child once they are here. In a way I am glad I didn't know for sure at the start of the labour that she had definitely died, as the thought of giving birth to a baby I knew was dead would have been too much to stand, that little bit of hope that she might be alive got me through the pain of labour. That's the awful reality of stillbirth – being told there is no heartbeat and the baby is dead is heartbreaking enough, but it is easy to forget that the baby needs to come out and you have to give birth.

I stayed in for two nights and once I was strong enough they discharged me and Ralph took me home. We got back to a bedsit full of baby equipment but no baby to use anything – the Moses basket, the little white vests and Babygros, the bottles and steriliser – all there staring at me but, ultimately, useless. It was like walking into a ghost bedsit. Just days earlier we had left for the hospital so full of excitement and anticipation and now there was only the grim reality of loss. Putting the key in the front door and seeing an empty basket where my darling daughter should have been nearly finished me off. I remember so clearly thinking, *Today is the worst day of your whole life, Denise. It will never get worse than this.*

Surely nothing could be worse than giving birth to my dead baby and leaving hospital without her, leaving behind all the dreams I had for her and all that she could have been. But two years later, leaving The Strand shopping centre on that pitch black and freezing February night without my little boy's hand in mine, well that was the worst thing of all. Then I became a mother of two children, but without either of them by my side.

We buried our daughter in a tiny coffin after a small and simple funeral service. No fuss, and once it was over we went straight home where I stayed for a while. I would walk around the bedsit imagining what it would be like to have her there with me, what we would be doing now if she hadn't died. I spent the first few weeks in a total trance, not really taking anything in or caring much about what was happening around me, a bit like floating through the motions. I couldn't form any clear thoughts apart from one: I knew right after Kirsty died that I needed to fill that basket with another baby.

We didn't really talk much about what happened. It was hard to get Ralph to open up about his feelings generally, although he did support me as much as he could. But my body ached for my baby and was confused by the fact I'd given birth and now had nothing to nurture. Long after the actual birth, things happen biologically that you have no control over, like producing milk, which was devastating. Even though I hadn't planned to breastfeed – it wasn't as popular back then – it was another very physical reminder of the emotional trauma and all that I had lost.

The one thing that became immediately clear was that I couldn't deal with being around other people's children, even my own nieces and nephews. Friends and family would offer to come and see me but I would turn them down flat as I couldn't even look at a baby for those first few weeks – it was all too much. People often ask if I had any counselling – either for Kirsty or for James – the answer is no, as it just wasn't the done thing. I can't even remember if the hospital offered it to me and I declined or if I was just sent home to get on with things, but my family rallied round and I slowly got back on my feet.

Not too long after I came home from the hospital, I agreed to let my sister Barbara visit with her new baby, Natalie. She had been born just a few weeks before I lost Kirsty. Looking back she must have been so nervous about how I would handle seeing her baby – a little girl the same age as my daughter should have been. But one thing that runs deep in our family is loyalty in a crisis – and if anyone could pull me back into the 'now', it was my family.

Another reason for her wanting to come over was the fact my brother Gary was due to marry the following week and the family wanted to know if I would be attending. It was only going to be a small affair in a registry office with close family and friends, but there was no way I could face being at such a public event so soon after the birth. I had barely left the bedsit since we had got back from the hospital; Ralph was going out and about to keep family and friends updated on how I was but I seemed to spend all of my time shut up inside.

Even though I wasn't up to going to the wedding, I wanted the rest of my family to enjoy themselves. I refused to bring everyone else down, which is why I kept myself to myself in those early days. I definitely didn't want to go to such a happy day and be the one in the corner not really joining in. It wasn't fair on Gary and Pat, his fiancée – they had saved so hard for their big day and every bride wants their wedding day to be perfect. That said, I had a brilliant suggestion for how I could help out – I would offer to have Natalie for my sister so that she could go and let her hair down and have her first day out since the birth. My sister had been so good to me during those early days, it was the perfect way to say thank you. Also, truth be told, I was desperate to spend time with the baby on my own.

I think Barbara could see how much good this would do me, plus she knew the baby was safe and so she could really relax and have fun. The wedding was only up the road, meaning she could pop back and see Natalie whenever she wanted to check all was well.

From the minute the baby arrived on the morning of the wedding, I couldn't put her down. I sat in the chair feeding and hugging Natalie, I was in my own little world, but still with one foot in reality. I knew she wasn't my baby and wasn't pretending or anything like that, but it felt so good to have a baby in my arms. After an hour or so, there was a knock at the door, which was unexpected. I reluctantly opened it and standing there, with her mouth open in shock, was the midwife who had come round to do my post-birth check-up. Her face was a picture – she looked like she had seen a ghost and it very quickly became clear that she thought that, in my wild and grief-stricken state, I had gone out and stolen a baby! She started giving me the third degree, asking loads of questions as she furiously scribbled notes on a pad – it was almost funny! In the end she refused to go until I got my sister to leave the wedding, come back to the bedsit and confirm that Natalie was hers and that I hadn't kidnapped her! That was a rare humorous moment after the stillbirth.

Looking back I am not sure how I coped, I don't think you ever really know that's what you are doing at the time – it is more like putting one foot in front of the other and surviving for those first few months. It doesn't occur to you to give it a label like 'coping'; it's just not going under, I suppose.

We packed away the baby things and drifted from one

week to the next, trying to be 'normal' and like everyone else. Although I was drowning in grief, I was also determined to stay together and build the family I longed for. Losing Kirsty was the worst thing possible, but I knew that I had to carry on. I know that Ralph felt the same even if he didn't always show it. The loss of a baby is such a different experience for a woman as you have carried the baby, there is a physical pain that is hard for men to understand, but he did his best even if we dealt with it in our own specific ways. Then suddenly there was a ray of hope when, four months after losing Kirsty, I discovered that I was expecting my James.

* * *

As soon as I realised I was pregnant, Ralph and I decided to get married and we arranged it for my birthday, 16th September 1989 – somehow it seemed fitting that he proposed on Kirsty's birthday and we married on mine. It was a small do, nothing fancy as we couldn't afford much, plus I was in the early stages of pregnancy and wanted to keep the news quiet until I got to the 12-week mark and felt sure everything was okay.

Looking back I realise we were still so young, I was 22 and Ralph was a year older, and yet so much had happened. I was determined this would be our fresh start and the beginning of proper family life, all I wanted was for us to be happy and raise a family together.

Everyone was happy to see us tie the knot after everything that we had been through and it was a lovely day. My mum made my wedding dress and it was the most beautiful thing I had ever seen. I loved it and, despite the beginning of a bump, I felt so glamorous. We had a little party afterwards at Mum and Dad's but it was all very low key, just as well as it didn't take much at that stage of the pregnancy to exhaust me. It felt good that the baby would be born into a stable home where Ralph and I were man and wife, and I was sure that he or she would complete things.

I started to feel like myself again, as if the fog was lifting slightly after all the sadness. It helped me to reconcile what had happened because I now had another purpose: I was going to be a mum. We had lost our beloved daughter, but I was determined that nothing would ever happen to this second precious baby. I wouldn't let him or her out of my sight. But, as soon as I told everyone the happy news, the worry set in immediately and what followed was an angst-ridden second pregnancy. All I could think was that it had happened once, without warning or explanation – why wouldn't it happen again? You hear about some people who just have such bad luck – in the back of mind I thought, *Perhaps that's me.*

I spent nine months haunted by Kirsty's death, but the hospital staff were amazing with me. I decided to have my second baby at the same hospital so they knew my history and they kept such a close eye on me – making it clear that I could come in any time and have a check-up or scan if I was worried. The main issue I had was not knowing why Kirsty had been perfectly active and healthy one minute and then died the next. In my mind, I had no way of making sure it didn't happen again as I didn't know the cause. After I had Kirsty the hospital did offer me a post-mortem but there was no way in hell that I wanted my precious baby put through any more – a post-mortem was obviously something I couldn't avoid with James, and it broke my heart.

In truth I would say that all of my pregnancies were psychologically hard – there is no way they wouldn't be after all that happened. Dr Abdulla, who works at Fazakerley Hospital, was amazing and delivered James and my subsequent babies, which gave me peace of mind. But there is no doubt that my pregnancy with James was heightened by the stress and anxiety that something would go wrong again. I tried to focus on the good things: I was having my longed-for baby and I had just married Ralph, I just had to get through this pregnancy and everything would be fine.

I checked every detail. I was given a kick chart by the hospital and I was obsessive about logging every single movement – even the hiccups! I must have driven the hospital demented, but they were so understanding, I suppose they must see it a lot. However, not even filling out kick charts relentlessly gave me any peace of mind.

After all, Kirsty had kicked right up until I was in labour. No, for me, until that baby was in my arms and crying, I took nothing for granted. In a way, I was dreading going into labour too – for most people that is the final hurdle, the finish line, and the pain is made bearable by the fact that you get to hold your perfect baby in your arms. For me, labour was the moment my baby had died and so the whole process was the wrong way round.

However, apart from my anxiety, the pregnancy was actually very straightforward and it seemed to pass quite quickly. After the wedding it was the build up to Christmas and anyone who knows me will understand why I mention this. I am the biggest fan of Christmas, I cannot get enough of it – for me the build-up starts in September. I am a nightmare! Then suddenly the new year arrived and our baby was due. This time around I knew better than to plan anything at all – I didn't get anything ready, no Moses basket, no washed little clothes ready, no pram in the hallway. I didn't want to jinx anything so all I had at the bedsit was a Babygro to bring the baby home in and a shawl. I kept everything else at my mum's. I didn't really even think too much about how I wanted the birth to be – it was like I couldn't plan any bit of it just in case it all went wrong again. I had given birth to Kirsty naturally, and all I knew was that I wanted to do the same this time round, but the doctors weren't going to take any chances. With Kirsty I went into labour during the early hours of a Wednesday morning and she was born the same day. With James they didn't want to let me go full term and decided to take me in two weeks before he was due and induce me, which was reassuring – though it could have been because they couldn't face another two weeks of me popping in for a scan!

* * *

The day finally arrived and off we went. We were both really quiet on the way to the hospital, excited and terrified all at once, and both so aware that this was exactly how we had set out a year before when I was expecting Kirsty. We were taking the same route and I had packed the same hospital bag, but this time we had a whole different set of hopes and expectations. This time we knew all too well that the ending wasn't always a happy one.

I got to the hospital and Dr Abdulla was there to greet me, he flashed me a reassuring look and told me everything would be okay. I am sure he could see the fear written all over my face. I was taken into a different room from last time and they started the labour. I tried not to let my mind revisit Kirsty's death and kept reminding myself that this time, after all the pain, there would be a crying baby in my arms.

It was a tough labour and I remember being in the labour ward and suddenly being hit by an overwhelming need to sleep. Ralph started panicking and asked the midwife, 'Is she going to be okay, is the baby going to be okay?'

The midwife explained that I was fine. Thanks to the

pain relief I would have a sleep and, once I woke up, I would be ready to give birth. The joy of an epidural! The needle had gone in and I fell asleep straightaway and then, just as she said, I woke up in full-blown labour. Eventually, after about 36 hours in all, I was ready to push. After what seemed like forever, with Ralph by my side, out came James and I remember the doctor saying, 'It's a boy, Denise!'

My beautiful James Patrick Bulger – named after Ralph's dad who had died before I gave birth – was born on 16th March 1990. He was biggest of all my babies, weighing in at 6lbs 3oz. He had blond hair, blue eyes and the most perfect skin. I was overwhelmed by this beautiful, pink, perfect, screaming bundle. I often think back to that moment, when I first held my baby boy and vowed he would never leave my sight.

Chapter 3

Forging a Bond

James came out screaming and didn't stop from the minute we got him home as he had terrible colic. It is no exaggeration to say that he screamed the house down all day every day for the first four months of his life and it was a nightmare because nothing I did eased his pain. I had him over my knee, rubbing and patting his back, I sang to him and rocked him as I cried too because I felt so helpless. There is nothing worse than not being able to make things better for your baby. This was one of the all-consuming thoughts I had in the days immediately after James' murder – that when he needed his mummy more than ever I hadn't been there. I was haunted by the idea that in his darkest hour he had been calling for me and I didn't come and make it okay. That thought doesn't really ever leave me.

After the birth I stayed in hospital for five days. It wasn't like it is now where if everything goes well you can be in and out within 12 hours. It was a long time to be in and I hated it because I just wanted to get James home and settled. I have a clear memory of being on the ward, lying in bed with James in his plastic cot next to me and hearing the clink of the glass formula bottles as the nurse pushed round the metal trolley at feeding time. It was all very regimented and there was no 'feeding on demand'. I didn't really consider giving breastfeeding a go. The hospital certainly didn't encourage it in the same way they do these days. The bottles would come round, they had long dark brown teats and the milk was always so cold. I remember thinking it was far too cold to give to James and sitting there rubbing the bottle in between my hands to warm up the milk before his feed. I actually ended up doing that for all four of my boys when I fed them in hospital – I had it in my head that their little tummies couldn't handle the chill. It's funny the small things that run through your head when you've had a baby. The maternal instinct is overwhelming.

During my hospital stay I was definitely lulled into a false sense of security as James was fairly quiet and fed well – then, as soon as we got home, the full-blown colic kicked in. He wouldn't take a bottle, he wouldn't settle, all he did was scream. It was awful to watch him having one of his episodes, as he would bring up his little legs and his face would go purple. I knew he was in agony and there was nothing I could do. I took him for long walks in his pram to the park, up and down the road or to my sister's. Come rain or shine I walked him for miles and hoped that the rhythm of the pram would soothe him. Sometimes the motion helped, sometimes it did nothing and I walked in circles as he carried on screaming – I tried everything, including industrial amounts of gripe water.

Often I ended up at my sister's front door desperate, knackered and crying and she would say, 'Give us him', and then start pacing the floor with him. When she couldn't manage it, her husband would have a go, and eventually James tired himself out after all his screaming and dropped off. But then we would go home and he'd feed and the cycle would start all over again. It was relentless.

The only way I could settle him during the night was by propping him up in his little bouncy chair. If I put him in that and positioned my legs underneath the chair to rock him, he would drift off, but as soon as I stopped he'd wake up and start screaming. We were in the bedsit and so all in one room – Ralph was good at sleeping through it but, to be honest, that didn't bother me. It was down to me to comfort James. When he was upset, James wanted his mummy, and that was that.

As a result, in those first few months we forged the most incredible bond. I look back now and I am so grateful for all those late-night cuddles and the extra time we had while the rest of the world slept. After he was murdered, I remembered those long nights together and wondered if, somehow in a weird way, the universe had given us the chance to cram in as much time as possible before he was taken from me. There aren't many mums who look back fondly on sleep deprivation and long, broken nights, but I do.

Once James got over that colic he was like a different baby, so smiley, and we spent every minute together. Don't get me wrong, it was hard work and in those early days I would have loved some time to sleep. Ralph started going out a bit with his mates and sometimes I wouldn't see him for a few nights in a row. He loved his son and doted on him when he was at home, but all his mates were young and single and it was a big adjustment. All new parents have their rows in the early days – both of you are tired and feel like one is doing more than the other, it can become a competition about who is more exhausted! But, like a lot of mums then, I did most of the feeding and changing on my own, something that made my bond with James even tighter.

James' first year passed in a sleep-deprived flash and was punctuated by milestones that I savoured: his first smile, lifting up his head, his first tummy roll, sitting on his own for a few seconds, crawling and bum shuffling, and then finally his first steps. I know every mother is biased but I do think he was very advanced for his age (though I would say that!) He walked quite early and once he was on his feet there was no stopping him. Everything had to be put out of reach and the bedsit fully baby proofed. From the minute the colic disappeared, James had the sweetest nature, but he was also full of energy from the moment he woke to the second he fell asleep. As every mum knows once a baby becomes independent and starts moving around, it is non-stop.

Because we were still in the bedsit, it was cramped and it got worse once James was mobile. He had slept by our bed since we brought him home from hospital and the lack of space meant that we were side by side all day. I loved every stage. I know some mums prefer the baby bit, or love it once their kids start interacting and they can have a conversation, but there was nothing I didn't adore about being James' mum.

From the very start, my daily routine with him was simple – we would get up together every morning and potter in the bedsit. When he was small he sat in his baby chair or would lie on his mat while I did my chores; once he was older I propped him up with cushions and his toys, and eventually he crawled around after me. After we were both washed and dressed, I would put James in his pram and we would either go to my mum's or get together with my sisters and their kids in the park. Mum used to joke that she couldn't actually keep us away, me and my sisters all piled round to hers with our kids and there would be prams blocking the hallway. In fact, it became a hilarious competition to see who could get there first because that person got the prime pram parking spot and the rest had to leave theirs out in the rain!

As I had so many family members with babies, I didn't go to classes or baby groups – there was no spare money for outings and it wasn't like now where you all meet up for coffee and cake. Lots of people we knew were unemployed and just about surviving, it was hard to get work and so every penny counted. I preferred to spend time with my family. All the cousins played together, a couple of times a week one of us had the rest round, and I saw Mum and Dad every day as they lived round the corner. Life had a reassuring rhythm to it and everyone just made the best of what they had. I didn't go out drinking with friends because we didn't have the money, and also I didn't want to leave James while he was so small – everywhere I went he came with me. I could count on one hand the number of things I did without him in his short little life. When he was gone, I felt like I had lost my other half.

* * *

Despite the lack of money we were desperate for space, so we went on the list for a flat not far from where we already lived. The bedsit became impossible as James approached his first birthday – it was just a room with a bed along one wall and then a couch and TV on the other. It was particularly hard in the winter or when it was raining. So, once James was on the move it became more and more pressing to find somewhere bigger. The waiting list was long and I got really disheartened as I wanted James to have space to move around more freely. However, the quest for a new place was put on hold when my father died suddenly.

On 16th December, as usual, James and I went round to spend the day with my parents. The visit passed without incident – everyone seemed fine. Dad made a pot of his special soup for lunch, we all ate together and he was full of good humour. Dad and James played endlessly together with little cars and James' other toys, just as they always did. My parents idolised all of their grandchildren and made each of them feel special, and it was so lovely for me to see the close relationship that Dad and James had. We said our goodbyes late in the afternoon and I put James in the pram and set off home to do bath and bedtime.

The next morning my brother-in-law came round to tell me that Dad had been taken ill the previous evening and rushed to hospital. Because Ralph and I couldn't afford a telephone it had taken a while for the news to trickle down to me, especially as it didn't seem serious. He had a bit of angina but I was told he was stable and not in any immediate danger, so I decided to go up to the hospital later that afternoon and, in the meantime, to pop to Kirkby market with my sister to get him some bits for his hospital stay – we had no idea how long he would have to be in.

I remember that I had James in the pram and my sister had her little girl in hers too. We needed to pop into Ethel Austin but there was no room to take in the prams so I left James outside with my sister as I nipped in. Once I was inside I bumped into the stepson of my older brother John, and it became clear that we had to get home as something had happened.

We raced back to my mum's where all the family had just arrived, gathered in the front room, working out how to find me and my sister to tell us the news. As I looked at all the faces around me I immediately realised that the news was true. If I'd been in any doubt, it was quickly confirmed by the sight of my mum slumped in her armchair. She looked awful – no colour in her cheeks and in a complete trance. She stayed that way for a really long time. Truth be told, she never really got over the shock of his death.

Apparently Dad sat up that morning in his hospital bed feeling much better than he had the night before. In fact, he felt so good that he decided to indulge in his favourite start to the day – a big cooked breakfast, which he didn't do often but he loved. Within an hour of him finishing and being washed and dressed, everything failed on him and he died, just like that. It was 17th December, and the whole family was rocked.

No one knew what to do but it soon became clear that Mum wasn't coping and so began a long line of health troubles that plagued her right up until her own death eight years later – a series of strokes eventually put her in hospital, and a general dilution of her health meant that things were hard for her towards the end.

James was nine months old and my mum's saving grace

– we carried on our routine of going round there all the time, and it was obvious that seeing James was one of the few things that made Mum seem like herself again. She looked brighter and more relaxed the moment we entered the room – James made her light up, but then he did that to everyone he met.

We all rallied round – I guess that's a benefit of having so many children, there was always one of us on hand to pop over and see that she was okay. I would do a big cooked dinner for us all and try to make it as normal as possible for her. She did her best to be strong for us and we tried for her, but sometimes things happen that you can't get over. Not everything is meant to be dealt with, I suppose, and there is only so much the human heart can take, something I came to know all too well only two short years later.

Once Dad's funeral was over it became clear that Mum was desperately lonely and wasn't coping with living on her own, so Sheila decided to move in with her. Ralph and I decided that it made sense for us to move into Sheila's flat. It was the perfect solution – Mum wouldn't be on her own and we would have more space. I had a real battle on my hands with the council though, who were reluctant to give me the flat, so in the end I just moved in! I took the view that they couldn't really kick me out with a baby. I needed that flat for my family and that was it. James settled quickly and it instantly felt like home.

My sister's place only had one bedroom but it felt like

a palace to me as it was so much bigger than the bedsit. Me, James and Ralph all still shared a bedroom, but that's how I liked it. The flat had a wide hallway, a living area, a bedroom, kitchen and a bathroom. Just as I had done with the bedsit, I went about making it a cosy family home and set aside special space for James' toys; I couldn't have been happier with our first proper family home.

We were still strapped for cash as Ralph had casual jobs that didn't pay regularly. I didn't work as I had James to look after and I didn't feel happy about leaving him. I am sure my mum would have had him, but I wanted him with me all the time. I know all women are different and I would never knock any mum for doing things her own way, each to their own. I just felt the need to be at home. I didn't miss a minute and, as it turned out, I thank God every day for that. It was precious time – I just had no idea it was also borrowed time.

It wasn't long after we moved into the flat that my baby became a one-year-old. I couldn't believe that time had passed so quickly and it had been the happiest year of my life. I set about planning a little tea party for James and it followed the pattern of other family parties we'd had for the kids: loud, messy and chaotic, with buns, sausage rolls and cupcakes. He and his cousins adored each other; they were like siblings really and the age difference didn't really seem to matter as James was so easy to play with.

Everyone said it, mainly because he shared everything

– even from a young age. He was never one of those boys to hold on to a toy if anyone else wanted it – he would hand it straight over and find something else to occupy him without any fuss. I can't stand kids who don't play nicely with others, but I didn't need to worry about James as his nature was never like that – he was never a greedy child. He was a sharer and he was trusting. You only have to look at the CCTV footage of him being led away from The Strand to see that.

Chapter 4

Fizzing With Life

P art of the reason I wanted to write this book was to tell the world about the real James, my baby boy. Not the murdered toddler who made headlines and sold papers, not the media's version of James Bulger, but the baby I gave birth to.

The media came to love one particular image of James that they used over and over again – the blurred photograph of him frozen in time and looking straight at the camera, with a serious face, a few strands of fair hair falling into his wide eyes and what looks like milk around his mouth. I would often get asked what that was around his lips – it was actually yogurt he'd had for his tea just before the photo was taken. That image has been used on the covers of other books about the crime and to publicise documentaries and various programmes about what happened that fateful day – but that isn't my baby. James became immortalised in death and the world has only ever known him because of the way he died, meaning he is often talked about and remembered in the same breath as Thompson and Venables, an association which I hate.

To me there is so much more to my baby than the grainy images that are recycled by newspaper desks to mark an anniversary or a similar news story – my James was real and fizzing with life. James lit a room up – he was never grumpy, there were no tantrums and he wasn't naughty; he was a cheeky little ray of sunshine. That said, I won't try and portray him as an angel – he had a really mischievous side to him that's for sure. It has been so important to remember the fun times as well as the sadness.

I remember one particular day we were at my mum's and my sister asked if she could take him to the shopping centre to pick up a few bits she needed for tea that night. As usual the answer was no, because I wouldn't let anyone take him anywhere, and so he stayed behind with me at Mum's. I was folding some clothes and he was playing in the room where my mum had a shelf of ornaments, all the precious bits she had collected over the years. James was tearing around, running in and out of the room when, suddenly, he reached up with his little hands to grab one of the ornaments and ended up pulling the whole shelf down. He watched wide-eyed as every single ornament smashed to smithereens. I ran over and checked to see that the china hadn't cut him

(I didn't care about the ornaments!) and James was just staring at me, laughing at the commotion and slightly amazed he had caused all this drama. Meanwhile, Mum was shouting, 'I've had those for years!' – although James was soon forgiven as no one could be mad at him for long.

James went at life with gusto. He never really walked anywhere, he ran at you and everything in his little life was done at 100 miles an hour. Even if he was just going from one room to the next in our tiny flat he would sprint. As he came at you all you could see was bouncing hair, followed by that cheeky James smile. His beautiful hair was thick, blond and curly, until I took him for his first haircut. I still have his first lock and his hospital band in a special box. Once I'd had his hair chopped, I kept it quite short and it went darker in his final winter months, making him look like a proper little boy rather than a baby.

I absolutely adored dressing James in lovely clothes. I don't think I bought myself a single thing once he arrived – every penny went on making sure he looked smart. My favourite outfits were the lovely white sailor suit he had with matching socks and his denim shirt tucked into jeans, white Adidas trainers and a denim cap turned to the side, with his blond hair poking out of the side. He looked so adorable and people always commented when they saw me walking him round to my mum's all dressed up.

James celebrating his first birthday was one of many moments we treasured. There was a family holiday in

Wales with James and Ralph as well as my mum, sister, her husband and their kids for a week. It was a real adventure as we all got the coach from Liverpool to Wales and then stayed in a caravan – the kids loved every minute of it and we made some wonderful memories as they all played together outdoors for hours on end. It reminded us of our own childhoods, running around in the fresh air until we were exhausted but not wanting to come in for bedtime. It ended up being the only holiday James went on, which makes the photos all the more precious.

For James' last Christmas we bought him a go-kart which we thought he would love to speed around on. He opened it up, all excited as he tore off the paper. and Ralph set to work putting it together for him. As soon as we turned around we found James sitting in the box it came in and he stayed there for hours, far more interested in that than the actual present! After we had opened all our presents we decided to go round to my mum's and I asked James if he wanted to go on his new go-kart like a big boy. He nodded his head in agreement, so we got on our boots and coats ready to set off. As soon as we got outside we saw the tiniest dusting of snow on the ground, so fine you could barely notice it. James saw it and refused to climb on and so Ralph ended up having to carry the go-kart all the way to Mum's as James happily held my hand and walked, stamping his feet into the tiny bit of snow that had settled!

Everyone loved to treat James and he certainly collected

a few sets of wheels in his short life: a Noddy sit-on car that also acted as a baby walker for his first birthday, a little blue tricycle from my mum for his last birthday, his go-kart – he loved going fast, and they all helped get him to where he needed to be in a rush. After he died I couldn't part with anything so I still have all his clothes and all his toys. I don't look at them but I just know they are there in loft and nearby. There is one jumper in particular that I have kept in a drawer under the bed and that has to stay there, directly underneath where I sleep. I sometimes take that out and smell it or hug it. It just makes me feel close to him.

I have always been someone to make a fuss on Easter Sunday, too, and I definitely passed that on to James, as he adored it. For his last one I lined up all of his eggs in size order, right in front of his little stool. Because I had such a big family there were so many treats and his eyes were out on stalks when he saw them all laid out, he couldn't believe his luck when he walked into the living room! Actually, looking back, it took months to get through the stash and we had chocolate for a long time afterwards. As a treat he was allowed some chocolate for breakfast on Easter Sunday, and that last year he had quite a bit. He was absolutely covered in chocolate and I took a series of photos as he slowly lowered his chocolate-covered hands towards my pristine white carpet, made his imprint and then raised them up again, posing for the camera the whole time and looking delighted. Those hand marks were hell to scrub out but it is still one of my most vivid and happy memories of him.

As well as chocolate he also loved Chipsticks – they were his favourite food. One time I walked into the living room to find him chucking them like darts at my curtains and laughing so hard as they stuck there, hanging from the fabric. Of all the toys he had, that was how he preferred to spend his time, just like the cardboard box. He loved simple things and would spend hours playing. He was easily pleased but also very bright – though I would say that as I am biased – but he was very quick at picking up new things. By the time he died he knew his ABC off by heart and he loved me reading to him; he would sit on my lap and he knew exactly when to turn the pages at the right time. I would tell him how clever he was and he would beam back at me, delighted.

When James was murdered he was out of nappies and wearing grown-up pants in the day and through the night; it was another milestone that had passed without a huge fuss, something I was proud of, especially as everyone told me potty training a boy would be a nightmare. With James I found it really easy and adopted the praise method, as he loved any kind of positive affirmation and being told he was a good boy. Whenever he did a wee he got a great big kiss and a cuddle and a round of applause, which he adored – he was such a happy and positive little boy and he loved it when he felt he'd pleased you. Even if it was just the tiniest bit, I clapped enthusiastically and he joined in, adding in a little dance too. I can still see him waving his arms in delight. Once he started wearing pants at night, I would wake up every morning and the first thing I did was to check his bed and then give him a round of applause when it was dry. I picked him up and swung him round, and he clapped himself, and then we would go and have breakfast. It became one of our morning rituals right up until his very last morning.

I was particularly proud that he started using the toilet immediately too, so that I didn't have to deal with a potty in every room and emptying it out the whole time. Eventually I got him little boxer shorts – I couldn't get over the size of them. They were so tiny because he was tiny; they were the cutest things in the world.

Anyone who knows me will be familiar with the fact that I am obsessed with Michael Jackson and James felt the same way even at his young age. My final Christmas present from James was a behind-the-scenes look at how they made the music video for 'Thriller'! James and I used to watch it together and then James would get up and start imitating the moves perfectly – he would spend ages with his nose pressed up against the TV studying the dancing and then get up and put on his own little concert for me. I actually spent more time watching James than Michael Jackson! His favourite song just before he died was 'Remember the Time' and he loved the video with the magic beans; he would get up and do the whole song from start to finish, trying to get the words right. But the moves were definitely his thing and he was a great little dancer.

Like all small children, he had his cartoon favourites and they included *The Smurfs*, *Teenage Mutant Ninja Turtles* and *Thomas the Tank Engine* – he had a duvet and matching pillow on his little bed, which was at the end of ours, and he loved climbing under that each night. He also had t-shirts and pyjamas with his favourites on them, and it was often a battle to bribe him into wearing anything else. Because of how much energy he used up during the day, he was often so exhausted at bedtime that I would bath him and get him all ready and then he would play with Ralph while I nipped out to the shops to get a few bits. I only went across the road and wouldn't be any more than half an hour, but I liked going when the shop was empty. I would get back and unpack before doing story time and tucking James up safely in his bed. Once he was asleep I cooked for Ralph and me, if he wasn't going out, and then would tidy up and watch my soaps before going to bed. It was a simple and quiet life really and was all about being James' mum; I didn't really think about anyone else.

James bounced out of bed like a whirlwind but he was a boy of few words, especially in the morning when he first got up. I honestly think he decided not to bother talking as he could use his own pointing language with me and that seemed to get him exactly what he wanted! James was a gorgeous toddler and became a proper little companion – he was so funny.

He and I were always up first in the mornings and enjoyed our quiet time. He would run in from the bedroom and sit down on the floor right in front of the TV, almost with his nose touching the screen. He'd look at me, then at the TV, nodding with a big smile, and I knew that was his way of asking me to turn it on. I would go over to the TV and point at it and he would nod again as if to say, 'That's right! Well done Mummy!'

Then he would point to the VCR and nod again. Sometimes I didn't respond just to see what would happen and if he would actually talk! He never did, but if I didn't do what he wanted quickly enough he would simply do it himself, which always made me laugh. He was clearly capable of doing all these things on his own and just preferred to keep me busy and running around after him.

Once he was sorted I would say, 'Right, I am going to do your breakfast now. What would you like?'

He had no trouble finding the words to tell me that – he would look up with a huge smile and say, 'I want Frostieeeeeees!' really stretching the word out on the last bit in a sing-song way. It was his signature phrase and the family used to tease him at meal times, saying, 'What do you want for your tea, James? Do you want Frostieeeeeees?' and everyone would fall about laughing, including James. Sometimes I made James have a change and he would have

Rice Krispies, but everyone knew Frosties were his thing – he was obsessed!

He had a little plastic football bowl that he insisted on using for all of his meals, and he would sit with his cereal watching his favourite video before we got ready for the day. When it came to teatime, we ate together, and he would be with me in the kitchen so that he could watch me cook. He would sit at the table on the other side, well away from the cooker, and watch as I chopped and stirred. But never one to miss a trick, he often helped himself to food when I wasn't looking. Once I put down a plate of buttered bread on the table as I finished off cooking the meal, dished up, and when I turned back the bread had all gone, apart from a pile of crumbs – James had eaten the lot! It wasn't surprising because he'd always had a brilliant appetite and ate whatever was put in front of him; he definitely skipped the fussy eating stage.

James didn't actually ever go to nursery, none of my kids did, mainly because I didn't want to leave them, but that didn't get in the way of his ability to socialise. James was pretty much at the heart of whatever was going on. He was so excitable and able to see the fun in life, he would give anything a go and loved joining in with his older cousins – he certainly didn't let his age hold him back and was pretty fearless. While writing this book I obviously had mountains of stuff to sort through and one of the things I found tucked away in a photo album was my application for his primary school place. I have no doubt he would have loved school life, which was another 'first' he didn't get to experience. It is hard to tell at that young age what he might have enjoyed, but I have no doubt that whatever it was would have involved climbing, chocolate, Frosties, being sociable and being fast!

He absolutely loved being around other kids but was equally happy playing on the front room floor with his cars – like most boys he also liked clambering over furniture. He had his own little stool to encourage him not to climb over the sofa, and eventually Ralph built him his own wooden chair to sit in and watch TV. He loved sitting there; I could tell he felt like a big boy and would be up and down, getting on and off like a yoyo, as he couldn't sit still for long. He was always up to something, getting every last drop out of every day.

Chapter 5

Final Hours

It's not often now that I allow my mind to dwell on those final hours with James by my side. In the early days, when I replayed every little detail over and over in my head, I often couldn't breathe. There was a time when I could recite every last minute – always praying it would end differently. Ultimately, the only way for me to survive has been to compartmentalise it so that the guilt and anger doesn't completely swallow me.

As with so many terrible stories, the day started just like any other with no hint of what was to come. It was Friday, 12th February 1993, a freezing cold winter's day. James woke up full of beans at the crack of dawn ready for the day ahead. The whole flat sprang into action as soon as he was up – there was never any chance of 'just five more minutes in bed' with James around! Right from when he was a baby, we loved our relaxed mornings together and that day was no different. After inspecting his bed and giving him the usual round of applause for not wetting it, we went into the front room so he could watch TV as I got him a bowl of his beloved Frosties. He had his own little table and chair so that he could make as much mess as he wanted because, as with all toddlers, meal times were carnage! I had my breakfast with him but, much as I try, I can't remember the cartoon he got to watch on his last morning.

I remember Ralph being at home and, as it was a Friday, I didn't have any specific plans apart from my list of usual chores. Ralph had agreed to help my brother Paul put together some new furniture, so I hoped he might take James along. I thought James could spend a few hours playing with his cousins and I could nip to the shops and get everything done in half the time without having to bribe a bored toddler. As we were all getting ready I suggested this to Ralph but he said no because he didn't want James to be around the heavy wardrobe doors and all the tools, screws and dangerous bits. It made sense as James was a real livewire and definitely at the age where he was into everything, so in the end I decided to take James to my mum's.

I got myself ready and then washed and dressed James – his outfit is something I've had to describe so often that it will be etched on my brain forever: a silvery grey tracksuit with a white stripe down the side, white socks and his white trainers with a black inlay and white laces.

Once he was dressed I zipped up his padded blue jacket, which had a hood at the back for extra cosiness. All three of us set off on the short walk to my mum's – just another unremarkable start to a very ordinary Friday. We arrived to find that Mum had already left to do a bit of shopping with my older sister, Joan, so I settled down to have a cup of tea with my brothers while the kids played. Ralph stayed for a bit and then set off to Paul's to start the work. As he shut the front door, he shouted back at James, 'Ta-ra' – that was the last time Ralph ever saw his son and the final time we were a family of three.

I sat with Ray and Gary for a bit – it was a typical day where we all congregated at Mum's to catch up, even if she wasn't there. We all lived so near to each other, it was impossible for me to walk down the street and not see a brother or sister! Sheila's little girl, Antonia, and James were really close, like best friends really, and it was great how they occupied each other. It could get a little bit spirited, so we always had to keep a close eye on them, but they loved each other like brother and sister and it was so cute to see. We stayed until about lunchtime when Nicola arrived – she was engaged to my brother Paul at the time and they lived together round the corner. She was looking after my other brother John's little girl, Vanessa, that day as a favour and had obviously come round to escape the mess, dust and noise at hers as Ralph and Paul got on with their DIY.

Nicola had come to ask Sheila if she fancied a trip to The Strand shopping centre but Sheila was out meeting a friend that afternoon, so Nicola asked me if I wanted to go with her. I had a list of chores but thought I could easily do them at The Strand rather than the local shops, and it would be nice to have the company. James would probably also prefer to go shopping with Vanessa to amuse him – it would make the whole thing easier if he was occupied. So I said, 'Sure, why not!' and we started to get the kids ready.

Whenever I look back on the day that James was taken, I am haunted by so many 'what ifs' – what if I had taken a buggy to the shopping centre? What if I had left him at Paul's with Ralph? What if I hadn't gone shopping at all?

Although there are many moments from that day that I have buried deep, there are some that remain resolutely vivid – the first is the memory of me getting ready to leave my mum's house. I was dashing around putting on James' shoes, tying his laces tighter so his trainers stayed on, pushing his little arms into the sleeves of his coat as he protested and tried to run away. All as I worried that I was keeping Nicola waiting. I knew she had lots to do and James was being cheeky, so I was a bit flustered trying to get him out of the door. It is hard to be focused when you are rushing but I paused to do my usual checks – keys, buggy, handbag, etc.

What I will remember until my dying day is walking over to James' pushchair, putting my hand around the right handle ready to collapse it to put it in Nicola's boot, and thinking to myself, *No need to bother with that, Denise – we will only be nipping in and out. You can just hold his hand.* Nicola confirmed this thought by telling me there wouldn't be room for it in her small boot once all the shopping was in. So, fatally, I left it behind.

I didn't ever take James anywhere without his pushchair. Ever. I'd even put him in it to get to my mum's that morning, despite the fact it was such a short distance. I will never understand why I decided to leave it behind and it is the first of many details that I have spent years analysing. I even remember thinking it would be the first time we had gone anywhere without James safely strapped in so he didn't run about and cause chaos. He was at that age where he tried to run ahead a bit and it was hard to keep hold of him. I dithered for a minute or two and then realised how late we were so I left the pushchair in my mum's hall, where it remained for months, even when I knew James wasn't ever coming home to use it. It's now folded up in the loft with all of James' other things that I've never been able to part with.

We set off in Nicola's car to The Strand and arrived at about 1:45pm. We parked up outside, rather than in the multistorey car park, as we thought it would be easier for getting the kids in and out of the car, and off we went to get what we needed. I remember it felt like it was getting colder as the day went on and I was wearing a heavy flying jacket to keep warm – it's funny the details that stick in your mind.

The shopping centre was packed full of people getting food for the weekend and rushing about. James couldn't believe his luck that for once he was in among the crowd. I held on to his hand but inevitably he would run a yard or so in front of me, always where I could see him. If he strayed too far I rushed ahead and brought him back to my side, holding on firmly to his hand. All that running after him meant that I was soon sweating in my heavy coat, but he was so quick that I had to watch him like a hawk. I remember saying to him, 'Stop running away! You're getting naughty now and I'm not happy.'

And that seemed to calm him down a bit. Lively as he was, James never liked to think he had upset you or made you cross, and he held on to my hand a bit more after that. In reality having another toddler there didn't help. Vanessa was a tiny bit older and the two of them together were giddy at being out and about. In a bid to keep him calm in one shop, I sat him on the counter, and he must have stuck his hand in the communal sweet bowl next to the till and helped himself to a stash. I didn't notice until I walked out of the shop and saw he had stuffed them all in his mouth. I said to him, 'Where did you get those from?' and he just laughed as he struggled to eat the mouthful he was chewing. I was mortified and went back into the shop to pay for the sweets he had taken.

I hope this puts paid to the unforgiveable rumours that circulated afterwards that I had been in The Strand shoplifting with my mum. Firstly, I have never stolen a single thing in my life and, secondly, my mum wasn't even with me that day. If there is extra proof needed, my whole shopping trip was captured and examined frame by frame once the police went through the edited CCTV footage. It clearly shows that before 3:39pm I was shopping and after 3:39pm my world was crashing down around me as I frantically tried to find my boy.

It was clear that both children had reached their limit, so we decided to make a quick and final stop to buy some meat for tea at A.R. Tyms, the butcher's we used a lot as the meat was great quality but not too expensive. There has been so much written about what happened next and so many opinions given, but I want to make one thing clear: I absolutely did not leave my baby outside the butcher's on his own – I would never have done that. He was with me and holding my hand as we went inside. The only time I let go of his hand was to pay for the chops I had bought, and he was standing right beside me. I picked out the meat I wanted and took my bag from my shoulder, got my purse out, opened it to count the right money and, when I looked down, James was gone.

I paid at the counter nearest the door while Nicola was being served by another butcher in the corner, just in front of the chiller cabinet. As soon as I realised James wasn't standing by my thigh, I spun round and shouted, 'Where is James?'

Nicola looked back and said, 'I don't know.'

I could see Vanessa, but no James – if they weren't getting into mischief together, where was he? I shouted, 'He was just right there!'

Nicola tried to calm me down by reassuring me it would okay and he would be playing just outside the door. I looked immediately outside the shop doorway and all I could think was, *Which way, which way?* I had a 50:50 chance of picking the correct way and no clue at all, so I turned left frantically to start looking, another seemingly small decision that was to have the most earth-shattering consequences. I stepped outside the shop and couldn't see anyone who looked like James. The crowds were beginning to thin out a bit at that time so it was easier to get a clearer view, but whichever way I looked I couldn't see my little James.

I took another left turn and went towards the ground-floor security information centre, which felt like the most logical thing to do in the midst of a nightmare that made absolutely no sense at all. Perhaps someone had taken him there, or he might even have been clever enough to get himself there once he realised he couldn't see me. I kept telling myself that James was bright; he understood things and there was a chance that he might find someone friendly to help him. I remember losing sight of Nicola immediately – I just got caught up in a swell of deep fear that saw me running around frantically trying to find any trace of James, and she carried on manically searching too.

God knows what they must have thought of me as I approached the information desk, sweating, panicked and screaming that my baby was lost. I tried to calm down a bit to describe what he was wearing, what he looked like, his name and address, and they immediately started putting it out over the tannoy. It was only five minutes after he'd gone, so I was desperate to keep looking for him before we lost too much time. I remember telling them to shut all the shopping centre doors in case he wandered out as surely it would be easier to find him if we could somehow keep him inside. Obviously that wasn't possible but I was clutching at straws. My only thought was finding James as quickly as possible. They offered me a seat in the security room and I remember really clearly thinking to myself, *I'm not sitting around here doing nothing*. I started my own frantic search, running in and out of shops asking if they had seen a little boy. I lost count of the number of people I stopped to ask if they had seen James – it felt like thousands. I couldn't even begin to tell you what shops I went into – the whole thing was a blur – but I remember just after the announcement went out over the tannoy, I was searching under clothing rails and an assistant came towards me and asked if she could help. I told her I was looking for my little boy and she looked at me with a big smile and said, 'Oh yeah, I know. Don't worry love. They have found him. He's on the second floor in such and such a shop.'

My heart leapt – thank God he was safe. I raced up the

escalator two steps at a time, ran into the shop and shouted, 'Have you got my little boy? Have you got him?'

The woman behind the till looked at me, 'No, we haven't, but I think they've got him two shops down.'

So I ran down there only to be told they didn't have him either, and so began a wild goose chase of well-meaning people and a shopping centre that didn't seem immediately to grasp the severity of what was happening. I ran up and down that shopping centre, from top to bottom, more times than I thought would be humanly possible. I even went to the car park to see if he'd made his way back there, but no one else seemed panicked. I suppose they were used to kids wandering off and being found. One security guard even said, 'Come on, I'll take you back downstairs to the security office. Don't worry about it. He'll be in Woolworth's – we always find them in Woolies playing with the toys. We've never lost one yet.'

There are whole bits from that afternoon that I simply can't recall but one thing that stands out is suddenly remembering how much James loved the ride-on cars that you had in shopping centres back then. His favourite was a fire engine or racing car and they used to be dotted around the shopping centre and at the entrances and exits – you put 20p in and it would go up and down, sometimes playing a tune or a nursery rhyme. His little face would light up when it started moving, and as soon as it stopped he would point to tell me that he wanted another go and I needed to put more money in. As I was running from shop to shop, I started slowing down to see if the little blond head going up and down in one of the cars was his.

The only accurate word to describe me at this point is hysterical – I felt like I was in a computer game, everything was in slow motion with people just coming at me the whole time. My eyes were darting around everywhere and soon they started throbbing from the strain of jerking my head in every direction to see if I could spot his mop of hair or a flash of his jacket. I just kept screaming James' name, running around in circles and almost falling over other shoppers in my desperation.

Everywhere I looked I prayed that I would see my boy's face peeking out from under a fitting room curtain or see him running towards me as he spotted me through the crowd. The scene was right there in my head: he would hurtle towards me with his arms wide open for a cuddle – he would be crying because he'd scared himself and he would want his mummy. I would scoop him up and my initial anger would fade because I would just be so relieved to have him back. I would tell him that he must never leave my side again and eventually my thudding heart would slow down and I would get him home and bath him and put him to bed, all the while so desperately grateful because it could have ended so badly. I would exhaust myself with what might have been and eventually fall asleep – grateful and with my baby safely tucked up.

My dream was suddenly interrupted when a kindly shop assistant placed her hand on my shoulder and said, 'You look awful. Come on – sit down and have a coffee.'

I must have looked at her like she was mad – coffee? I think I said to her, 'I'm not sitting down for a bloody coffee – I'm looking for my son.' I know she was only trying to help and, actually, she was great. She got a crowd together to help me search all the small places he might have crawled into and got stuck. At this point I genuinely felt like I was losing my mind; the security staff did not understand my sense of urgency or my panic, and I was becoming frustrated because I couldn't make them see how serious this was.

Finally, at 4:22pm, 40 minutes after James went missing, PC Mandy Waller received a message over her patrol car radio that a child had gone missing. But that's when the nightmare really began. As the police began their own search of the shopping centre, James was already on the journey towards his death, having been spirited out of the shopping centre 35 minutes earlier – just four minutes after he left my side and after the alarm had been raised. As Mandy herself went on to say years later, 'We were just looking for a missing boy when in fact it was an abduction.'

Chapter 6

The Hunt

Of course, no one had any idea of the evil forces that were at play that day, but to me it seemed like people were just walking round and talking about the fact he was missing but not actually finding him. I know that wasn't actually the case, but at the time my desperation clouded everything. Mandy was out and about on patrol and was the nearest officer to the scene, but as soon as she arrived two young boys smashed the glass door into the shopping centre and Mandy ran off after them to make sure they were caught. Looking back I can see that she was only doing her job and she couldn't let a young yob smash things up in front of her and get away with it, but I knew about things like 'the golden hour' after a child goes missing – it is called that for a reason because every minute counts and I couldn't have given a damn about some broken glass. All I knew was that it was cold and dark outside and my baby wasn't safe; this policewoman was supposed to be here to find him. Suddenly I heard a voice that I realised was mine, 'You are here to look for a two-year-old baby, not fix a bit of glass.' I just couldn't help myself.

I later found out that Mandy had been concerned even before she got to the shopping centre – 40 minutes was a long time for a small child to be missing if he or she had just wandered off. But at that point she was calm and reassuring, and we retraced my steps with James, even if it was frustrating to be looking in all the places I had already searched. Everyone was convinced he had got himself stuck somewhere and that he was still inside the shopping centre, so we kept looking.

The Strand is a big shopping centre with over 110 shops. It is split-level and altogether it has five entrances and exits plus ramps and stairs that lead to the car parks. I knew that I couldn't have scoured every inch, but it still felt like we were going round in circles. I remember saying, 'You should be searching from the outside in, because if he was inside we would have had him back by now.' I had no idea what to expect, what was normal really – how would I know the best way to conduct a police search for a missing child? I was struggling to keep it together, in a bubble of horror. Obviously I knew something was deeply wrong but I was almost floating above it, watching all these people, and the only thing that could burst that bubble were the words I longed to hear, 'Don't worry! We've found him and he's safe and sound.'

Soon it was 5:30pm. The shops started closing and that's when deep fear settled in. We had searched high and low inside but I just knew he was out there somewhere and he needed me. Once everything was shut, Mandy and some other officers took me on another tour of the shopping centre – it was so eerily empty. Precincts are such strange places without the hustle and bustle of everyone going about their daily business. It was like a movie really: the lights were starting to go out, everyone was locking up and it was pitch black outside – how could this be happening to me and where was my baby?

Eventually Mandy suggested that it was time to go down to Marsh Lane Police Station and that was when I really got upset – I was crying so much I couldn't breathe. I knew he wasn't there because we had all looked everywhere, but the thought of leaving the shopping centre without him was crushing. I knew that walking away from the place where he had gone missing, without any idea where he now was, meant that things were really bad.

* * *

We got to the station and I was told that Ralph was on his way; my brother Ray was bringing him down. I knew that Ralph would be thinking the same as me, that we needed to get out and start looking for our boy, but first we both had to give statements. It soon became clear that police procedure dictated they had to be sure neither one of us was behind James' disappearance, especially me as I was the last person to see him. From the very beginning I felt that I was a suspect and nothing they did or said really lessened that in my mind.

Obviously it was a highly emotional time, and perhaps you could argue that the only thing anyone would have been able to do right at that moment was find my son, but I remember quickly feeling that they thought I was to blame. There was a female officer in the interview room with me asking all sorts of questions about James and our relationship, and it just felt to me as if she was trying to catch me out; it was so upsetting and stressful. I don't remember everything that was said but I do recall some really stupid questions, such as, had he ever been on a bus on his own. I was barely holding it together and suddenly I just lost it, 'You can sit here questioning me all you like but it won't help bring my son home. I will answer anything you want to ask me but at the end of it, you'd better walk in with him. Why the hell are you asking me questions like, "Would he get on a bus on his own?" He is two years old!'

What kind of bus driver would let a two-year-old board a bus on his own and not raise the alarm? His legs would have been too short to even get up the steps! The poor woman was only doing her job, but as far as I was concerned every minute stuck in this room answering silly questions was another minute James was out there on his own. Ralph was being questioned in another room and he later told me that the interviewer had repeatedly asked about my state of mind and if I had ever hurt James. Of course I know that this is standard police procedure – when a child goes missing they always check out the parents first – but it felt insensitive and a waste of time when I had repeatedly told them what had happened. I hadn't yet seen Ralph and had no idea how he was. I think that after his statement they took him back to the flat in order to get some up-to-date photos of James which they could circulate.

It must have been about three or four hours after I first got to the police station that I was finally allowed to see Ralph. I was in the interview room with Nicola and I burst into tears when I saw him come in through the door. He came barging at me, almost running at me, and I truly thought he was going to hit me, but he just pulled me into a bear hug. I don't really remember what I said but I know I kept saying that I had only let go of James for a second and repeatedly begged Ralph to find him and bring him back. I had tried my best to keep it together and give a clear statement. I would have done anything to help find James, even if the questions were irritating, but I was losing control and everything felt like it was in free fall.

I had no idea what was going on outside but I later found out that a huge search with police, family and friends was taking place. There were loudspeakers, helicopters and traffic patrols looking up and down the Bootle area, as well as over a hundred officers and our families out on foot searching for James along the streets. In the meantime, Ray drove me back to The Strand for yet another look and all the shops were searched again as I retraced my steps. By now everyone was sharing my panic that a baby was still missing at bedtime. I couldn't stand even to think where he could be when he should have been clean in his jammies under his duvet, safe and asleep.

We went back to the station again and I think Ray was asked to give a statement too. By this time Mandy had been assigned to look after us and was our main point of contact for anything we needed. Despite a rocky start when she first arrived at the shopping centre, Mandy did her absolute best for us. She was by my side the whole time and I know she was determined to find our boy alive. She looked after us brilliantly and I will always be grateful for that.

I think it must have been around midnight when we were taken back to The Strand yet again. This time it was more promising as we had been told there was some CCTV footage that the police wanted us to look at – there was a chance that the child in one of the shots might be James. Ralph and I arrived there with the police team and I am sure Mandy must have been there. It felt so reassuring to see things happening and the team working so hard.

They had started to go through the footage from that day – there were 16 security cameras placed throughout The

Strand and they had all been recording, which was a huge relief as sometimes cameras can just be for show. Police had been working round the clock to build up a frame-by-frame sequence of what had happened to James after he left my side. The cameras were on a time-lock system, meaning that they operated in short bursts rather than offering continuous footage. There were hours of footage to sift through, and that huge task had begun, but what they did have right now was a first frame. That sequence came from a camera placed right outside the butcher's shop and showed a very blurred image of a tiny boy running through the door out into the main precinct at 3:39pm. I didn't need to look twice – that was my James. I shouted out confirmation and I felt sick to my stomach but also strangely buoyed up – it was James, he was right there – so if we could follow the frames then surely they would show us the crucial minutes we were missing. We would see where he had gone and it would lead us to him.

So the first frame showed him leaving the butcher's. The next frame, timed at 3:40pm, showed me leaving the butcher's to begin my frantic search. I have no doubt that at this point the police were convinced James had wandered off out of the shopping centre and had got himself into trouble. If that was the case then we needed as many people out there to find him as possible. I kept saying to myself, *Someone must have seen him*. I didn't need to worry as, by now, the search was in full swing with loads more volunteers, and all our nearest and dearest, out searching every inch of the neighbourhood and the canal. I remember thinking it was such a bitterly cold night they must be freezing.

The police kept trying to persuade me to go home and get some rest. Initially, I absolutely refused but eventually I let Ray drive us back to Kirkby on the understanding I would shower, change and come back to the station whenever I wanted. I was taken to my mum's and I didn't last more than an hour before I begged to be taken back to the station. It was the only place I felt close to James and there was no way I wanted the comfort of home while James was still out there all alone. Ralph and his brothers went out to join the search and I told my mum to stay at home by the telephone in case there was any news. My brothers were also out searching everywhere they could – building sites and derelict housing estates. Everyone was out all night, determined to find him alive.

The police had started knocking on doors as well as leading wider searches but I had no real idea of what was going on. I was put in a room with Mandy and told as little as possible – I am sure this was for my own good as I was in a terrible state. I sat in that small room all night long, only leaving to go to the toilet – I couldn't eat or sleep and, as every hour passed, everything felt bleaker. As dawn broke, my family and Ralph came back from the search and we spent some time together.

* * *

I didn't know it but, in the early hours of Saturday morning, the officers who had been stationed at The Strand to view every single piece of CCTV footage had discovered more surveillance of James. There were now multiple images that told a whole new story.

As we knew, the first frame showed James leaving the butcher's at 3:39pm, the second frame showed me leaving the butcher's at 3:40pm, but while I was beginning my frantic search downstairs, another camera, timed just after 3:40pm, showed James on the upper floor apparently following two boys. The next frame timed at 3:42pm became the most haunting of the case – that infamous grainy image of my baby holding hands tightly with his killers. The final frame, timed at 3:43pm, showed Venables, Thompson and James walking out of the shopping centre's upper exit, which went towards the Leeds and Liverpool Canal, just four minutes after he had left my side, just as I was frantically searching for him downstairs and reporting him missing. Two hundred and forty seconds was all it took for them to lure James away from me and get him out of that shopping centre.

Although the police initially thought James had wandered out of the shopping centre on his own and perhaps fallen into the canal, the discovery of this new CCTV footage meant that theory went out of the window. It became very clear that James wasn't a lost child – he had been taken. All the footage may have been blurry but I knew my baby and, as the police showed it to me, it broke my heart to see him there without me. But in reality, looking at that grainy imagery was also the first time I had allowed myself to feel a tiny bit of relief. Although I hadn't voiced it, I'd been imagining all sorts of horrific scenarios in my head from the moment James went missing, and my biggest fear was that he had been abducted by a paedophile. To see him trustingly clutching the hands of two young boys raised a lot of questions but also strangely reassured everyone, including the police. Immediately everyone went from fearing the worst to discussing the fact that they could be mucking around with him in a garage, feeding him Mars Bars and treating him like a kid brother.

I don't think I allowed myself to wonder why they would be wasting their time with a baby. All I thought was that, for the first time, I was sure I would get James back. After all, how could two young lads possibly want to harm my child when they were just children themselves? The theory was, the boys would get bored and then James would be found; he might be hungry, upset and tired, but he would be home. The police just had to find where he was and it would all be over. There was definitely a feeling of hope in the air that he would be returned unharmed – after all, you bring your kids up to be wary of strange men, not other kids.

This discovery meant that the police were busier than ever and I overheard them planning a press conference at 11am on the Saturday. I was still in the small interview room in a trance and numb with tiredness – my nerves were shredded and I wasn't really taking much in. Mandy was with me and there were people coming and going out of the room and lots of noise, but I suddenly became aware of officers talking to Ralph – they were trying to persuade him to do the appeal. I remember standing up and saying I would do it, but they kept trying to put me off. I think they wanted to spare me the stress, as I clearly hadn't eaten or slept in nearly 24 hours and I was in no fit state to face TV cameras and a barrage of questions. But if talking to the press could help find James I was determined to do it. I remember saying, 'Listen, he's my son. I was the one with him when he went missing and I will do whatever it takes to get him back.'

I wasn't given a script or anything but the advice was to try and stay as cool as I could. I can remember thinking, *But what does that even mean?* I was sitting in an airless police station with no idea where my baby was and desperate to get him back, I was clearly in a state – I couldn't stop myself from breaking down every time I talked about the moment I realised he wasn't standing next to me.

I don't remember much about the conference apart from the camera flashes and lots of noise. I did my best to describe what had happened but all I can remember saying is, 'If anyone has got my baby, just bring him back.' Then I crumbled – I broke down and I couldn't stop. The tears represented 24 hours' worth of exhaustion, terror, desperation and fear all coming to the surface. It was terrible and I had to be led away from the table and taken back to the room as the cameras clicked. Ralph stayed and the police continued to brief the media, saying that James had been led away from the shopping centre by two young boys. The CCTV images were shown and they instantly made headline news around the world, although no one had any idea they would become such a chilling representation of evil.

The investigation continued at a rapid pace and was now being headed up by Detective Superintendent Albert Kirby, head of the Merseyside Police Serious Crime Squad. Alongside him were Detective Chief Inspector Geoff MacDonald and Detective Inspector Jim Fitzsimmons. While I was tucked away in a side room with Mandy and my relatives coming in and out, more and more police were being drafted in: this was now officially an abduction. I overheard someone saying that divers were dragging the canal for evidence of my boy, and just one hour later I was confronted with the grim reality of what that meant.

Without warning, the door was flung open and a frogman, dressed in full retrieval diving gear, strode into the room and marched over to me. He was clutching a tiny pair of trainers and, without a word, dangled them in front of my face. I looked at Mandy and said, 'No, no, they aren't James'.' I felt such relief they weren't his until I realised it took us no further on. The frogman didn't utter a word, but left the room, slamming the door behind him.

Chapter 7

'Please Bring My Baby Home.'

By late Saturday afternoon, I was losing my mind and tensions were running high, so it was no surprise that the police were keen for me to go home. I had been at the station, apart from the further two visits to the shopping centre and my quick shower at Mum's, since Mandy took me there on Friday afternoon. Ralph was out searching with the rest of the family, my mum was at home by the phone and my sisters were taking it in turns to come up to the station and sit with me and Mandy. No one knew what to do for the best and we were all running on pure adrenalin – but as it began to get dark on the Saturday we were all acutely aware this would be our second night without James.

Everyone pushed on and my brother Ray says they refused to consider the worst – the fact we knew two boys had taken James meant it could easily be a prank designed to cause a fuss. James could have just been left somewhere once they realised the police were involved and the trouble they would be in. It was such an unusual situation that anything was possible. Late Saturday afternoon I was going stir crazy and begged Mandy to take me out in the car so we could join the search. She reluctantly agreed and so we drove around looking along possible routes James could have taken. It was highly unlikely to be effective but I felt so much better doing something. I remember repeatedly asking Mandy if she thought we would find him and she did her best to comfort me, but I couldn't tell if she believed herself or not.

As Saturday night set in the police advised me to go home and get some rest – a polite way of telling me they needed me to leave. I was all over the place but in my mind they made me feel in the way because I kept asking questions they simply couldn't answer. I can imagine the police frustration as they headed up their biggest inquiry to date and simultaneously had to keep me informed. I think it got too much for everyone and they told me the best thing was to go home and that I could keep in touch by phone. I cried uncontrollably as I left; it felt like my world was finished and that somehow it was admitting defeat and giving up on James simply to go home without him. As a parent you are in charge of your child – where they go, what they eat, when they sleep – but here, in this police station, I was at the mercy of two children who had taken my baby and an investigation that didn't want me hanging around. I was distraught.

Ray took us back to Kirkby but there was no way I could go back to our flat where I had last seen James – it was full of his things and I was so highly strung I knew I wouldn't be able to deal with it. Going back home without him would make it all real and I couldn't handle that while there was still hope, so we went to my mum's. There was actually a much more practical reason for not going home – we didn't have a phone in the flat and Mum did. If they weren't going to let me stay at the station then I was going to stay glued to a phone – and in fact I am sure they heard more from me via the phone than they had when I had been at the station. As I left they told me to call anytime and I probably called every 15 minutes, so the final time I phoned the response was, 'Don't call us, Denise. We will call you the minute we hear anything.'

I do remember still having hope that night – there had been so many sightings of James, lots of new reports by members of the public saying they had seen a boy like him by the canal, but the divers hadn't found any trace of him, which I took as a good sign. I am not sure what I thought at that point – I am not even sure I was capable of thinking at all as I was so wrung out. I seem to remember being terrified that he was stuck in a building somewhere, freezing cold, having been left there by those two boys. I couldn't help but think how scared James would be – he hadn't spent any time apart from me ever, never mind having been away for this long out on his own. What would he be thinking?

At my mum's we sat up for a bit talking through what might have happened, although I wasn't really listening. I was staring trance-like at the phone, willing it to ring. My mum was in a bad way; she stayed in her room mostly because she didn't have the words to deal with what was happening – no one did really. I do remember trying to help her stay positive when I got in. I was on my way to take a shower and knocked softly on her door, finding her lying on her bed. I said, 'We are going to get him back, I just know it. Two lads have got him, but it's okay because they are young. We will get him back.'

Mum just looked back at me, eye to eye, and said, 'Let's hope it's sooner rather than later.' She looked shattered.

After my shower I was on my way downstairs when the phone rang. My heart truly felt like it had stopped. As I raced down the stairs I reached the bottom step and the little square window that faced out to the front of the house. I will never forget glancing out and seeing hundreds of media camped there – all with camera lenses trained on the house and all waiting for the money shot of me. I recall thinking, *What is this and how is this my life?* It was a nightmare I could not wake up from or press pause on. I ducked under the window, grabbed the phone and shouted into the receiver, 'Hello! Who is it??' Desperate to hear the words that would end this living hell: he's safe. We've got him, Denise.

There was a pause and then a voice told me clearly and calmly, 'We've got your little boy.'

I started screaming, 'Who is this? Where is my baby?' And they wouldn't answer; they just kept saying it over and over again – 'We've got him.' I realised it was a crank and put the phone down, baffled at the fact that someone could do something so disgusting at such a dark time. I've no idea if they had found my mum's number in the phone book or if it was someone who knew us. Either way it nearly pushed me over the edge – and at that point I was clinging on by my fingertips.

The family tried to get some sleep and begged me to do the same but I knew I wouldn't be able to. In the end, to stop everyone fussing, I decided to lie down on the floor with one hand on the phone. I didn't close my eyes once because I knew, if I did, all I would see was James needing me and the only way to stop that was to keep them open. I wouldn't even put a mattress down as comfort felt wrong – feeling warm and cosy was the last thing on my mind and, in a way, the worse I felt the better I felt, if that makes sense. I refused to even lie on the couch and would have much preferred to be sitting in the plastic chair at the police station, where I could at least see what was going on. I was lying on the floor facing my mum's fireplace – it was white with engraving going down the front and there was a small wall light over the top. I was concentrating so hard on the pattern, trying to make out what it was, that I realised it had become an angel with wings. Suddenly I sat up with a fright, terrified that this was a sign James had died and this was his way of saying goodbye before he left this world. Perhaps that very moment was the moment he went? I remember saying to myself, *Stop that, Denise. Don't let yourself go there for God's sake, just don't*. I sat bolt upright until dawn and then begged to be taken back to the police station.

The police wanted to hold another press conference to keep the media on board and informed – I was too distraught to do it this time so they all agreed that Ralph would read a statement that I prepared for him. I tried to keep it as calm and straightforward as possible:

Me and my wife want to say to the lads who were seen with him, whoever they are, if they could come forward and get themselves eliminated or bring my son back, as long as he is safe nothing will happen to them . . . just as long as he gets back. If they could drop him into the nearest police station or somewhere safe or phone or something, or anyone can give information, whatever, no matter how small it is, just get in contact.

There had been a really definite sighting of James at around 4:30pm on the Friday. He was with two boys and the female witness had looked closely at the pictures and was sure it was James, but the police wanted anyone else to come forward who might have seen anything, however small. Apparently the witness asked the two boys about James and they said they had just found him, a mile away from The Strand, heading towards Breeze Hill. The police were also keen to reassure the lads who had him that they would not be in trouble as long as James was returned home uninjured. I am not sure who was at the press conference as I was too upset to go, but I think that DCI MacDonald was running the conference and I hoped he would update Mandy as soon as there was any news so that she could tell me.

Despite the fact I was determined to be upbeat, I wasn't stupid. James had been missing for nearly 45 hours and I could see the despair in the faces of the officers – I could also definitely feel it in the body language of Mandy. They weren't expecting a happy ending, but I couldn't let those thoughts in. That weekend, time stopped for me, and I existed in some kind of parallel universe. People often ask at what point I realised James being with two kids wasn't going to end well and the answer is never. Even after the funeral and the thousands of letters, even during the court case when those two boys were standing trial for his murder, even then I thought he was coming home. That last day in court I still told myself I was only going to have to suffer life without James for a while but that he would be home as soon as that trial was done. It was after the trial that my world truly collapsed and the reality of never seeing my baby again hit me.

But that Sunday I needed to get out and do something, especially after Ralph and the family went back out to search a new area. I told Mandy that I felt hopeless, stuck in that family room waiting, doing nothing, I had to at least try and find my baby, so Mandy agreed to take me out in the car again at about 3pm. I can't remember where we went but yet again I was quizzing Mandy on what she thought might happen. After all, she had more experience than I did when it came to missing kids. I was sitting in the passenger seat and I turned to her and said, 'Do you think I am going to get him back?'

Until now she had been upbeat and encouraging, but this time she looked at me and said very gently, 'What do you think?'

I refused to take the hint and remember just thinking, *You're the policewoman, that's why I am asking you.* My brain couldn't cope with any kind of gentle preparation for the worst.

We were quiet after that and carried on driving around – we hadn't been out very long, maybe 20 minutes or half an hour, when Mandy got a call on her police radio to come back to the station immediately.

I swivelled round in my seat, saying to her, 'They've found him, haven't they?'

Mandy just looked at me and said calmly, 'I don't know.'

I knew, though. I was convinced they had found him. What I didn't hear when she took the call was the instruction: 'Come back to the station immediately . . . and turn your radio off.'

We drove to the station in silence, got back to Marsh Lane in a flash, parked up and made our way into the station. One of my strongest memories of that day was being met by DS Albert Kirby, DCI Geoff MacDonald and DI Jim Fitzsimmons at the entrance. Just as we were going in, other police officers were running out and there were people everywhere. I studied their faces and it was hard to tell. I started shouting, 'Have you got him?' but I couldn't get a straight answer out of anyone. I asked Mandy and she didn't really answer either, so I became upset and was led back to the family room to wait for news. I don't even know who took me back but I think I was there for 40 minutes or so. I had no idea that Albert Kirby had driven to Walton to be sure it was James before I was told the devastating news. I just knew that the waiting was driving me insane. But there was still a big part of me that expected them to come in carrying James and for everything to be fine. I kept asking Mandy over and over again if they had James and she just kept saying she didn't know.

I genuinely don't know who else was in that room with me because I blocked it out – I think family started coming back from the search to see if there was any news and I just remember that suddenly the room felt very crowded and small. They were all still trying to be upbeat – they hadn't seen Albert Kirby's face; they hadn't seen Mandy get that call. What felt like a lifetime passed and the door kept opening and closing – I didn't take any notice of who came in and who went out, but suddenly I heard Geoff MacDonald's voice; I heard him before I saw him. I just knew, in my bones I just knew. I refused to look up thinking perhaps if I didn't look at him then it wouldn't be true. I felt Geoff kneel down beside me and he put his hand on mine.

My mind was blank – I still had to think hard about why I was even there. *Where is James? Why aren't they bringing him to me?* The room went silent and I heard the heartbreaking words, 'I'm sorry.'

I looked up and said, 'Sorry? What? Sorry? Why?'

Geoff looked at me and said, 'We've found him and it's not good news.'

And then I don't remember a single thing until I woke up on the floor. Later one of the officers on duty at the station that day said, 'I just heard an almighty screech, real bottom of the gut stuff, like an animal. I burst into tears because you just knew what that meant; you just knew her heart was broken.'

Chapter 8

Starting a Life Sentence

From the moment that Mandy picked me up from the floor and helped me onto a chair, all I remember is the air being filled with silence. It stayed that way for months.

As I came round, I looked up at the sea of concerned faces and I didn't hear or feel a single thing. Mouths were moving and hands were reaching out to me – to steady me, to offer comfort, to tell me how sorry they were. One thing I realised very early on is that people touch you a lot when they don't know what to say, it's strange the things you think about when your world has stopped turning.

Ralph was still out looking for our precious boy with my brother Ray and some of the rest of the family. I remember thinking I should ask if he knew that James had been found and then my mind went black again. I was like a statue, rooted to the spot and I have no idea how long I sat on that chair in the tiny police interview room – it could have been days for all I know. I think an officer went to find Ralph and Ray and insisted they should come back. Not knowing what had happened, Ray says that he and Ralph were frustrated at being brought in – they wanted to keep looking for James and didn't understand why the police weren't keen for them to do so. Eventually they were driven to a car park so that Ray could collect his car and, while they were getting ready to leave and come back to the station, Ralph's brother Jimmy pulled up. Apparently Mandy had told Jimmy about James at the police station and they all decided that it was better for a family member to find Ralph and break the news in person. So that's how Ralph found out our baby had been murdered: sitting in a random car park on Valentine's Day.

In truth, this is where a lot of the detail is lost for me – I either can't remember because I have blanked it out or else the facts were kept from me for my own sake. They say that the brain filters out what we can't cope with and that is certainly true in my case – it became immediately clear I could not process what I had been told. I remember saying over and over in my head, *But where is James and when is he coming back? Why weren't they bringing him to me now they'd found him?* It didn't sink in and I certainly hadn't allowed my mind to compute the fact that, if James was dead, that meant the two boys in the CCTV footage had murdered him. I remember being offered a visit from the police doctor, which I declined, and I remember Ralph coming into the room and putting his arms around me. That's pretty much all I can recall of the day I was told my beautiful baby, who loved anything to do with trains, had been found dead on a railway track in Walton.

A group of boys had found his body on the line, nearly three miles away from The Strand shopping centre where I had last held his hand. Ironically, even though hundreds of volunteers and police officers had been searching round the clock for James, his body ended up just 100 yards away from Walton Police Station. I wasn't given any information about how they thought James had died, only that the way he had been found immediately ruled out accidental death. It is important to say here that I have never found out the exact nature of all that was done to James in his final hours and I never will – I know as much as my heart can take.

I don't remember who drove me back to my mum's. I didn't even know if she had been told as I sat in the back of the car, hugging my knees and totally wound in on myself. All I do recall is walking straight into the kitchen and seeing my sister standing there, eyes full of tears. She grabbed hold of me and yanked me into her chest and we stayed there, completely still, neither one of us saying anything. I can't remember if I cried, I do know that I was utterly numb.

Everyone meant well and people started coming round

with food and cards and kind words, and I watched them like it was happening to someone else. I didn't eat, I didn't sleep, I didn't shower, I didn't talk – it was like I was floating. I'd wander round the house and suddenly become aware I was in a room I couldn't remember walking into. I was just shuffling aimlessly from room to room and there was no purpose or point to anything. Hours bled into each other, day and night were the same to me. 12th February 1993 was the day I stopped sleeping and I haven't had a full night's rest since. The nights were always the hardest time – they still are.

A few things stand out from the first days after James was found: I recall walking into my mum's washing room the morning after and being aware of how cold it was. Even though it was the middle of winter, the window was open and there was an ice cream van outside – I remember thinking how strange it would be to eat ice cream all bundled up in winter coats, mittens and hats. The driver turned off his jingle alert, which meant I could hear his radio. The news was on and it was loud, lots of chatter about all that was happening in the world, and suddenly this chirpy newsreader announced that the two-year-old boy who had gone missing in The Strand shopping centre had been found dead. I was standing by the window looking out and I clearly remember thinking to myself, *His poor mum, she must be in bits*. Then I heard my brother storm outside and bang on the window of the van. He shouted, 'Have some bloody respect – that two-year-old all over the news had a mum. She's in that house right there and she can hear every damn word.' They both turned to look at me and my brain finally caught up with the reality of what was happening: *if I was that poor mum then that meant my baby was dead.* I remember turning around and climbing back up the stairs to lie down and try to block it all out.

On the second night I had an overwhelming need to go back to the flat and be around James' things but none of my family thought that was a good idea. I hadn't been left alone for a second (in fact, I didn't spend a single night on my own until well after the trial was over), my family just wouldn't allow it. Looking back I know they were terrified of what I might do and they had every reason to be scared for me: the days passed and I wished them all away. People talk about returning to normality after a death, but to me that meant going back to the way things were before – and that meant being at home with James. I was desperate to hold my baby and feel close to him and the only place I could achieve that was the flat where we had been together all the time. That was the place I fed him, cuddled him and snuggled into him as he watched cartoons on my lap. Every night I would bath him, read him stories and tuck him into bed. I would whisper 'I love you' as I turned the light out and I would sink into the sofa, exhausted, but content that my baby was all clean and safe in his bed. The flat was where I had protected him.

That night I waited until everyone had gone to bed and my sister had made her usual check on me before she turned in. Once the lights were out I got dressed. I knew it was unlikely that anyone would hear me leaving, we were all so wrung out and exhausted from living on our nerves that deep sleep came easily to the rest of the family, even if the misery had the opposite effect on me. I snuck out the back in order to avoid the photographers camped by the front door and set off for home.

It was a journey I had made thousands of times, that walk from my mum's back to mine with James all safely strapped in his buggy. We would chat away about what he was having for tea, sing songs and recite his ABC as he pointed out things along the way – more special time for the two of us that was gone forever. I got to the flat and put my key in the door. I didn't dare turn on the outside light in case that alerted the paparazzi, so it was dark as I went inside. I shut the front door, switching on a lamp, and it just hit me like a sledgehammer – so hard that it actually took my breath away. I hadn't even gone right inside; I felt it immediately as I paused in the hall. The place was full of James at every turn and it was like I could physically feel my heart shattering inside my chest as my eyes took in each thing of his: his tiny trainers, his coat with string mittens dangling from the sleeves, his go-kart parked by the door and ready for a trip to the park – every glance was like a bullet to my chest. I wanted the feel of James back and this was where I felt closest to him, this was where I had been his mummy, but it was breaking me to see all the things he would never use again.

I looked at the TV he danced in front of, the special chair that he would never eat in again. I ran my hand over his pile of books and smiled at his bike in the middle of the room – right where he had left it as I chased him round that Friday morning trying to put his shoes on and get over to my mum's. I had been in such a rush to get him out of the house, I wondered why now. Why didn't I slow down so I could savour those last moments? I went into the bedroom – there were his clean jammies neatly folded on the end of his bed, all ready for the night he never came home. It was like being frozen in time. I sat down and I tried to soak in the feel and the smell of him – it was everywhere as I breathed in, as I touched the sofa and the walls.

The living room door was always wedged open because James would hurtle through it at a hundred miles an hour, I had to keep it secure as I am sure he would have crashed right through it otherwise! I sat, eyes fixed on that door, waiting for him to come spinning round the corner, big smile, hair bouncing like mad. The crushing feeling of knowing I would never see him again almost suffocated me. As I went to close the door into the living room I saw his hand smear on the glass door, and right then I knew I would never be able to live here again. It was impossible. This flat had been a home for the three of us, now it felt like there was no one left. It was like we had all died with him.

I curled up on the sofa and stayed for a few hours, creeping back early in the morning – no one had even noticed I'd gone as they were asleep, and I felt like the loneliest person in the world. Ralph was with his mum and had no idea I had been missing, and the one person who would have immediately noticed my absence when he woke up in the morning was my baby. He would have climbed out of bed, his little feet scurrying across the carpet as he called my name, but now he was gone and it felt like I had no one at all.

It was as if I'd started a life sentence – a veil came down and I just retreated from everything and everyone around me. I was staying at my mum's but we could barely find the words to say anything comforting to each other. She retreated to her bedroom for hours on end and I did the same in my sister's bedroom, which she had given up for me. When we talk about it now, my brother Ray says that Mum and I were so similar in how we handled our grief – we both closed up and didn't let anyone in. It was a house weighed down by anguish – my mum hadn't long buried my dad and now she was faced with a daughter who had lost a child. But she had lost James, too, and they were so close, especially after Dad died – she saw him every day; he adored her. I didn't know how to comfort her and she didn't really know what to say to me. I think it broke her heart to see me catatonic with loss and aching for the one thing she couldn't give me back. As a mother, no matter how old our children get, all we want to do is make it okay, and knowing you can't do that for your child is the most devastating feeling in the world. Suddenly it felt like loss and despair were all we had in common.

I was in my own bubble and had no concept of the brutal realities others were dealing with – I didn't know what had happened to James' killers and I wasn't involved in the logistical side of things like identifying my baby's body. That devastating task fell to Ralph's brother Jimmy. I later found out that Ralph had asked to do the identification but had been prevented by the police as they decided it would be too much for any parent to stand. I know my brother Ray had also considered doing it but he was in pieces.

I talked to Ray a lot for this book – especially about those days, where I was in no position to take anything in. We had never really talked to each other properly about it all before. He remembers so much more about those awful days than me. Of the identification process, Ray says, 'When Jimmy stepped in and offered I was so grateful, I will always be grateful that he spared me from a sight I know would have haunted me forever. Now I can remember baby James on that final morning, standing on my dad's armchair and waving at the birds out of the window. Happy, smiling and loved.'

I think Jimmy went to see James' body a day or two after he had been found, but it's all a bit hazy as no one really discussed it with me. I do remember distinctly feeling utterly distraught at the thought of him lying there in a mortuary all on his own, no one to hold him or stroke his forehead. But inconsolable is the only word to describe me when it became clear that they had to do an autopsy on my boy. The thought of that sent me into a dark spiral – even now I have to shut it out of my thoughts if my mind goes there. It was something I'd been able to avoid with Kirsty, but, after all he had been through, I couldn't even protect my James from that. It felt like a final act of brutality.

I know it wasn't easy for anyone involved. The pathologist, Dr Alan Williams, has said, 'Doing post-mortems on young children can be so upsetting, especially if you have kids yourself. At that time I had a child only slightly older than James. Like all parents, you look at your own child asleep safely in bed and you pray it will never happen to your children. James had a large number of injuries and bruising and it was all very difficult.'

A lot of decisions were being made over endless cups of tea in the kitchen and I preferred to lock myself away in my sister's bedroom. Lying curled up on the bed and being still was all I could handle, but in the immediate aftermath of James being found and identified there were things I had to know and deal with whether I liked it or not. That started with a visit from DS Jim Green, the man who had taken my initial statement at the police station on the Friday evening after James had gone missing. He had been formally appointed as our family liaison officer, along with Mandy, and he had the job of coming to my mum's house to tell us that James' body had been severed by a train. Various sections of the media knew this fact and he wanted to tell us before we read it in the papers, not least as some of the media had been down to the railway track trying to get photographs of James' body being removed by the forensic team.

I heard the bell ring and, as usual, just turned over in bed and ignored it. Eventually there was a soft knock on the bedroom door and my sister told me that the police were here and I needed to come down. I walked into the kitchen to a collection of faces – some I knew, some I didn't – and Ralph. We stood there as they told us what had happened to James' body and I could feel Ralph tensing up. He was holding my hand and the grip got tighter as he struggled to keep himself in check. I kept my head down, staring at the tiles on my mum's kitchen floor, thinking how muddy they would get as people weren't taking their shoes off when they came in. I didn't look up once and can't remember what was said, I just wanted to be back upstairs wrapped in my duvet in the quiet. We spoke briefly about how to handle the press attention and they asked if I had any questions. I remember thinking, *Where on earth do I start?*

Chapter 9

The Arrests

We were advised to stay away from all forms of media in those early days, which suited me fine, although realistically that was impossible as my baby's sweet face was splashed across every newspaper and magazine up and down the country. The police were doing their best to keep us up to date on how the investigation was progressing and they moved quickly and efficiently during those first few days after James was found. I know that obviously the priority in those initial hours was tracking down the two lads seen in the CCTV images. Now that James' body had been discovered it was becoming even clearer that the security footage represented something very much out of the ordinary, but at this point I still don't think the police had any idea of the significance those images would take on as the events unfolded. I remember Albert Kirby saying that officers thought they were looking for boys of around 13 years old, but that it was very difficult to judge their height against anything in the precinct due to the grainy quality of the security stills.

Those first few days felt like purgatory: the police were still appealing for the boys to come forward and I was still locked away from the world at my mum's. I wasn't eating, I wasn't sleeping and my brain was burning with images of my baby needing me, calling for me, putting his arms out for me – I truly felt like I was going mad. I was wasting away physically and mentally. The doctor brought round dozens of Complan shakes and persuaded me to drink those as the weight was dropping off me. I couldn't even entertain the idea of food, the very thought of chewing defeated and exhausted me. It's funny what you can get used to and I soon forgot how to exist in any part of the house apart from my bedroom so, on the rare occasion I did come out, any room I walked into felt too big. I'd look around and be filled with panic that there was too much noise and too many people, I couldn't cope and so I would go back to my room and calm down – it became my safe haven.

Although I wasn't necessarily aware of it at the time, the commitment to finding those responsible for James' murder was overwhelming. Obviously I knew that Albert and his team were working night and day to find out what had happened to our boy, but the finer details were kept away from me. Ralph knew more than I did, along with my brother Ray, and everyone's focus was on making sure that I didn't have to deal with anything that might tip me over the edge. Ray says now, 'Although you said from the start that you wanted to know everything that was going on, it was such a fine line between keeping you informed and thinking about every word before you said it – the smallest detail could have been too much, never mind the bigger and more distressing stuff. The pressure was really on and that only got worse once the trial started. I was there as eyes and ears for you and Ralph, but I couldn't bring myself to tell you most of what was said.'

On the one hand I know I was very lucky to have a family so concerned with my well-being, on the other it meant that, once I was ready to hear more detail about what had happened, it was too late and would have caused more harm than good. It also meant that, though Ralph and I were united in our grief, a distance opened up in those early days that we couldn't close. As time went on it became harder to come together in our pain and we both sought separate ways of dealing with the overwhelming sorrow that almost drowned us.

* * *

In the days after James' murder, more than 50 young boys aged between 10 and 18 were called in, arrested and questioned immediately – some after being identified by witnesses, some who were picked up by police for being in the wrong place at the wrong time. That in itself was a roller coaster for us all. Ray said, 'When you hear the word "arrested" you immediately imagine they have the potential culprits, but it actually just meant they were questioning anyone and everyone.'

Albert Kirby's statement at the press conference after the murder had struck a chord: 'There must, somewhere, be somebody who knows the identity of the boys seen with James.' The amount of information that came in was extraordinary. One police officer said, 'In any other murder case you would put an officer aside to answer the phones and deal with the incoming information, but the phones were ringing off the hook and in the end we needed to set six or seven officers aside simply to deal with the queries and the amount of information flooding in.'

At that moment there weren't any concrete theories the police could share with us. I know that before they arrested and interviewed Thompson and Venables, they toyed with the idea of James' murder being a prank that had gone wrong. I suspect this was as much to do with the fact that no mind, not even a police one, could wrap itself around the idea that any young child could have deliberately lured James away and done what they did.

I became aware of a potential breakthrough on the Tuesday after James was found, raising my hopes that the monsters who had taken my baby had been caught. I was told that a boy of 12 had been arrested in Kirkdale. Lots of neighbours had seen the police activity at his house and immediately concluded that this must be James' killer. That meant that the press were tipped off and things descended quickly into a near riot.

It showed the level of emotion swirling around and the amount of people who wanted justice for James. But I must say that I have never wanted violence in James' name – not least as he didn't have a bad bone in his body. That has never changed, not even once Venables and Thompson were convicted – and very much contrary to reports that I organised vigilante groups to find them once they were released. All I have ever wanted for my boy is justice and so, even though my spirits were raised at the thought of an arrest, I didn't get my hopes up. We were getting all kinds of phone calls from friends and family keeping us informed of what was being reported in the press, so my brother Ray called DCI Geoff MacDonald to try and separate the facts from the emotional second guessing.

Geoff told Ray that the lad had only ever been a 'possible' suspect in the hunt and that he was one of many arrests – it just so happened that the journalists had found out about this one rather than any of the others. It was then that he told us, 'We are arresting anyone who fits the description if they don't come willingly to help us.'

It came to light that the boy in question, Jonathan Green, had aroused the suspicion of his father, who had called police to share his worries. Parents were so appalled by what had happened that they were questioning their own children. It soon became clear that Jonathan had nothing to do with James' murder but that didn't stop the harassment and, even though the boy was totally innocent, he and his family had to leave their house and the area.

The request for information continued and on the Thursday evening *Crimewatch* was aired: it was the first time the programme had featured a crime the same week it had been committed.

The programme showed new images of the boys enhanced using techniques favoured by the Ministry of Defence – they were still fuzzy but a huge improvement on the originals. What we didn't know was that, just before the show aired, two more boys were in custody being questioned. A woman, who had been away on holiday for over a week, walked into Marsh Lane Police Station late Wednesday evening saying she had information about the youngsters captured on CCTV. She told the police that she was a friend of the family of a boy called Jon Venables and that he was often in trouble for skipping school and causing general mischief. She could recognise him from the images that she had seen on the news and she was certain it was him. She was also able to give the name of a boy he often hung around with: Robert Thompson.

Armed with that information two teams went to arrest them in plain clothes and unmarked cars, marking the start of a new horror story for my family. Thompson lived in Walton, not far from the murder scene, with his mum and two younger brothers. The arresting officer recalls knocking on the door and it being opened by his mother. The officer explained who he was and why he was there and ended up speaking to Thompson's seven-year-old brother. The officer said at the time, 'He knew about the murder, so much so that he and Thompson had been down to put flowers on the tracks – I remember hearing that and wondering if we were making a terrible mistake. I mean, what adult could be that conniving if they had murdered someone, let alone a child behaving so cynically?'

Venables was arrested at the same time. His parents had divorced when he was three years old and they shared custody of Jon and his siblings. Teachers described him as an attention seeker – seemingly the very least of his issues once everything else came to light. When he was called to the landing by his mother the arresting officer recalled, 'I was so shocked to see his age and his size, I just couldn't get my head around the possibility that this tiny kid had committed such an evil act.'

They were taken to separate police stations and Albert Kirby travelled to London for *Crimewatch*, I am sure still believing that the two boys they had in custody were far too young to be responsible. I remember it being one of the hardest things to get my head around – they were just seven years older than my James, the baby they were supposed to have murdered. I have since learned that the arresting officers began their questioning on the Thursday afternoon and it was the first time any of them had interviewed murder suspects so young. There was no precedent for what was taking place, and so that had to be set at the same time as following protocol. One officer later said, 'We were aware that it would be going to the Crown Court whatever happened, so any mistakes could rob that poor James of justice. In that situation you have to shut off your own feelings and do your best to be impartial.'

The interviews were recorded but a court injunction now bans them from being broadcast to protect the identities of Venables and Thompson – a familiar pattern of protection for my son's killers that was established early on. Because of their young age, the first and most important thing to establish was if they understood right from wrong and the difference between a lie and the truth. I know very little about the ins and outs of the questioning – it's been the only way to survive really and protect what was left of my sanity. I know there are full transcripts that have been printed, but I try not to waste my emotional energy on the two boys who stole my world. There has been enough written about them and I would rather spend my time remembering James as he was, not for how he died. I do know that interviewing these two boys affected some of the officers deeply – that really came home to me years later when I met one of them at a police party. I could clearly see in his eyes that he was still hurting, that he was trying to tell me something but didn't quite know how to do it. Because he'd had a bit to drink he couldn't get the words out and was also terrified of upsetting me. He looked haunted and, frankly, destroyed – he later said of the interviews, 'The level of manipulation, detail and evil for such a young person to be involved in will stick in my mind forever.'

* * *

We had ongoing support from Mandy, Albert and the team and it was actually their suggestion that Ralph and I should get a solicitor on board to help us manage all the press, the paperwork and the general admin that I just couldn't engage with. I could barely dress myself and sit upright, never mind deal with any kind of process – all I wanted to know was if they were going to charge the two boys they suspected had murdered my son. I don't remember a thing about that first meeting with Sean Sexton, the recommended solicitor, who was known to the family (mainly by my brother Ray).

I spoke to Sean while writing this book, and he says of how he first got involved, 'I got a phone call almost one week after James' body had been found, it was Saturday, 20th February. I was 34 and had set up on my own four years beforehand. Until that point I'd done a whole range of what a high street solicitor would do – personal injury work, criminal work, dealt with family issues, but nothing that prepared me for this case. I got a call asking me to go to Kirkby in relation to the James Bulger case. Originally I thought it was to do with one of the kids who had been arrested, as that was all over the media at the time and I thought maybe one of them wanted representation from a solicitor.'

It turns out the response to James' murder was threatening to swamp Marsh Lane Police Station and the team knew that I wasn't dealing with anything at all. Ralph was also in bits and had started drinking to ease the pain, so they decided to enlist some help on our behalf. During the week between James' disappearance and the discovery of his body, there had been letters flooding in – some simply addressed 'James' Mummy, Liverpool' – so the police were having to vet them all to check there wasn't anything inappropriate inside. They were nearly always cards of condolence and most had cash inside, telling us to buy a teddy bear for James or buy some flowers for me. The generosity was overwhelming and reminded me how many good people there were in the world despite the horror we had encountered. The station had never seen anything like it and tried to put a team in place around us, and so the police arranged for Sean to come and see us on the Saturday morning. I was persuaded to come downstairs and meet him.

Sean remembers, 'I got there at midday and went to your mother's house, Ray lived in the same road just a bit further on. I walked into that house and the misery hit me, as soon as I crossed the threshold. I was introduced to you and Ralph, and you just looked through me. You didn't seem to be connecting to anything that was happening. You didn't hear anything that anyone was saying – you weren't really functioning at all. I remember that Ray offered me a cigarette. I had given up smoking that New Year's Eve – I was so proud of myself and had done so well, not a single puff since – but the atmosphere was so intense that I smoked two cigarettes in the first half an hour before I remembered that I had given up the fags. I couldn't see exactly what my role would be at that point but one of the police liaison officers suggested that I go down to Marsh Lane Police Station and see what they were dealing with. So off I went and, when I got there, I was led into this small room with four or five police officers sitting there opening mountains of envelopes full of donations and letters. It was almost overwhelming.'

The emotion, interest and press attention increased tenfold on Saturday, 20th February at 6:40pm, when Robert Thompson and Jon Venables were charged with my baby's abduction and murder. At Marsh Lane Police Station in Bootle the investigating team were in shock, one officer simply said 'it was utterly horrific' before welling up.

What did I feel? Relief they had been caught but not much else – my baby was still dead so what else could I possibly feel? I remember climbing the stairs to bed safe in the knowledge that, if I had my way, I would quite happily never get up again.

Chapter 10

My Baby's Funeral

What are you supposed to feel when two children are charged with the murder of your toddler son? There aren't any rules in a situation like this and a lot of the detail is hazy; I do recall Albert Kirby coming to my mum's house to tell us what would soon be all over the news. He wanted to do the right thing and tell us in person, although at the time the kind gesture was slightly lost on me, as I was just too numb.

I continued to stay away from the newspapers and TV at the time, but I now know that all the second-guessing started immediately: how could it be that two children had abducted and murdered a baby? What kind of childhood must they have had in order to commit such a heinous crime? What was wrong with our society that no one had stopped two young kids, sensing something was amiss, as they dragged my baby along the streets for three miles?

No one will ever know what drove those two boys to do what they did, but I want to be clear on one thing here: I know that Venables and Thompson went out to abduct and kill that day. What they did was no accident and their attempted abduction of another child that very morning proved it. I also know that some of the officers involved in their arrest and eventual charging agree with me, one of them saying, 'There was no remorse, absolutely no remorse. I won't ever be convinced there was a shred of remorse for what they did.'

I have had to work hard over the years not to let my feelings of anger swamp me, and I am not going to examine their backgrounds and the various theories out there to explain why they murdered my child. All I know is that they killed my two-year-old baby and took away his whole future, wrecking mine in the process. No amount of psychoanalysing is going to change those facts.

It seemed that we had started working with Sean at just the right time because, once it was public knowledge that the police had arrested and charged two ten-year-olds, the floodgates opened and everyone was in danger of being washed away. Sean was thrown in at the deep end when it was announced that the two boys would be appearing in Bootle Youth Court on the Monday morning. There was no way I could go and Ralph wasn't up to it either – we wouldn't have been allowed into the courtroom in any event, as it was a youth court – but we did both want to know what was happening so we asked Sean to go as our representative and say a few words on behalf of the family. Emotions were at breaking point in Liverpool. The idea that two of the city's own had done this to a tiny boy set off a fizzing anger that threatened to spill over outside the court.

The press were out in force hoping for the money shot: there were hundreds of cameras poised and ready for either a picture of the boys looking vulnerable in the back of a police van or a shot of the angry crowd boiling over. They ended up with neither as the police sent out a decoy vehicle as a distraction until it was safe for Thompson and Venables to be escorted out. For our families, the court circus took us one step closer to knowing when James' body would be released for burial. Thank God I didn't know it at the time, but the individual legal teams for Thompson and Venables had the right to decide if they wanted their own independent post-mortems because their clients had been charged with murder. They didn't do this, but I truly think if I had realised it was even a possibility it would have finished me off completely – it broke me enough to think of him being cut open once, never mind three times.

The house was at its busiest over the following week, people were in and out planning James' funeral and I would watch the activity going on around me, my head spinning. The only comfort I found was in my room away from all the noise and bustle. The last funeral planned in this house had been for my dad and I know it brought back all sorts of bad memories for my mum. We still couldn't really talk about what had happened, nor could Ralph and I. He was finding his solace in the bottom of a bottle, I was finding mine in silence, but between us we tried to plan the best send off for our son that we could manage. I will forever be grateful to my brother Ray, who stepped in and took over all the admin and planning. He was the person liaising with the police about what we could expect and it soon became clear this wasn't going to be a small family funeral as I'd hoped.

We had already buried one child, but with Kirsty the funeral was different, not least as the hospital had taken care of all the arrangements. I had also just given birth and didn't have a clue what was going on, so I'd been grateful to have it all sorted. Although the loss was heartbreaking, when Kirsty died we hadn't had the chance to get to know her for nearly three years – she didn't have a favourite toy to be buried with, a favourite outfit that I could dress her in, a special chair that she sat on or a special teddy she couldn't sleep without. We didn't know where to start with James – I should have been running behind my little boy as he drove his go-kart round the park, or pushing him on the swings, not picking out a casket for his body. A body that was so tiny that in the end we had to have one specially made.

We couldn't view James – as the funeral approached I did ask if I could see him one last time but I was advised by the police not to. I didn't get a chance to touch my little boy, kiss him goodbye or tell him how much I loved him.

Perhaps it was for the best as my imagination had already been working overtime at the thought of what he might look like after all that had happened to him. When I think back now, I am glad that I get to remember his cheeky face the way it always looked: with that wide smile and those mischievous eyes. At the time I don't think I could have survived any more agony.

It took every single ounce of strength to get through the planning stage, and the small details were the ones that nearly killed me. People were so generous – the funeral directors, Graham Clegg, refused to take any payment for burying James and it was the same with the coffin company. It was those acts of kindness that helped me just about keep my head above water. There was one thing that only I could do and that was to decide what James should wear for his final journey. I picked his outfit the day before he was collected from the mortuary and moved to the undertakers. I decided on the corduroy suit that he wore on his last Christmas Day – it had dark brown trousers with turn-ups and pockets and a matching waistcoat, I finished it off with a cream roll neck and some white socks. I decided not to put shoes on him, I'm not sure why.

I remembered the last time James had worn that outfit – I had taken him round to my brother's on Christmas morning and everyone said how cute he looked and called him a little Steve Davis. He looked so beautiful and grown up – and a bit like a snooker player! He ran around excitedly when he saw all the presents and did a little dance. Now, I couldn't face looking at the outfit so a member of the family got everything ready for the undertaker to collect. They packed the suit neatly into a bag along with his favourite teddy, a toy motorbike and a torch – I remember thinking that he always took his torch to bed so that he could see in the dark and not be scared, so it was really important he had that with him in his coffin. Once all his things were inside, the bag was handed to the undertaker and it would fall to strangers to dress my baby for the final time. I had dressed and undressed him every single day of his short life, we had never spent a night apart, and it killed me that it wouldn't be my hands touching him for the final time. But I was glad to know he was out of the mortuary and being looked after by a firm who knew our family really well. Once he was ready the casket was sealed immediately, as Graham Clegg was determined to protect James in death – as he said, 'His mum and dad and the family were not going to be able to see him and I didn't want anyone else to be able to say "I saw him" either.'

Mandy and Jim, who were still our liaison officers, paid a visit to my mum's a few days before the funeral to talk us through just how enormous the media interest had become and what we could expect on the day. I don't think I had any idea just how much had been written and said about the case already as I had been tucked away at home, but it slowly dawned on me that the world's media would be descending on our son's funeral and I was horrified and terrified in equal measure. Poor Ray was bearing the brunt of all the planning chaos: 'It was the hardest time – here we were planning a funeral for my baby nephew who had been brutally murdered and I was having to sit in police review meetings discussing air exclusion restrictions – all so that the press couldn't get shots of my sister burying her child. It was madness and so surreal.'

It became a case of damage limitation – doing what we could to give the press what they wanted so that they didn't take over the day. There was no way this could be done privately, much as I wanted to, so in the end we agreed to allow live coverage of the funeral mass from inside the church to satisfy the journalists and keep things civilised. We had every news organisation knocking on my mum's door wanting interviews, as well as access to the funeral. Merseyside Police were amazing and they organised a pool at the front of the church, like a pen almost, to contain the media so they didn't flow in and out in huge groups. There was a pool for TV and a pool for press – as well as a few designated photographers who would do all the photos and then make them available worldwide to the media. Basically it meant less people there getting in the way of our family grieving. Merseyside Police also imposed a three-mile air exclusion zone over the church and surrounding areas. What they couldn't stop were the few journalists who tried to pay the homeowners living opposite the church for access to their bedroom windows so they could get shots of us arriving with our son's coffin.

We decided to hold a Catholic mass and I don't know how we would have got through any of it without Father Michael O'Connell and his natural warmth and compassion. I am Anglican but Father Michael didn't even question it. I won't ever forget what he did for us, he was incredible. Along with Ray, he made sure the service was exactly what we wanted. It would feel like a private and intimate goodbye, even though hundreds of the world's media would be watching our every move. I had been in bed for two weeks torturing myself and now I had to face the world with no idea how to cope. But somehow, knowing that the service was in good hands, gave me a focus and some strength to get through it, it also meant I had no choice but to leave the house in daylight for the first time since James had been found.

We helped pick all the hymns and music and asked Albert Kirby to do a reading. It seemed only fitting that the man who had searched for our boy, and then his killers, should stand up and play a part in saying goodbye. We also decided to put the special chair that Ralph made for James, the chair he loved to sit on while he ate his meals and watched his favourite cartoons, up on the altar during the service. I picked out some of his favourite toys and decided they would sit next to the casket as we said our goodbyes, so they were close to James for one last time.

I knew that I had to go shopping before the service for

something black to wear. I was also advised by Ray's wife, Delia, that I should buy the biggest hat I could find so that the press couldn't take any pictures of my face. That was truly the best advice anyone could have given me and I chose one with the widest brim possible. I hadn't been out in Liverpool since that day at The Strand and I was terrified of being recognised and spoken to, so I went with Delia to Southport for the day. Despite our best efforts, we were recognised pretty early on and ended up going to Skelmersdale instead, where I picked a plain black outfit, a hat and some tights. I remember Delia driving me home as I thought to myself, *How can I be buying a new outfit for my baby's funeral?* We drove in silence and as soon as we got home I went straight to bed.

The next day Ralph and I, along with close family, went to the chapel of rest in Maghull so that we could spend time with James' casket. Father Michael thought it would be important to have a private moment, ahead of all the press on the actual day of the funeral. He also advised it would be a good idea to see the casket in advance of the service.

We had a few prayers and got to see some of the flowers that would be there on the day. I am not sure anything prepares you for the sight of a tiny white box that holds your lively, bouncy, funny, cheeky son's remains – I could have seen it a thousand times and it wouldn't have been any less shocking. I stood there, still not understanding how this was happening to me. I had taken my purse out of my bag to pay for some chops and here we were, touching a sealed casket with James inside – what was going on? Ralph and I cried until I didn't think there were any tears left. I just felt like I had let James down and, in all honesty, if I couldn't have him back then all I wanted was to be curled up in that casket with him.

Chapter 11

Falling Apart

Monday, 1st March 1993, was the day we put our baby into the ground. Fittingly, it was the coldest day we'd had that year so far – even the weather was outraged. I don't remember getting ready that morning, but I do remember waiting anxiously by my mum's front room window for James to come home for the final time. The service was taking place at Sacred Heart Church in Northwood, Kirkby, and James would be buried four miles away in Kirkdale Cemetery in a strictly private service. But first he was coming back to the place he spent so much of his life, his happy place. Our neighbours closed their blinds and curtains as a mark of respect and the procession of 14 cars arrived for us all to follow James on his last journey. The first three cars were completely full to the brim with flowers sent from all over the world by well-wishers. Behind those was the hearse carrying my baby – inside was his bright white casket along with some flowers, a large wreath spelling out his name and a teddy bear made out of carnations. Ralph and I got into the fifth car, the one right behind James' casket, and even though the church was only 400 yards away, I felt like we were in that car for hours. I don't think Ralph and I said a word to each other the whole day, we just clung on to each other for dear life. What did shock me was the number of people who lined the streets to see James on his way – there were literally thousands of people with their heads bowed, sharing our pain.

As soon as we pulled up to the church gates, I got out of the car and quickly stood behind the casket – I could hear the sea of clicking cameras and I put my head down – it stayed that way for the whole service. Ralph and his brother Phillip had agreed to carry James' casket along with my brothers Ray and Gary, so we all walked slowly into the church. Ray said to me for this book, 'To be honest all I can remember is looking down at my feet the whole time, desperate not to trip or stumble in any way. I was carrying the most precious cargo and I had been so honoured when you and Ralph asked me to help take James on his final journey. As far as I was concerned there was no bigger job and I wanted to do you and James proud. I had to keep it together for both your sakes, but my God . . . '

I remember a few things – the church was absolutely

packed and the seat Ralph had made for James was there at front on the altar waiting to receive James' casket. But what I remember most of all was walking down the aisle and seeing rows and rows of black shoes – some polished, some with laces, others with buckles, round toes and scuffs. All I saw was a sea of black and I didn't raise my eyes as I shuffled to the front pew to take my seat.

James was placed down gently at the front and Ralph sat beside me, holding my hand tightly. I tried to look at the casket holding my baby just once but I couldn't do it – because how could I look at a box with a lid on and know my son was lying in there, dead and cold and gone? His picture was on top of the casket – his big, beaming smile filling the church – and I remember saying to myself, *This is a fucking nightmare and I am going to wake up from it any minute.* The only way I could hold it together was to keep my eyes down – I saw a corner of white and a flash of a silver handle, the photo, the corner of his chair and some of his teddies and I thought, *No, that's not my son, that's not my baby.* And I didn't look up again, not once, I didn't trust myself.

I remember Father Michael's sermon starting with the words, 'Everyone's heart absolutely goes out to you,' and saying that he wished he could bring James back to us, but the words that really struck a chord with me were, 'We are going to miss him every day for the rest of our life because we never forget and won't ever get over him. Time does not heal. Time just helps us cope a little bit better.' I remember thinking, *Really?*

The hymns and readings we had so carefully picked out passed in a blur – I was inconsolable, taken over by deep and scarily dark grief. I remember 'Heal the World' by Michael Jackson coming out of the speakers and immediately imagining James dancing right in front of the TV, throwing his head back as he did another dance move. Extraordinarily, Michael Jackson actually got to hear about his song being played at the funeral and he sent us some flowers and a condolence note – I couldn't get over the fact that news had travelled so far, it was one of many touching moments in the dark days after the funeral.

Once the requiem Mass was over everyone stood up and started to file out of the church to Eric Clapton's 'Tears in Heaven'. Ralph and the others picked up our son for the final time and placed him in the car for the journey to the cemetery. Again we saw crowds and crowds of people bowing their heads and nodding as we passed through – even the traffic had stopped for us as a mark of respect. We sat in silence as we made our way to the cemetery and James' final resting place.

We had picked a plot under a tree as I thought he would be protected from the elements. Come rain or shine, a tree would offer a bit of shelter and comfort, as I couldn't stand the idea of him being there alone with no one to hold him. We only invited close family and friends to the burial –

as well as a few police officers who had been intimately involved in the case – because we desperately wanted a private moment. I was exhausted from being on show and having all those eyes searching for my gaze.

A few prayers were said and my darling boy was lowered into the hole that had been dug for him. Ralph and I placed a single red rose on top of his casket and I caught sight of the gold name plaque on top, glinting as he went down into the earth. I had asked that we be given rose petals to scatter on top of James' coffin instead of the traditional earth – I couldn't stand the thought of throwing mud on top of my precious boy. Whatever we put on top had to be soft and gentle, like a final, loving stroke.

By now I was in a total trance, being pushed and pulled into all the right places and positions but feeling nothing at all. The tears wouldn't stop flowing but somehow my brain wasn't engaged. *What were we doing here and when was I going to wake up from this hell?* If the finality of James going into the grave didn't break the last bit of my heart, then the poem we read as our final goodbye did.

Obviously there was no way I was able to say anything myself, I could barely stand up on my own let alone string a sentence together, but I had written something for my baby the day before. I'd been lying on the bed, thinking about James and all the things I wanted him to know, and I started writing down some sentences. It just all poured out and I decided to try and make it into a poem – I remember thinking that the rhyming would be soothing as he went down into that cold earth. As we stood in the freezing cold and listened to Father Michael reading it out, I thought that it summed up exactly how we felt at the moment:

James, our beautiful baby son.

We didn't get to say goodbye and that really makes us cry.

You brought so much love in our lives, that love for you will never die.

The only thing that we can do, is sit and pray for you.

In our hearts you will still be there, locked inside our loving care.

God, look after him as we would do, for we are sure that he is with you.

Goodnight and God bless, James Patrick.

All our love, hugs and kisses, Mum and Dad xxxx

We tucked the poem into the floral wreath spelling out his name and then we had to get in the car and leave our baby on his own, with just words and flowers surrounding him. I cried without any care as we pulled out of those cemetery gates – all I could think about was that in just 15 days' time we should have been going to his third birthday party with balloons and cakes and a pile of presents. Instead we were headed to his wake.

The wake was at the Sacred Heart Club and I don't remember much about it or how long I was there, but I do remember suddenly feeling desperate to get away, back to my bedroom and away from all this endless chatter. I made my excuses and headed back to Mum's, where I was also greeted by a sea of faces. I went into the kitchen but soon escaped upstairs and I didn't come down again for days – I remember rather irrationally thinking, *They didn't even know my boy, why are they here?* I also felt anxious, as there were people in the house I had never seen before. I was beside myself and I just wanted it all to end – quite literally. If someone had offered to help me kill myself right then and there, I would have done it without thinking twice.

Ray has said, 'They were such dark days, we were all beside ourselves with worry for you – it was like this veil had come down and no one had any idea if it would ever lift. My little sister was unrecognisable when I looked at her – the grief had altered you physically in every way. I look back now at photos from that time and I think, *That isn't my sister*. It was like looking at a stranger.'

The weeks that followed were actually some of the worst – people often say that there is a sense of release and relief after the funeral of a loved one, but that's certainly not something I recognised. If anything the abyss just felt bigger and deeper than ever. There was nothing practical to be done and not a shred of hope to hold on to – I knew where James was now and he was lying in a cemetery. I went there a bit but I certainly didn't get any solace from my visits. In fact, in the very early days when I did go there were often strangers paying their respects and leaving flowers, gifts and teddies for James. I actually found it very touching that people would go out of their way like that for my son, they still do in fact. All these years later there is one family who send money to the flower shop opposite the cemetery on James' anniversary. They ask the florist to make up a bouquet, put it on James' grave and take a photo for them so they can see the flowers in place. I can't tell you how touching that gesture still is, every year I go there to mark the day that James was murdered.

In the immediate weeks that followed the mail continued, as did the flowers and toys. After a while all the soft toys that had been left by the railway where James had been found were collected up and sent to local children's hospitals and maternity wards. I found it too hard to keep anything associated with where he had been left to die but I knew other children could benefit hugely – at least some good could come out of it.

The funny thing about earth-shattering loss is that, much as it kills us inside, we quickly become used to it, and so the weeks after the funeral took on a weird sense of normality. I was never left alone and my family took it in turns to sit with me. We never talked about what had happened, it was just the comfort of another human being there with me.

Nobody knew what to do or say for the best when it came to talking about James. If I brought him up then people would listen and join in, but no one initiated chat about him and I understand why. In reality, no one knew how I would react and who could blame them, I am not sure I would have asked me either.

There was one person I couldn't reach and that was Ralph. I think those initial weeks after the funeral saw a distance set in between us that just got bigger as time passed – it was like rot setting in. Ralph had never been a man to talk about his feelings – it just wasn't something that came easily to him, and it was particularly hard in awful circumstances such as this. What could we possibly say to each other that could help the other or make it any better? Our son would still be dead and those boys would still be in custody waiting for their trial date. As James' third birthday approached, just four short weeks after his body had been found, I think we both hit absolute rock bottom, I certainly felt I had nowhere left to fall. Not only did I have the grief of losing James, but Ralph just stopped coming home. The best way to describe how I felt was like a wind-up toy that hadn't been fully activated – I was trying to go through the motions but sinking fast.

I suppose a trauma like the one we suffered with James was bound to highlight all the cracks in a relationship that was becoming increasingly fragile. We couldn't communicate, Ralph was either drunk or out. And none of this was helped by the fact that, when I was at my lowest ebb, I felt Ralph blamed me for losing James and taking my eye off him. Would I have done the same to him if the roles had been reversed? Probably. But I also know that, believe me, there isn't a single person on this earth who could have added any misery or guilt on top of the mountain I was already buckling under. I know it was the grief talking, but for him to throw that at me in a row felt unforgiveable. How were we supposed to move on if we couldn't stop hurting each other?

James' birthday passed and so did the rest of March, thinking back now it is simply lost time that I waded through. I was still staying at my mum's and – apart from the night I went back to look at James' things – I hadn't been able to face the flat. I was still sleeping in my sister Sheila's room, she was on the sofa, but I knew it couldn't go on indefinitely. Sheila had a little girl, Antonia, and because I couldn't face being around children she had been sent to live with her dad. I felt terrible that me staying there meant that mother and child were separated, which is something I knew I'd never have contemplated with James. It was unfair of me to expect it of her.

After a few weeks I decided to try a couple of nights at the flat, I think one of my family went ahead to tidy away some of James' clothes and toys so it didn't hit me again as soon as I walked in. I really tried to be okay there because I knew that life needed to get back to normal for the others around me. I managed three nights in all, one on my own, but I knew that I could never live there again. I saw James everywhere I looked and I knew that wouldn't ever go away, no matter how much time I gave it.

Sean contacted the council to explain that I had tried to go back to the flat and make it work but I just couldn't do it, and that it would be great if they could find me somewhere else to live. They refused, so I moved in with my sister Rita, though I still felt like I was putting people out as she gave me her son's room and he had to go in with his sister, which he hated. I pulled my weight by cleaning the house, ironing and making dinners. In fact that gave me a real sense of purpose and I loved being able to look after people again, but it wasn't my home. In a way it made the sense of loss all the harder because I had gone from running my own house and having a family to feeling like a child again.

I truly felt like there was no point in living and it was hard because the person that I wanted to talk to wasn't there. Ralph was coping with things his own way – he had his brother Jimmy and he had the pub. I had lost my son and now I felt like I was losing my marriage. I spent nights on end wondering where he was and if he was okay. I could barely help myself so I had no idea how to see him through his grief. We were imploding and neither one of us had the tools or the energy to do anything about it. We were both angry as hell and so very tired of trying to understand what was happening to us – he wanted to drink to forget and I wanted to go to sleep forever.

And then, just like a gift from God, at the end of March I discovered I was pregnant again. I truly felt like we had been saved from ourselves.

Chapter 12

The Eye of the Storm

There are no two ways about it: finding out I was pregnant saved my life. I was drowning in grief and anger and going under quickly. In fact, I would go as far to say that waking up every morning became a deep and real disappointment.

I was all over the place mentally, but I also had no idea if my body was up to the physical challenges of pregnancy. I couldn't sleep – all I saw was James when I closed my eyes so I stopped closing them, it hurt less. I couldn't swallow any food – how could I be concerned with fuelling my body when my baby was dead? People kept telling me I would get ill if I didn't eat and I remember thinking, *Good, I hope I get so ill that I die*. It sounds dramatic but it was truly how I felt – I wanted my body to give up on me, to take the decision away from me. The only way I could see the pain disappearing was to feel nothing. The weight fell off at an alarming rate, I was a tiny size six and looked like a skeleton with some skin just about covering my bones. All I wanted was my son and I couldn't have cared less about a single thing.

Obviously the pregnancy wasn't planned and I was initially completely stunned. But the shock soon turned to terror and I began to suffer from extreme anxiety about the new baby. All I'd ever wanted was a family and twice it felt like God had decided that it wasn't my path. Now that I was pregnant again, I was terrified something would happen to this child too – this was my third pregnancy and I had buried two babies. What if motherhood wasn't meant for me and, by wilfully carrying on trying to be a parent, I was putting this baby in danger too? I became obsessed. Grieving for a child is a complicated and hideous enough process, but when you add pregnancy hormones into the mix too, everything becomes much more difficult. However, once I got used to the news, the idea of holding a baby in my arms again helped lift me out of the deep pit of grief that had been consuming me – it was the lifeline we all needed.

I knew immediately that I was expecting and told Ralph my suspicions – he was shocked but, once the surprise had worn off, he was as delighted as I was. Our hearts were broken by James' death and we were both still pretty much incapable of feeling anything, but I hoped this pregnancy might give us a chance to start healing.

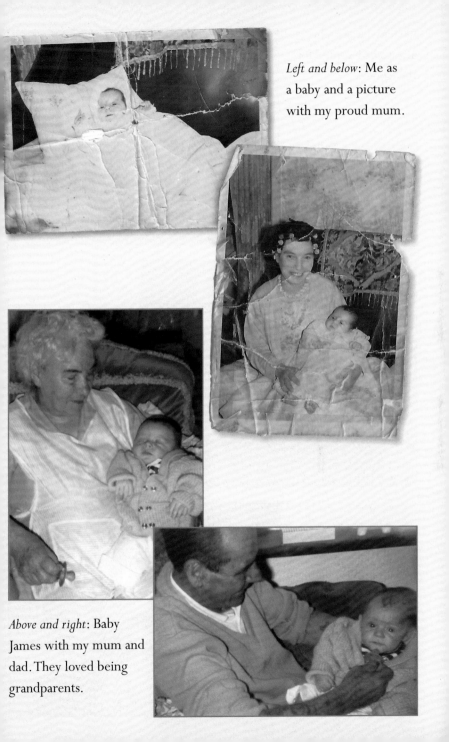

Left and below: Me as a baby and a picture with my proud mum.

Above and right: Baby James with my mum and dad. They loved being grandparents.

Cheeky James – he always had a smile for the camera.

Caught in the act and covered in chocolate after an Easter treat.

One of James' favourite games – turning the TV on and off!

Above: Celebrating my sweet boy's first birthday.
Below: Kisses for my baby – the best feeling in the world.

Above: I loved dressing James up in little outfits and his denim look was one of my favourites.

Below: Me and my boy – he made me smile every single day.

James and my mum – we saw her almost every day and they were so close.

James was such a homebody and loved pottering around
and causing mischief.

He always loved bath time,
even if most of the water
ended up on the floor!

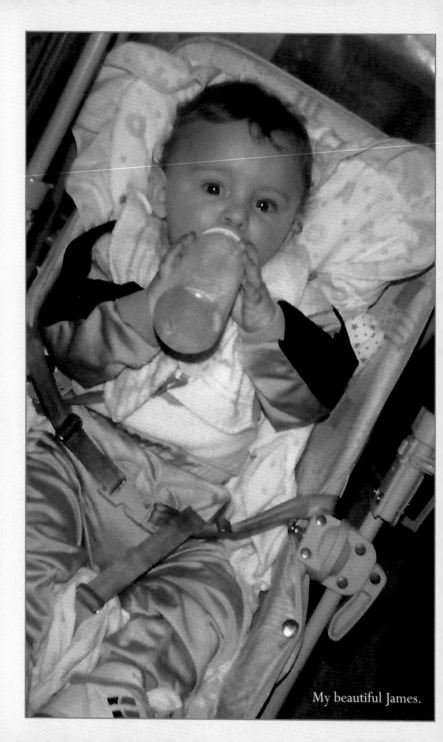

My beautiful James.

However, it soon became clear that the pregnancy was no magic solution – when people say a baby isn't a plaster to hold together a broken relationship, boy are they right. My news changed nothing; it certainly didn't stop Ralph's love affair with alcohol, if anything, the drinking sessions became longer and more frequent. In those early days, as I weighed up the world I would be bringing our baby into, I would watch him stagger home, a few days after 'popping out for a quick drink', and wonder what the hell we were doing. Instead of talking about it and working together, we both carried on doing whatever got us through another day: me growing our new baby, him blotting it out in the pub and spending time with anyone who wasn't me.

It was so soon after James' funeral, we were all still in the thick of deep, dark grief. It certainly didn't feel like a remotely nurturing or positive time, more like battling with quicksand. It was that early denial stage of grief – I kept pretending to live life, but really I was waiting for someone to tell me it had all been a terrible mistake, that it was some other poor mother who would never see her baby again. Random people were still arriving at my mum's house – they came to bring food and comfort; they offered to run errands or to take me shopping. People were only trying to help but I would look at them blankly and think, *You can't give me the only thing that will fix me, so why are you here?* No one could click their fingers to wake me up from this endless nightmare and bring me back my baby, so what was the point?

I still didn't really interact with anyone – not even with the family members who sat with me for hours on end. That didn't really change after I discovered I was pregnant. If anything I became even more desperate to be on my own. I decided to wait until my 12-week check before I told anyone apart from Ralph about the baby. I felt a bit nervous announcing my news – even though I knew the family would be happy for us, I also knew they were desperately worried about me and they would wonder if I was strong enough for another child. My mum and I were still finding it really hard to talk about James and what had happened – she didn't have the words and I didn't have the will or the energy. It sounds awful, but I just couldn't be bothered with anything at all, so finding the strength to tell Mum my news was harder than I imagined.

I took a deep breath and went into her room, sat on the end of the bed and told her she was going to have another grandchild. She looked at me for a long time; it was hard to work out what she was thinking or going to say, and finally she told me she thought it was too soon after James. I wasn't surprised. Of course she was anxious – it was impossible for any of us to contemplate the joy a new baby might bring when our beloved boy had just been murdered weeks before. But, in a way, Mum's concern and anxiety made me realise for the first time that this was meant to be.

I took her hands and I said, 'Life is planned for you.'

It didn't matter that I was trying to convince myself as much as my mum; I had to believe it – it was the only way to try and explain the pure torture we were all living through. I had to convince myself that I was meant to have this baby and be its mother. It was the only way I would survive the pregnancy and not feel as if I was betraying James.

I knew that the press would go into overdrive once the pregnancy was announced – we had been of interest before but, with this news, I had no doubt it would be off the scale. However, I was completely unprepared for the pressure and scrutiny. We all were. Actually, although he didn't dare say anything at the time, Ray was terrified for me. My baby had been murdered, his ten-year-old killers were going on trial and I was a pregnant six stone recluse too terrified to open the curtains in case the reporters who were camped outside saw me – it was no way to live. Ray didn't know how I would last in such a pressure cooker environment and he woke up every morning wondering if this was the day it would all disastrously collapse. Each day there was a new story and nothing was off limits, especially my surprise pregnancy.

I had been kept away from the press since the day James went missing, whether it was good or bad. I now understand there were all sorts of things written about me and, once the pregnancy story was out, that started happening again. Everyone seemed to have an opinion and there were definitely people who thought that I was having a new baby too quickly – as if we were trying to replace James immediately. That couldn't have been further from the truth – I was barely functioning – but that didn't stop the detractors from thinking: *Look at her, she's lost one and gone straight on to have another*. Yes, it was very soon after James' death but, in all honesty, if I hadn't been pregnant with Michael in those early months after James' funeral I wouldn't be here today. The baby became my lifeline – before I found out the news I didn't know how low it was possible for a human being to go. Did I try to kill myself? Not quite. Did I think about killing myself? Absolutely. Very often and in great detail.

Once everyone knew, the family stepped in to try and protect me as much as possible because the press couldn't get enough. They were still printing pictures of James on a daily basis and they wanted interviews about the pregnancy. It was a strange thing to fixate on, but one of the things that upset me most about the coverage was the fact that the papers kept calling James 'Jamie'. I have never understood why they did that – perhaps it sold more papers? But whatever the reason, I hated it. It was one thing to feel that the world had hijacked your child in death, but when they started calling him by a different name, it felt as if he wasn't mine anymore.

I felt I was constantly firefighting, and I look back now and realise I had no time to grieve. I couldn't keep my head above water and so it was decided that I should leave the area for a while. The police and my family thought this might help calm down the press intrusion and encourage them to move on from my mum's doorstep. They were also very worried about my health and the well-being of the baby too – the strain was immense and it wasn't doing either of us any good. I felt terrible for the rest of the family – they were being doorstepped at work and my sisters were harassed as they took their kids to school – it was endless. I hoped that if I wasn't around they would lose interest, so I went off to stay with some friends in the south of England. It didn't really help the situation with Ralph, as he didn't come with me. And it didn't stop the press – the interest just seemed to get worse.

* * *

As the months passed, I grew bigger and the pregnancy progressed well. But the elephant in the room was the imminent trial. I look back now and I find it extraordinary that the entire time it took me to grow my baby, the police were pouring over every small detail of our son's death preparing their case against Thompson and Venables – talk about a parallel universe. As with my pregnancy with James, this third one was an angst-ridden time as I spent nine months convinced I didn't deserve a new baby. The stress was immense and my emotional state was worrying – the grief was so deep I didn't ever think the wounds could heal and I was guilt-ridden because I was looking to the future. If I felt the baby kick and got excited or laughed and smiled, I immediately felt disloyal to James because for a split second I was focused on the new baby and not him. I practically lived at the hospital and probably had a scan almost every week. I was so paranoid that something would happen to the baby, that somehow the misery I felt would seep into my unborn child.

Ralph and I tried our best to carry on as normally as possible as the trial date approached but, if I am brutally honest, it was clear that there wasn't much in the way of a marriage to salvage. Everything died with James that cold February day, including the closeness Ralph and I had shared. The initial distance that set in with Ralph's drinking would have required some serious effort to undo and we just didn't have anything to give. The problem was that all our energy was taken up surviving a day at a time and preparing to see our boy's killers get what they deserved – there wasn't an ounce of anything else left over. We were both so focused on getting justice and making sure those two boys were punished for what that had done to our family, we ignored each other.

We still didn't have a home, as I couldn't go back to where James had lived, so we were pretty much living separately – me at my sister's and Ralph at his mum's – and the months rolled by. I found the arrival of summer really hard. It sounds silly, but as long as the weather stayed cold and wet it was the same as when James had been here, so he was close to me. Watching the leaves and flowers coming out and the days getting longer meant time was marching relentlessly on and my baby wasn't here. I found one of the scariest things about those early months was the worry that James was getting further away from me and that there would come a point where he had been dead longer than he'd been with me.

The police were still being fantastic – Albert, Mandy and the whole liaison team kept in close touch and that contact increased as the trial grew closer. As with James' abduction and murder, the details given to me were sketchy – it was very much a need-to-know basis. That suited me fine, although as the trial date drew closer I suppose my interest intensified – I was absolutely terrified that Thompson and Venables would get off because they were so young. The thing about me is that I can't help asking questions and I am quite good at reading people, so there were a few awkward moments where I asked for an answer that was clearly hard for the police team to give without adding detail they knew would deeply upset me. It was a delicate balancing of what would come out in court (and therefore be all over the papers) and their wish to protect me.

By the time the court date arrived, I would be eight months pregnant, and there was great worry that the stress of the trial would bring on early labour. The pregnancy had been relatively straightforward, which felt like a miracle, all things considered. It had been such an emotionally complicated experience – grieving for one baby while knowing another one was coming along. With the trial a couple of weeks away I was deeply sad. I tried to be hopeful and look to the future so the baby being born would feel joyous – yet there wasn't a shred of happiness in me. I couldn't get Kirsty's stillbirth out of my head. That had happened when we were carefree and happy, so goodness knows what might happen as my son's murderers went on trial.

It was decided early on between the police, my family and my doctors that it would be best for me to stay away from the trial. I didn't put up much of a fight – I had no idea what to expect but, whatever it was, deep down I knew I couldn't face it. I especially didn't want to be under public scrutiny, hearing terrible details about my son's death for the first time in front of the boys who killed him. I most definitely would not do anything to put my baby's health in danger.

That said, I was determined that James would be properly represented, so in the end we decided that Ralph, Ray, Phil (Ralph's brother) and Dennis (my brother-in-law) would go and they would report back at the end of each day. A week or so before the trial started, we had a long visit from Albert Kirby and Mandy Waller to talk us through what we could expect. I had lived the past eight months in a bubble – my family had swung into action any time I walked into the room and the TV was on with people talking about James.

The radio stayed switched off in the kitchen now, just in case, and everyone stopped having newspapers delivered. Friends knew not to bring up anything they might have read and they also closed ranks on the press who tried endlessly to get stories from them by feeding them bits of information about Thompson and Venables, hoping they would get angry and speak out. I was so well isolated and cared for, but now, not even my nearest and dearest could protect me from the circus that would surround us for the next few weeks.

On the one hand I felt relief that the date was finally here, the eight-month wait for James to have his day in court had been torture, but now it was here all I felt was dread and fear all over again. When Albert and Mandy came round they sat Ralph and I down and gently talked through the process. I remember clearly watching their mouths move and thinking, *I shouldn't be sitting here talking about James like this; I should be talking to him.*

Sean was there too, on hand to try and explain anything we didn't understand. It was explained to us that, because both boys were ten years old, the law presumed they were incapable of committing an offence like James' murder, so it was the job of the prosecution to not only prove that they knowingly killed James, but also that they knew it was wrong. The law was changed in that regard in 1998 by the new Labour government, I believe as a direct result of James' murder.

It seemed that anyone charged with murder, particularly

when that person is ten years old, rarely puts up their hand to say, 'Yes, I am guilty.' Obviously two such young children would have been advised to plead not guilty, so in reality there was always going to be a trial. Some people assumed it would be a formality and that a guilty verdict was a given, but that was never the case.

As the date drew nearer it was decided to move the trial out of Liverpool to Preston, mainly because of heightened feelings, but also because the defence for Thompson and Venables argued they wouldn't get a fair trial with so much anger swirling around.

It was obvious that detail would start to emerge of James' last hours and the police wanted to make sure we were prepared for that. It had been Ralph's intention to go every day and look his son's killers in the eye, so the police wanted to make sure there were no surprises in court. As I decided not to go and didn't want to know the detail at that time, Albert Kirby took Ralph aside and explained what they would be putting forward as evidence. Albert Kirby and the team had led a very thorough investigation and he was also sensitive to what Ralph and I did and didn't need to know. I only found out afterwards that the decision was taken, in conjunction with the Crown Prosecution Service, not to use all the evidence they had for the trial because they thought it would be unnecessarily upsetting for us. They selected the evidence they needed to secure a conviction but didn't put everything in the public domain.

Sean was also heavily involved during this time and knew far more than me. He comments, 'It was a police decision to keep back the detail from you and that became doubly important once you discovered you were pregnant with Michael. Did Ralph know everything? I don't know and to be honest I am not sure I know everything. Albert Kirby was very concerned with the welfare of the two of you; he is a Christian man and he felt strongly that he didn't want to cause the family unnecessary distress by making public information that pointed to a possible sexual motivation, especially if it wasn't necessary to secure a conviction. There are some things that I genuinely don't know if you know, because we haven't ever talked about it.

'The prosecution was represented by the very senior and experienced Richard Henriques QC. Everyone went through the evidence with a fine-tooth comb and said, "This is relevant, we are going to use this. This isn't, so we won't use that." Albert was always keen not to upset you unnecessarily, so if the jury didn't need to know something he made sure they didn't and he didn't volunteer anything extra.

'Perhaps, as things subsequently turned out, there is an argument that, had everything Venables and Thompson did to James been put in the public domain, then they would have been given longer sentences and James might have had the justice he deserved. At the very least they would have seen the inside of an actual prison.'

Either way, everyone did what they felt was right at the time, and Ralph and I were as prepared as was possible given the circumstances. As 1st November arrived, the reality of it all suddenly hit me: we were about to hear the terrible truth of how our son had died at the hands of two ten-year-old children and we also had to share that with the waiting world.

Chapter 13

The Trial

Just before it started, the police took the time to explain again the realities of the trial. You'd have to be on another planet to even question if those two were guilty of the crime, but that wasn't the issue or what needed proving. Getting a guilty verdict rested on whether it could be proven that Thompson and Venables understood that abducting and killing James was wrong. So the job of the prosecution wasn't to prove the crime – that was obvious from the fact that the only time I could spend with my son was in a cemetery – but it was to establish that Thompson and Venables knew right from wrong, good from bad, truth from lies. If that could be proven beyond doubt, then it followed that they knew full well what they were doing and understood that their actions would hurt and kill James. The irony was not lost on me that in the end, it all came down to whether or not the two boys who murdered my son had any understanding of morality.

At that time, English law demanded of its juvenile killers an ethical awareness that adult murderers are not required to possess. The trial became a slightly odd forum for discovering the intensity of Thompson and Venables' malice. Some argued that being children actually played against them – the jury was able to hear details of their characters and behaviour patterns in a way that wouldn't have been allowed in an adult trial – so the court was told about their shoplifting and truancy and their torture of animals.

I can't really remember the exact detail of the first morning of the trial, although I do recall everyone being worried about setting off in good time, as it was 40 miles away. I think I went to my mum's to spend the day there with her and my sisters as Ralph, Ray, Phil and Dennis set off with the police and a group of family and friends. Everyone was very quiet and dressed in smart suits. Other than that, nothing really stands out. I have since found out bits and pieces about that day – the press were swarming everywhere and, most bizarrely, there was a queue of normal people wanting a seat in the courtroom to hear the grisly details of what had happened to my son. To this day I still don't understand why anyone would queue from 7am to be given one of the 48 seats available in the public gallery. It is incomprehensible to me that anyone would willingly subject themselves to hearing awful information about unspeakable things being done to a baby they had never met. In a way it made me all the more certain I had made the right decision to stay away. Ralph, Phil, Dennis and Ray had reserved seats in Court One, which also meant an uninterrupted view of Thompson and Venables as they walked up the 23 steps to take their seats in the dock.

Ray said that first day passed in a bit of a blur. The morning was taken up with legal arguments and the actual trial didn't begin until after lunch. One of those legal arguments was from David Turner QC who tried to argue that the judge should grant a 'stay' due to 'abuse of process'. Basically he was arguing that because of excessive and biased reporting by the media, the boys would not receive a fair trial – that would have stopped the case there and then and meant all charges were dropped. Thankfully that was overruled and things carried on as planned. For our family, and Albert Kirby and his team, that would have been our very worst nightmare.

It was a huge relief to my family to know that things would be proceeding, but any sense of calm was soon put to an end once Thompson and Venables entered the courtroom. Ray often describes his sense of shock at seeing them for the first time and it was something I shared when I faced them both on the final day of the trial. It is almost impossible to explain how small they looked in such a grown-up and severe environment, like little toys on a grown-up canvas. They were just two short kids dressed in their school uniforms.

That initial sighting was so extraordinary it was like being punched in the chest.

As Ray has told me, 'I went into that courtroom every day, representing our baby James, taking the burden as much as I could from you and Ralph. Ralph went on the first day but couldn't go back in after that until the final day, when he came with you for the verdict. Every single day was a living hell, finding out certain terrible things right there in public and having to sit on your hands, it was the hardest thing ever. All I kept thinking was, "How could anyone do to a child what those two children did to my nephew?"'

I don't know how anyone associated with James could have spent days on end just yards from the boys who ended his life. It was so brave of my family to do that for us and I will always be grateful to them for going through it.

On the surface at least, the court proceedings appeared to be civil and polite. This was in direct contrast to the animal-like awfulness of what those two boys had done to my son, and that became obvious as the trial got going. David Harrison, who covered the trial for the *Guardian*, said the 'descriptions of what happened to James Bulger whisked us off to a darker world. And the emotions of the case exploded into the courtroom. Witness after witness broke down, sat down, drank water, struggled to regain their composure. At times it felt like the whole court was on the verge of a nervous breakdown.' One witness, when asked why he didn't intervene as he saw Venables and Thompson dragging James along the road, said, 'It's usually grown-up fellas who do that sort of thing, what kid kidnaps a toddler to do him harm? What normal person would even think that's what was happening if they saw it?'

David Harrison's article continued, 'The Bulger family are wise to stay away. There is no catharsis to be had at Preston Crown Court. Only incomprehension. And misery.'

As I didn't attend the trial my grasp of the ins and outs isn't as detailed as some other accounts, but I was told how the proceedings worked. The jurors were sworn in and the charges were read out. There were three charges in total and Ray says Thompson and Venables didn't even flinch as those crimes were recounted to the court: the attempted abduction of a child belonging to Mrs Diane Power; the abduction of my James; and the murder of James. Venables and Thompson had already entered a not guilty plea at an earlier hearing, so there was no need for them to speak. Apparently, as the charges were read out they carried on fidgeting and generally mucking around, the severity of the words having absolutely no impact whatsoever.

Richard Henriques QC did not mess about as he opened the trial – he went straight in with the cold, hard facts of what happened to my boy on that bleak February day and he spared no detail. I don't know all that he said, as some of his opening argument contained information about what they did to James that I choose not to know, but the message was stark and unavoidable:

James Bulger was two years and eleven months old when he died. He was the only child of Ralph and Denise Bulger and they live in Kirkby. They always called him James and we will refer to him as James throughout this trial. He died on Friday, 12th February this year.

In short, these two defendants abducted James from his mother in a shopping precinct in Bootle. They walked him some two and a half miles across Liverpool to Walton, a very long and distressing walk for a two-year-old toddler. James was then taken up to a railway line and subjected to a prolonged and violent attack . . . Both the defendants are now eleven years of age. On Friday, 12th February, they were both ten years and six months old, both born in August 1982. Notwithstanding their ages, it is alleged that they both intended to either kill James or at least to cause him really serious injury and they both knew that their behaviour was really seriously wrong.

Not only is it alleged that they both abducted and murdered James, but that they attempted, prior to abducting James, to abduct another two-year-old boy. He was in the same shopping precinct three hours earlier.

Ray says that you could have heard a pin drop as all this was read out, the crowd already transfixed by the grim details and the sheer calculated evil of which these two primary school children stood accused. The forensic evidence was then outlined, including bloodstains on shoes belonging to

Venables that matched a DNA sample taken from James. There was also other forensic evidence that tied in directly to the objects they used to kill James. That first day was a barrage of information – none of it welcome or easy to process – all of it only underlining the fact that everyone in that courtroom was in the presence of pure evil.

Henriques cited the attempted abduction of Diane Power's child before James, and other evidence that, at 12:30pm, three hours before they took James, a mother of two children saw Thompson and Venables and overheard Thompson say, 'We will take one of these.' She thought they were going to shoplift, but Venables confirmed in his interview that they were referring to taking a child out onto the road, where the buses and taxis pulled in and out, and pushing the child into the oncoming traffic to make it look like an accident.

* * *

While all this was going on, I was at home with my mum and sisters, where we all edged around each other – terrified of a real conversation. I know now that Mum was desperate to ask questions but didn't dare, so silence remained our friend. We had no idea what was going on inside that courtroom and, although I was grateful for it, having to rely on a second-hand account was still hard. When Ralph came home after that first day and said he couldn't go back, I think that's when I really allowed my mind to engage with all the possibilities. He had been so determined to go every single day – what on earth was being said in that courtroom that meant he couldn't go back? To be honest, I didn't ask. I don't remember much about that first evening but I know that Ralph changed out of his suit and went straight to the pub, leaving poor Ray to fill me in as best he could.

Ray says now, 'My job was difficult. I had to almost protect you from yourself – from your inquisitive nature. I definitely had to filter what the police were telling me. They were giving it to me in a hard way and my job was to take that information and dilute it so that you could process it, and then live with it. Every conversation started with "it's possible this has happened" or "there's a suspicion this has happened". Relaying that back to a grieving mother who doesn't even know the half of it was such a responsibility, sometimes I felt like I was sinking. There was also the way that James was found. Knowing that you didn't know that, it felt like I spent my whole time trying to find ways to relay the most terrible information to my broken baby sister. Just that one extra word could have tipped everything over the edge and the sense of responsibility was huge. Sometimes I am surprised I'm still alive myself really if I am honest: the funeral followed by the trial and having to sit and hear all that pure evil, it nearly finished me off, so God only knows how you are still standing. You are like a statue – so strong, amazing really.'

I will always be grateful to Ray for shouldering that burden.

All my brothers and sisters rallied round me brilliantly, but it was different for him as he was on the front line finding out things that I still don't know. My other brothers and sisters were able to provide a safe cocoon, as they also didn't know the details; ignorance really was bliss for them.

* * *

Having the first day out of the way didn't really bring any great relief, just the knowledge that it would have to be endured all over again the next day, where more awfulness would come to light. Worse than that for Ray, more air would have to be shared with the two boys who had caused all this pain and yet seemed utterly incapable of internalising what they'd done. They were sitting almost within touching distance of the family they had decimated and appeared oblivious to the consequences of their evil.

Day two focused on Richard Henriques reading out portions of police interview transcripts belonging to Thompson and Venables. I am not sure if that's the first time that each of them heard what the other had to say about the day in question, but they both soon realised that each of them was blaming the other for everything. I am sure that listening to the slow shift in their stories as they each tried to save their own skins is fascinating for psychologists writing papers on child killers and psychopaths – to my family it just reinforced how sly these two ten year olds were and how there was no doubt they had the mental capacity to understand what they had done. The level of manipulation and deceitfulness was beyond comprehension – they went from complete denial that they had even been at The Strand shopping centre to simply trying to pass the buck, all the time forgetting that this was my child's life they were playing with.

They were talking about the baby I had grown and loved more than life itself, the child I had nurtured but taken my eyes off for a split second. They had snuffed out everything he was and all that he could have become, and they had no care – as if they were arguing over who had stolen a bag of sweets. I found it particularly hard that we were all supposed to genuinely question if two ten year olds might not know good from bad – James was two years old and he knew right from wrong. It seemed inconceivable to me that we should even be questioning it in two boys so much older.

The interview transcription went on and on. What became clear to everyone was that they both definitely had a clear understanding of DNA and the implications of having James' blood on them. This was backed up by a police officer involved in their interviews, who said: 'Venables and Thompson admitted being in The Strand and that they saw James. They described the clothes he was wearing in great detail, proving that they were in his company for a long, long time. The breakthrough was when Venables asked if you could get fingerprints from skin. It was obviously playing on his mind after he had given his fingerprints on arrival at the station. Thompson later confessed that he and Venables had taken James from the shopping centre. It was obvious he was telling the truth as his feet twitched violently whenever he had to say anything about James – it was the most obvious giveaway and the only time I truly believed anything he was saying.'

The court was then told that Venables admitted to his own mother that he had killed my baby, but only once the tape was off. He later repeated this admission to the police at the same time as implicating Thompson. Ray describes it as being surreal – listening to childish 'he said, she said' and knowing it was about the life and death of my son. I believe that jurors were then shown very graphic photographs, inducing tears in some, and then witnesses were called – there were 37 in total. That meant there were 37 strangers who had seen my baby after I last had – seen him on the way to his death while I was still searching frantically, hoping he was inside the shopping centre. The last person saw him just minutes before he lay dying on a railway track, possibly at the same time I was running from shop to shop shouting his name.

Obviously the witnesses were a key part of the prosecution case. Albert Kirby and his team had organised identity parades for the nearly 40 witnesses who had seen Thompson and Venables dragging James along that day. Thompson had agreed to do his, but Venables requested to postpone his twice as he was too upset.

It was hard to know that my baby had encountered nearly 37 people on the journey to his death, all those individuals who could have intervened and saved his life. Do I blame them? Of course not. They weren't the ones who had woken up that morning with evil on their minds. They didn't end my baby's life, and I know many of them suffered hugely as a result of what happened to James – I wouldn't wish that level of guilt on anyone. I will never forget my own initial relief the first time I saw those boys leading my son away, convinced that two children could never do anything bad to him, so why should they have thought any differently?

The witnesses' testimony was combined with the CCTV footage, and was the only time that Ray had to leave the courtroom. He says that for him that was the moment James started to be murdered and he just couldn't sit there and watch it knowing there was nothing to be done, 'What you wanted to do was reach into that video, grab hold of James and get him to safety. But you knew it was too late.'

I know that some members of the press echoed Ray's sentiments, with one journalist remarking, 'I think what made it so perfect for the front page was that we were almost getting to see a murder unfold before our very eyes. As soon as those pictures were released, it was like watching it happening in the moment, because those images of him being led away came after we already knew the outcome. When the police saw footage of James being led over the dual carriageway, it was then that they realised he hadn't been taken by the two boys, dumped and then picked up by an older man. It was those tiny boys who couldn't get over a wall, they were the ones who had taken him and killed him. I think even the police didn't have a clue how to understand that and we were watching it all happen live. As soon as I saw the video footage I knew this was going to be huge – for the first time we had seen a murder on TV. That is definitely part of what makes those stills so hard to look at.'

Further on into the trial the court heard from the psychiatrists assigned to the case. Thompson, on the advice of his lawyers, didn't see the Home Office forensic psychiatrist, but shortly before the trial he was interviewed by Dr Eileen Vizard, a child psychiatrist who has worked for over 35 years with children and families when serious abuse and violence has occurred. Her clinical interests include forensic child and adolescent psychiatry, including expert witness work in both family and criminal courts. Her evidence was called by the prosecution and she was asked whether, in February of that year, Thompson would have known the difference between right and wrong and, specifically, whether it was wrong to abduct and injure a child. She said that she did not know categorically but that, 'If the issue is based on the balance of probabilities, I think I can answer with certainty.' Of course in criminal cases evidence isn't based on the balance of probabilities, it is reasonable doubt. But Dr Susan Bailey, the Home Office forensic psychiatrist who saw Venables on several occasions, had no doubt that he knew the difference between right and wrong.

The evidence read out was mostly devastating, no matter which side it came from, but I have been told that some of the most poignant words of the week were mine. My statement, made just after James went missing on the Friday night, was read out by the barrister, and one newspaper reporter said, 'Those words were enough to crack the flintiest of hearts.'

I remember very clearly being asked to describe James, to help the police and volunteers frantically searching for him, and I'd said: 'James' hair is ready for cutting, his eyes are really blue, but in his right eye he has a brown streak. He also has a full set of baby teeth.' I think I added that he loved anything to do with trains – something that turned out to be horrendously ironic – and described his outfit in great detail. Those words were said when I still had so much hope that this nightmare would end; they were the words of a mother who believed, against the odds, that her child was still alive and would come home. As another person in court that day later said, 'It was the use of the present tense that finished me off.'

As witness after witness took the stand there were only two people who remained unmoved by what they were seeing and hearing.

Those who took to the stand included the Home Office pathologist who described how James died and other experts who went through the evidence to explain exactly how the forensics put Thompson and Venables squarely at the scene. There were also testimonies from other various child psychologists who tried to climb into the minds of these two child killers and then, finally, the evidence given by the police who had fought so hard for our son. This also involved airing more of the lengthy interview recordings – the hours of painstaking questioning carried out by the force. I remain so grateful that I didn't have to listen to their childish voices denying all they had done to my son. I can only imagine how hard it must have been for those officers to survive hours of questioning children about the most heinous crime and then going home to their own. To know the true depths that people can sink to is a terrifying thing and means you can easily exist in a permanent state of fear – I know that more than most.

* * *

Meanwhile, life outside the courtroom took on a familiar pattern – Ray came home every night, accompanied by either Mandy or Jim, and between them they would debrief me and Ralph as much as possible on what had happened that day. I would wait for them by the window, then let them come in and get their shoes and jackets off. I'd put the kettle on and deliberately wait, careful not to ask them anything straight off; they all walked in looking pale and exhausted, as if they had aged in that courtroom and on the journey home. They would tell me all that I could stand, then Ralph would go to the pub and I'd go to bed. Sometimes Ralph and I discussed what we had been told, but most of the time all we could manage was a quick hug or a look. Often there was simply a silent acknowledgement that this was hell on earth; not living, just survival really, ticking off one day at a time.

The press presence was more intense than ever. There was no way I could even go out for a pint of milk, so I didn't leave the house at all unless I had a hospital appointment. I can count on one hand the number of times I went out in six months. As Ray says, 'You became a proper recluse, terrified to go out in public, terrified of life really.'

I actually had an antenatal check-up scheduled for the first week of the trial and Ralph came with me. It was a rare united moment and we couldn't help but sneak a smile at each other when the consultant told us that the baby was doing brilliantly. Despite everything, it seemed that this baby was a fighter and determined to be part of our family come what may. During that trial, as I felt my baby kick defiantly, it certainly seemed as if our unborn child was stronger than all of us put together.

Chapter 14

Guilty

Wednesday, 24th November 1993, was the day that 12 complete strangers decided if my son would get the justice he deserved. The morning of the verdict felt as flat as any other – every day since the one James went missing had felt as pointless as the next. Obviously my biggest fear was that they'd walk free; it was a terror so deep that I could feel it eating away at my insides. A not guilty verdict would truly render every single hour of pain worthless. It was so awful that I couldn't even entertain the idea, but at the same time I was aware that a guilty verdict wouldn't give me what I really wanted – James was dead and nothing would change that.

If I am really honest, my hatred for those boys was deep and I was dreading confronting them, I had no idea how I would feel and what would happen. Ray had warned me not to expect any kind of suitable reaction from Thompson, Venables or their families – if their behaviour throughout the trial was anything to go by it would be the opposite.

I certainly had no idea how much contact Ray had had to endure with the families of Thompson and Venables. Early on in the trial it had all got far too close for comfort. Ray told me, 'Late morning on the second day of the court hearing I decided to do the coffee run – anything to pass the time while we were waiting for the court to reconvene. I was getting impatient. So I asked Jim Green and the rest of the police team if they wanted a drink and in the end I had a request for 12 teas and coffees! I went off to place my order and was leaning over the counter when I felt somebody brush past me, knocking me sideways.

'At first I just thought the person had accidentally barged into me and I turned around to see one of the boys' mothers staring straight at me. I knew immediately she had done it on purpose and I just had to take a deep breath and say quietly to myself, *This is wrong*. Their camps were sticking together and stood lined up against the opposite wall looking at me, pointing me out as your brother.

'I kept telling myself I was there for James and I didn't want to let anyone down by losing my temper. Sean was fantastic and kept reminding us to maintain our dignity. I was proud of how we all handled it looking back; we did baby James proud.'

The world had gone mad: their children were on trial for

killing my baby and their mothers didn't even seem sorry. These feelings only got worse as the trial went on and my family saw their behaviour in court; I was repeatedly warned that I would find it hard.

Ray says now, 'People often ask me what it was like seeing those two children sat there – on raised, padded stools because they were so small – in a big adult dock, accused of murdering my nephew. But I didn't see them as children. I couldn't see them as anything. I didn't expect to feel anything really but what I did think I'd see was something etched on their faces to tell me that they understood what they had done, some kind of shame or guilt, but there was nothing there to say, "I have done something terrible and I am being punished for it". There didn't even seem to be any kind of worry at their surroundings, just nothing, and I couldn't get my head around that. They just looked out at the crowds with no care for who anyone was and the devastation they had caused or the little baby they had needlessly murdered.'

I think everyone expected them to at least find the court intimidating and oppressive – courtrooms are scary places and this one was very grand. It was really old-fashioned, like the ones you see on TV with lots of woodcarving, dark oak panels and lights. It was no place for children, especially when you added into the mix the 30-odd journalists who'd been allocated seats in order to cover the trial. That was enough pressure without also knowing that the judge had allowed the case to be transmitted to a room in a nearby office block where the rest of the media could listen live.

Perhaps Thompson and Venables felt more relaxed than expected because they'd been shown around the court before the trial in order to familiarise them with the room. It seemed that there were lots of measures in place to make things as easy as possible for them. For me it felt an over concern for their feelings that I have never understood or have really been able to deal with – my baby's comfort was of no concern to them as they dragged him to his death and away from his mummy, so it followed that theirs would be of no interest to me. No one would have known about this visit had a national newspaper not obtained the story and splashed it across their front page just before the trial began. Naturally there was outrage in Liverpool and it added weight to the argument put forward by Venables and Thompson's legal counsel that they would never receive a fair trial due to the excessive media coverage. To me it just felt like another blow to James.

On the final day of the trial, Albert, Mandy and Jim arrived at the house to find nothing but silence. Everyone was terrified the jury would find in favour of Thompson and Venables, but also worried about how I would cope with seeing them. I was told repeatedly that I didn't have to go, that I could be kept up to date in other ways, that it would be too much, but I was adamant that I had to look them in the eyes. Part of me wanted to curl up in a ball and keep my unborn baby as far away from their evil as possible, but I knew I had to do it for my James. I couldn't help him when he needed me, they had robbed me of that, but I could be there as his killers learned of their punishment. It was also really important that Thompson and Venables could see I was there and that they hadn't won – they'd taken my most precious thing, but they weren't going to take the final bit of strength I had left.

I had been reassured that I wouldn't have to hear them speak. In fact, Ray said that throughout the trial no one had addressed a single word to either of them. Apart from a few whispered remarks to their lawyers, it was like they were silent participants in their own trial as it went on around them. It seemed strange to me that witnesses would be standing just a few feet from them, describing their depraved behaviour as they sat there listening. The severity of the words had absolutely no impact whatsoever and they didn't seem to react to anything they heard, as they both looked straight ahead, still fidgeting. They kept their interaction to a minimum. I am sure their lawyers would have warned them that they each had to save themselves – perhaps it was also a final attempt to show the evil partnership was well and truly over.

It was a relief to know that I wouldn't have to say anything on the verdict day – the jurors had all the evidence and now it was up to them to make the right decision – but I still felt sick to my stomach. As we drove to the court all I could think was, *What if they are found not guilty? What if they are let out?* I had no idea how I would cope knowing they were free to walk the streets and live the life they had denied my son. I imagined them waking up in their own beds, having breakfast, maybe going to school, maybe setting out to cause someone else the pain they had caused us. That was the point – if let free they could do whatever they wanted.

Freedom would give them choices and, as far as I was concerned, that was the most dangerous thing of all. They had left their respective houses early on 12th February 1993 and had decided they would take a child; they had decided to beckon my boy away from my side; they had chosen to spirit him away and out of that shopping centre and drag him to a place where they could torment him. They had wilfully decided to kill him and place him on that track – these were two people who didn't deserve the right or power to choose anything at all, and I prayed to God the jury would see that.

* * *

We arrived at the court and I felt overwhelmed: I was only weeks away from my due date and so everything felt slower, as it always does in that final stage of pregnancy. I took in my surroundings as my family stood by my side and felt all the emotions it was possible to feel – the main one was anger. I should have been at home with James excitedly chattering about the fireworks from the week before; he should have been thinking about the presents he wanted from Father Christmas and the letter he would send to the North Pole. He would have been four months short of his fourth birthday, talking ten to the dozen and becoming so grown up. He would have been counting and dressing himself, maybe even reading – these were all the things he had just started to do when he died, tiny examples of the many milestones he didn't get the chance to achieve.

Given how outgoing he was, I was sure he'd have been popular with other kids – our home should have been noisy and chaotic, full of chatter and parties. There was so much I could imagine doing – like getting ready for him to start reception class; in fact I'd registered James for Sacred Heart RC Primary School a few weeks before he died. But most importantly, he would have been so excited about becoming a big brother and he would have been amazing. But he wasn't doing any of these things. Instead, he was lying beneath a marble slab and a pile of weather-beaten teddy bears and flowers – the very opposite of the lively three-and-a-half-year-old boy he should have been.

It was decided that I shouldn't be in court any longer than necessary, so the court set up a waiting room, allowing me to sit with family as the trial drew to a close. I decided not to go in and listen to the judge summing up, mainly because it would mean hearing details I didn't need to. The closing speech was expected to be as stark as Richard Henriques' opening argument and, at 33 weeks pregnant, it might have been too much to take. Ralph and I stayed close that day, putting on a united front for our son, but we also genuinely needed each other.

There was a big part of me that hoped, once we got the guilty verdict we needed, we could step out of this toxic state of mind we were in. Maybe a guilty verdict would help us rebuild what we'd had and allow us to raise our new baby in a united house full of love, like we had done with James. We had loved our son and we had loved each other, but we'd just been ripped apart by grief, anger, silence and alcohol. As we went into that courtroom, I realised that we had survived so much and had been happy once, maybe now we would have the strength and the will to rediscover how that felt. I wanted my marriage to work and I wanted Ralph to want to fix things too. We held on to each other, just as we had done the day we had buried James; this was the final step and I wanted to take it with him.

I could feel the nerves of the police and legal team; they were so desperate to deliver us the justice we needed and that they had worked so hard for. Sean, our solicitor, and Albert, Mandy and Jim, and all the other officers involved, looked as nervous as we did. It was a huge moment for all of us – they had grown to love James in death as much as we had in life, and I will always be grateful for the care they showed him and us.

We were warned it could take forever as the jury had retired with an exhaustive list of questions that would form the basis of their eventual verdict, but in the end it took just six hours. We were also made aware that while all of that was being taken into consideration, there was a separate argument taking place elsewhere. The judge was also hearing from counsel representing various newspaper groups who wanted the judge to lift his ban on identifying Thompson and Venables in the event of a guilty verdict. Until this point their names hadn't been released to the public; they were simply known as Child A and Child B.

It was made clear that the court was already preoccupied with their potential rehabilitation and the fact that it would be difficult to give them a clean slate if they were identified to the wider public. It felt like the world, and Liverpool in particular, was thirsty for details and justice, and I can see that the court wanted to act responsibly. But there was a strong counter argument put forward that James' murder was a crime so despicable that it was in the public interest to try and understand the circumstances that led to two now eleven-year-old boys, the youngest people on record to stand trial for murder in the UK, committing such an evil act. In the event, it was decided that the issue of identifying Thompson and Venables would be dealt with after the verdict. It was to become one of the most controversial parts of the whole case.

All thoughts of their names being released were put to the back of my mind as, some time after 5pm, we were invited into the court to hear from the jury – they had reached their verdict. I wrapped my big white cardigan around my bump, as I didn't want anyone looking at my growing baby. I clutched Ralph's hand tightly and we walked slowly into the courtroom and took our seats in the front row. Albert, Sean and the family all filed in behind us and sat down. I felt Ray squeeze my shoulder as the judge called for the boys to be brought up. My mum hadn't felt strong enough to come, but everyone else was there to hear the outcome.

To be honest all I could focus on was the moment I would see my son's killers for the first time. Suddenly there they were, my worst nightmare come true – two podgy, unremarkable children who had stolen and murdered my baby. I had built the moment up so much in my head that nothing was ever going to feel enough. Looking at them, it all seemed so pointless, such a waste for such an inexplicable and evil kick. My stomach lurched and I felt sick, but I was determined to show the same restraint everyone else had. I was here to do James proud and I wouldn't let him down at the final hurdle.

Just as I was getting used to the sight of them, I turned to look at their families, imagining how I would feel knowing my son had committed such a disgusting crime. So imagine my surprise when I saw smiles and laughter coming from their supporters as they interacted with Thompson and Venables in the dock. I just couldn't believe my eyes really and, as I looked to one side, I could see the police liaison officers in as much shock as I was, shaking their heads in dismay. They were feeling every inch of our grief, but on the other side of that little partition where evil sat, there was nothing at all to indicate why we were here – we could have been discussing the weather for all the remorse being shown. Then I saw their shoulders start shaking and I thought, *Finally, some tears*, but as I looked closer I saw they were laughing at something that had been said to them. I have no idea if they knew who I was, but that image of them is burned on my memory and will be with me until my dying day. My son was dead and they were chuckling without a care in the world.

I am sure I must have been holding my breath in anticipation and you couldn't hear a sound in the courtroom. We thought the deliberation would go on overnight but, as the 12 strangers filed back in, I prayed that their speed was a good sign. I was sure the whole room could hear my heart thumping inside my chest, aching with the stress of it all, but I tried to stay calm for the baby, who was kicking away. The court clerk asked the foreman if they had reached a verdict on count one, the attempted abduction of Diane Power's son. 'No,' came the clear voice. I remember thinking, *Oh God, they can't agree on that. Does that mean they will let them off with everything?*

Before I could think anything else the judge asked, 'On count two, have you reached a verdict on which you are all agreed?'

'Yes,' was the clear reply. The foreman was asked if they

found Thompson guilty or not guilty of James' abduction. The clear reply rang out around the courtroom, 'Guilty.' It was the same clear verdict for Venables.

I felt my shoulders lower ever so slightly as we waited for the next bit: they were guilty of taking him from my side but were they going away for my son's brutal murder?

'On count three, do you find the defendant Robert Thompson guilty or not guilty of the murder of James Bulger?'

I held by breath. I just kept thinking, *Please God, please, please, please.*

The clear voice rang out for all to hear: 'Guilty.'

'Do you find the defendant Jon Venables guilty or not guilty of the murder of James Bulger?'

'Guilty.'

* * *

I don't remember much else, apart from a jubilant 'Yes!' from someone in my family. I looked at those boys and, initially, there wasn't a trace of anything, although afterwards Venables started to sob. I remain convinced not one of those tears was for my son, more to do with the fact he had been caught and was about to be punished – his evil acts out there for the world to see. I felt Albert Kirby put his hand on my arm and lean in to kiss my cheek, leaving his tears behind. He reached over and shook Ralph's hand before embracing the rest of the family and his colleagues – they all looked exhausted. I watched Thompson and Venables preparing to be taken down as the jury left to try and reach a verdict on the attempted abduction. Not long afterwards the judge dismissed the jurors, stating that he would leave the abduction charges on file and not press them for a decision. I often wonder if being found guilty of that third charge would have meant a longer sentence.

There was chatter about revealing their identities again – the press was keen to get their evening issues to print and they would obviously sell far more newspapers if they could print names and details. The judge said he would deal with that later. For now he wanted to turn his attention to my son's killers. I don't remember everything he said, though it has been quoted often, but I recall he shifted round in his seat and looked at them squarely as he said:

Robert Thompson and Jon Venables, the killing of James Bulger was an act of unparalleled evil and barbarity.

The child of two was taken from his mother on a journey of over two miles and then, on the railway line, was battered to death without mercy and then his body was placed across the railway line so that it would be run over by a train in an attempt to conceal his murder. In my judgement your conduct was both cunning and very wicked.

The sentence that I pass upon you both . . . is

that you should be detained during Her Majesty's
pleasure, in such a place and under such conditions
as the Secretary of State may now direct and that
means you will be securely detained for very, very
many years, until the Home Secretary is satisfied that
you have matured and are fully rehabilitated and
until you are no longer a danger.

Let them be taken down.

I was clutching on to Ralph's hand, my body shaking
steadily. I finally thought that these murderers had got what
they deserved, especially when the *Guardian* reported the
following day that they were 'expected to be kept locked up
for at least 20 years'. So imagine my heartbreak when we
found out later how little time they would actually have to
serve – it was like James being murdered all over again.

Chapter 15

A Reason to Live

Once Thompson and Venables had gone down, the judge continued talking to the court, 'How it came that two normal boys aged ten of average intelligence committed this terrible crime is very hard to comprehend.' He commended Mrs Thompson and Mr and Mrs Venables for trying at all times in the interview process to get their sons to tell the truth. He went on to say, 'The people of Bootle and Walton and all involved in this tragic case will never forget the tragic circumstances of James Bulger's murder.'

He then wished me well with the new baby and said he hoped we could find some peace over Christmas – highly unlikely given this would be our first without our beloved boy. I was only half listening to the words, still in shock that it was all over but wondering why I didn't feel more jubilant or that a weight had been lifted. That veil of sadness was still there and it seemed nothing would shift it – not even James' killers being locked up.

Outside the court was a media circus – people were booing and jeering as Thompson and Venables were driven away and we were under siege. Everyone wanted to know how we felt, wanting a statement and a picture of us leaving court. I suddenly felt so very tired. I just wanted to be away from there, away from the whole world. We managed to get out of court quickly and set off for home – I remember it started snowing and thinking how ironic it was that James had died in the winter, been buried on a freezing cold day and now it was snowing on the day his killers were found guilty.

I am not sure what I expected to feel after the verdict came in, but in all honesty I just felt dead inside. Perhaps I imagined that somehow, after the trial, I would finally understand why they had murdered my baby. It is human nature to look for reasons, but I quickly came to terms with the fact that there weren't any – the police and the court had established the truth about what had happened and they had uncovered their guilt, but no one could answer my only question: why did my baby have to die? As soon as we arrived at my mum's, Ralph and I reverted to our usual patterns of shutting everything out – he reached for a drink and I went to lie down in a dark room.

We then found out that the judge decided to remove

his original anonymity order that banned reporting of their names. He replaced it with gagging orders relating explicitly to information about their whereabouts and care since 18th February 1993 and any photographs taken since that day. Put simply, the wider world would finally get to know that two boys called Robert Thompson and Jon Venables had murdered my son, but no new information about them after that date could be released.

In the absence of any juicy new details about Thompson and Venables, the press set their sights on us. The number of reporters and photographers outside our house tripled overnight and the interview requests came thick and fast – every newspaper and magazine under the sun wanted to talk to us. I coped by staying in bed, desperate for some peace before my baby arrived.

In truth I was very scared by the interest: how could I bring a baby into the world and protect it if I couldn't even get out of my own front door without hundreds of whirring cameras and flashing bulbs blocking my way? It is really hard to explain what it's like suddenly to become the focus of intense press attention like this – your every move scrutinised and reported. If you don't smile enough you are described as 'hard-faced' – a label I was given very early on and one I have never really been able to shed. If you cry hysterically then you are 'fragile' and 'on the edge' – two things that I couldn't afford to be with a baby on the way. I have never really known how you are supposed to act with cameras in your face asking you how you feel about the fact your baby was tortured and murdered after you took your eyes off him for a split second. There is no right or wrong way to deal with such horror and yet I felt judged. Somehow all the press interest just added to the feeling that we had been plunged into a nightmare world we had no idea how to navigate. I often thought back to my simple mornings with James as we watched cartoons and he ate his beloved Frosties and I would weep for every bit of normality I had lost. I had been a simple mum with a baby I adored, enjoying every minute with him. Now suddenly everyone wanted a reaction from me and all I wanted was my baby.

I eventually went back to stay at my sister's and we all tried to regain some normality as we waited to hear exactly how long Thompson and Venables would actually serve. But the interest was relentless for all of us and it felt as if James was everywhere I turned.

Sean was there every step of the way and he remembers those stressful days better than I do, 'I remember in the months after James was killed, leading up to the new baby being born, just being so aware that you and Ralph were still in the thick of Kirkby, right where it had all happened, and you hadn't been able to catch a breath.

'We persuaded you both to go to Jersey for five days, just to get out of the bubble, but there was no escaping the fact that your son had been murdered practically on your doorstep. Around the time of the court case there were times I had to drive you both into Liverpool city centre. The first day that I drove you into town from Kirkby, I realised as we approached Queens Drive that we were about to cross the route on which James had been marched to his death. I froze for a second and thought of taking a massive detour, but it would have been too obvious and would just have drawn more attention to where we were. So I turned up the radio, gritted my teeth and drove on. God alone knows how you felt!

'One day we were in the car and the radio was on. You were in the back as usual and the presenter on air was talking about the new Robin Williams film, *Mrs Doubtfire*. There had been some controversy surrounding the certification of the film. They were having an innocent enough conversation about it when suddenly the presenter said: "Well of course, in the wake of the James Bulger murder these things now take on far more significance . . . " It was like a knife through the heart for me so goodness knows what it was like for you and Ralph – you couldn't do anything or go anywhere without being brought up short. The other thing that people forget is how young you were to be going through such trauma: you were only 26 years old. It was so much pain to bear.'

Years after James' murder it was also clear that the police officers who still worked in the area found it hard taking that same route that had been James' last. Albert Kirby has said previously, 'Driving past the railway bridge you are just aware that you know in minute detail what happened on the right, on the embankment and what happened on the left. Even now, all these years later, if there is another route to be taken I will do so. Even after all this time the markings that the scene of crime officers made are still there, visible reminders of pure evil.'

* * *

That brief closeness Ralph and I experienced at the verdict resurfaced as we got ready to hear the tariff that would be set by the trial judge – this was the minimum sentence that Thompson and Venables would have to serve. We were hoping for life sentences. I felt strangely nervous – it was as if the importance of my son's life would be measured by how many years Thompson and Venables got. I was also determined that those two monsters shouldn't be allowed to destroy another family.

Late one afternoon we opened the door to Jim, Mandy and Sean, expecting triumphant faces from the people who had worked so hard to bring this case to a close. Instead what we saw were measured looks – it didn't take a genius to work out that things hadn't gone our way, but I had no idea how bad they were. There was a lot of small talk and then I couldn't wait any longer, so I asked them straight for the details.

After that whole trial, all that irrefutable and tragic

evidence, after Judge Morland's chilling promise that they would be detained 'for very, very many years', Thompson and Venables were each given a minimum of eight years. I sank down into the sofa and put my head in my hands. It had been decided that eight years was all my baby's life was worth – that wasn't even a year for every hour his severed body had lain on the track. It was nothing and it was a disgrace.

Ray was with us when we heard the news: 'When the minimum sentence came back I was reeling: it was the most ludicrous thing I'd ever heard. If somebody goes out and robs someone at knifepoint they get a longer sentence. For you, it was like they took the final bit of life you had left. It was the final insult, especially after the words of the judge – it turns out that he meant "a long, long time" in the world of two eleven year olds, not for a murdered baby in a grave or two parents ruined for life. I remember you looking at me and saying, "It's like losing him all over again". The life that you had left, they took the final bit and they left you with nothing.'

They had snuffed out my baby's life and they would be free to start theirs at the ages of 18, when they would be eligible for release. That was the age when most people flew the nest anyway and set out on their adult paths; it was as if they were being rapped on the knuckles and sent to boarding school – I just couldn't accept it. The recommended minimum sentence of eight years had come from the judge and that could be increased or lowered by the Lord Chief Justice, Lord Taylor of Gosforth and the Home Secretary, Michael Howard. The former immediately made a move to increase the minimum tariff to ten years, which made no difference to me, as Thompson and Venables would still be free at 20. I was reeling and Ralph was fuming too – it was a huge kick in the teeth and I couldn't let it go.

I knew we had to do something, but I also knew that I had the new baby to focus on. There were practical issues that needed addressing – I couldn't live with my sister forever and, when the baby came, Ralph and I needed a home so that we could be a family again. I was still clinging on to the hope that, now the trial was over and once the baby was here, we would be able to piece ourselves back together as a couple and as parents.

* * *

Ralph finally accepted that it would be too hard to go back to the flat so we started the search for a new home – we went to view lots of places not far from my mum's and the area we had been in before. It was important that we had family support with the new baby and I wanted him or her to have the special relationship that James had enjoyed with his grandparents, aunties, uncles and cousins.

After a lot of searching we found a three-bedroomed house in Kirkby and I left it to Ralph to decorate and get things ready – the last thing I could face was the idea of excitedly nesting for the new arrival when I was coming to terms with everything the past nine months had brought. I knew I had to focus on the baby now; these last few weeks of pregnancy were crucial and I had to be calm and present in that moment, as I owed it to the new baby.

I suppose that this was the start, for me, of living parallel lives: doing what was right for the people in my new post-James life, but also balancing that with the fight for James and getting him the justice he deserved. From the moment we got the ruling on the minimum sentence, I vowed that as long as there was breath in my body and a fight to be had for James, I would be the one to lead the way. Someone had to stand up for him and it didn't seem as if the courts were going to rise to the occasion.

I spent a quiet few days packing up my things at my sister's and trying to rest, but I was scared about the birth and terrified that something would go wrong. I still hadn't managed a full night's sleep since James had gone missing. I was exhausted and didn't really know which way was up. I'd been monitored so closely and the doctors were really happy with everything, but my mind was spinning. There'd been stress at every turn and not a single moment where I'd felt truly relaxed or at peace – the very opposite of how the end of a pregnancy should be.

For that reason the doctors advised me to go into hospital early for a caesarean section. I wanted to try and control things as much as I could, so I was happy to take their advice. I was anxious about having a caesarean for the first time but in a way it was reassuring that this birth would feel completely different from the others – any connection would have been too heartbreaking. The date loomed in the distance and Ralph and I tried to prepare ourselves – we were going to be parents again and we were excited, sad and terrified in equal measure. I had all my baby bits ready in my hospital bag, but I was still haunted by the idea of tempting fate – after all that had happened, any chance of further tragedy was too horrifying for words.

We went to the same maternity unit as before and were met by Dr Abdulla, who had delivered Kirsty and James. I felt at home and relaxed in his care and it was a huge relief to know that the professionals were in charge. I tried my best to keep calm but there was no escaping the fact that I was about to become a mother again and the one person I most wanted to share it with wasn't there.

I couldn't help but dwell on all that James was missing – he would have been so excited. We would have made him feel included, talking to him endlessly about the baby coming and how grown up he was now that he was a big brother. We should have been a family of four – James should have been excitedly hurtling down the hospital corridor to meet his new sibling. I could just imagine him stretching out his arms to stroke the baby, intrigued, excited and maybe a little bit jealous. Instead I would be carrying our new baby to the cemetery to meet his big brother –

Thompson and Venables had truly stolen everything that my family could have been.

* * *

Michael James Bulger was born on 8th December 1993, weighing 4lb 14oz, and I fell in love immediately. He was named after both the wonderful Father Michael, who had seen us through so much pain, and after Michael Jackson, whose music James had adored. I had spent a lot of time wondering if I'd have enough love for another child. I know that's a normal feeling for some mothers when they have a second child – your first child turns your world on its head and then becomes everything so that you can't imagine having the ability to love another in the same way. With James dead it made those feelings doubly complicated – having a new baby felt as if I was moving on without James and that wasn't something I was ready to face.

I didn't have to worry – words cannot describe the joy and relief I felt when Michael was pulled screaming into the world. I felt as though I had been holding my breath for nine months and could finally let everything out. Once they had stitched me up, Dr Abdulla put Michael straight into my arms and I studied every detail of this perfect baby who had come from so much sadness. The love I felt for him was instant, but what took my breath away was his little face – he was the image of his big brother, and that was comforting and utterly devastating all at the same time. Ralph was by my side and I think we were both overwhelmed to have another son; we had chosen to keep the sex a surprise and I'd had no idea what to expect. I am not sure if another boy made it more or less bittersweet, but I was smitten and exhausted. Michael had lots of dark, fine hair, beautiful blue eyes and rosy smooth skin – I wouldn't let the nurses take him from my arms.

I couldn't help but think back to the moment James had been born, not long after I'd lost Kirsty, and how I'd thought that everything would be okay now that he had arrived. I had truly believed that him being born alive meant that the worry was over. Now, as I looked down at Michael I realised that I had no innocence left because I had truly experienced all that was bad in the world – all the evil it had to offer – and I had no idea how I would protect this precious baby from it all.

I knew that Michael could never replace James – I didn't want him to, as that would diminish all the joy that James had brought. But, as I held my new baby tightly, I felt like I had a purpose again – finally I had a reason to live. I can hand on heart say it was the first time I had smiled since 12th February.

Chapter 16

Petition for Justice

After the birth of James I had been impatient to leave the hospital, but with Michael I didn't have much choice. It became impossible to stay at the Fazakerley maternity unit due to the large groups of paparazzi stationed outside the entrances and exits. As I'd had a caesarean, Dr Abdulla was initially keen to keep me in for a few nights, primarily so that I could rest and repair but I also think to give me a little bit of respite from the public glare. From the moment Sean had released a statement to the press announcing the pregnancy, the world had wanted to be part of our happy ending. I know all our well-wishers had the best of intentions and we were so grateful, but it was as if people thought a new baby would fix everything. Perhaps for some the idea of a new life meant that somehow innocence was restored, that the depravity of two young boys could be erased and replaced with good news.

Whatever the rationale, Michael's birth was front-page news: a lead story pretty much everywhere and generally a much-celebrated event – especially in Liverpool where the outpouring of love was immense. The night Michael was born I was sitting up in my hospital bed giving him a bottle, when I switched on the television to watch the ITV *News at Ten* headlines. Suddenly, Trevor McDonald announced Michael's birth and added, 'Both mother and child are doing well' and I remember thinking, *How do you know?!*

Just as we had been when James was murdered, we were inundated with flowers, teddies and good wishes from all over the world. It was humbling and overwhelming, but it soon became clear that all this attention was too much for the hospital. It might have been manageable if it hadn't been combined with journalists posing as patients and family members in order to gain access to my ward. There were banks of photographers waiting outside, trying to talk to my visitors and get the scoop on the new baby and how I was doing – one photographer even gave Ralph a huge bouquet to pose with outside the entrance and tried to make a story out of that. Luckily I was cocooned upstairs away from all the action, but I know that people visiting other patients found it intimidating to deal with.

It was hard on Ralph and me too. Just as the pregnancy didn't offer any kind of instant solution, neither did Michael's birth. I was in the hospital for three days and I didn't see much of Ralph. Looking back I was preoccupied with recovering from surgery and the emotion of finally having Michael; I probably didn't notice much. But my family did and they were quick to see that the gap between us was widening, even at this special time. When I asked Ray about it he said, 'It is hard to explain exactly how your marriage fell apart, from the outside the best way to describe it is that you just weren't together like you used to be.

'The love just went and it was replaced with raw anger and grief. You were hardly together – he was out drinking and you were in your bedroom, crying for your boy. You either get closer or distance sets in and you can't get back. I became aware just before Michael was born that things weren't good. Once you had the baby, we would all pile up there to see you, desperate for cuddles and to reassure ourselves that you were coping okay, and Ralph just wouldn't be there. I had been convinced that, after James, he was going to smother this new baby with love and adoration, but he was nowhere to be found. That's when I knew he either wasn't dealing with something or the marriage was on its way to being over. You were still living under a huge burden and it weighed you down; you even walked like you had the weight of the world on your shoulders; there was nothing else to go round.'

Perhaps it was inevitable as we had shut each other out, but we had Michael and he deserved two parents, so I buried my head in the sand and concentrated on bringing our baby home and making us a family of three again.

On the third day after I gave birth, the hospital staff politely came round and told me that having me there was disrupting how they functioned. I was mortified, and we arranged that I would leave the next morning. My departure offered a rare moment of humour as the hospital staff smuggled me out of the back exit. I shuffled to the waiting car with a blanket over me like I was some kind of celebrity, rather than a new mother with a caesarean scar that might give way at any time.

We were driven home by Ray and taken straight to the new house so we could settle Michael in. Mum had helped get everything ready, as there had been some baby bits at hers – I didn't want to see them in case it jinxed anything so she only brought them over once Michael had arrived safely. I had helped pick the house but had left the decorating to Ralph, as I just didn't have the will. He had also said that having something practical to focus on would help him to drink less, which was music to my ears. I let him decide everything and only had three requests: nothing dark or green, as green was for grief, and no Christmas tree up when I got home. Ever since I had met Ralph, he'd had to suffer the fact that I adore Christmas and I had hoped to pass that on to James. James was alive to see three Christmases and I went to town on each one – the build-up started in September and I loved getting everything ready. But this year was going to be different – it was our first without James, our first with Michael and the first one I had dreaded. I knew we had to get through it but I didn't want to celebrate in the slightest – a tree felt carefree and happy and neither of those descriptions applied to my state of mind.

We arrived home and I went inside to find wall-to-wall dark green – the furniture, the walls, even the curtains, and when I looked to the far corner there was a huge Christmas tree all twinkling and decorated. I didn't have the energy to protest, all I wanted was to get Michael inside and sorted – I was drained of everything. The initial post-birth euphoria was now mixed with deep sadness because I felt so lonely, guilty and sad. This wasn't how it was supposed to be, tucked up in our warm house with our new baby and James lying cold and alone in the ground. I still felt a real sense of shock whenever I thought about what had happened and I wondered if that would ever pass. I was delighted Michael was here and I wanted to be happy, but it all felt like such a betrayal of James.

* * *

We soon fell into a rhythm with Michael and he was a much easier baby than James because there was no colic. He fed well and settled quickly, which meant I got some sleep and he was very calm, almost as if he understood the sadness we felt. Right from being a tiny baby he would have this way of looking up at me that could reduce me to tears, as if he was a wise old soul sent to try and heal us all. As was the case with James, Michael's carrycot never left my side, day or night. I have always been one of those mums who keeps newborns with her at all times and Michael didn't leave my eyeline for a second. As with James, I adored those night feeds where it was just the two of us awake while the rest of the world slept soundly. I savoured those early days, but they were also filled with anxiety and pain. Having Michael there was a godsend but it also intensified my grief in a way that was difficult to describe.

Once we got home from hospital there were only two weeks until Christmas and I tried desperately to get into the festive spirit for the sake of the family. Michael had already brought so much joy to everyone – all the family loved piling round for cuddles and it was only natural we should want to celebrate that. But my heart ached for the boy who should have been excitedly getting ready to rip the paper from his presents with glee. As 25th December approached I did pop out to buy some presents but ended up just wandering around aimlessly, picking toys and clothes for baby Michael, watching other toddlers excitedly running around. I was on autopilot really and buying things I knew Michael couldn't play with, but I needed to cement him being there and distract myself from the fact that James wasn't.

Was I trying at this point to save my marriage? The honest answer is not really. Deep down I knew there was probably no way back and I suspected that Ralph had found comfort elsewhere because he was hardly ever at home. If I really think back to that time, I was so tired I don't have the words to describe the exhaustion. I was grieving, had a new baby to look after and I had a husband who would rather have been anywhere than with me. Having Michael made us both so happy but it also brought a magnifying glass to the deep, deep sadness we both felt. I am also a great believer that it takes two to fix things and both parties have to want the same outcome, but when you are both deeply traumatised no one can take the lead.

I wanted to be alive and with Michael, of course I did, but what had happened to James still had a vice-like grip on my thoughts – whether I was awake or asleep I thought about his final moments all the time; my brain never stopped whirring with the awfulness. My body was in shock too – I'd had three babies in four years; my hormones were raging and I was still so angry. I didn't give myself the time to come to terms with what had taken place – in truth it has taken me over 20 years to give myself a break and the space to process what has happened to our family, and writing this book has been a part of that. But back then I battled on, not ready to give up on my marriage or on justice for James, as well as wanting to be there for Michael – it was too much to handle.

All our previous Christmases had been big family affairs with James and his cousins running around squealing with delighted excitement and glee. James was so sociable and loved a party. At Christmas time he was in heaven with lots of food, music blaring and surrounded by all his gifts. I knew if we celebrated in our usual way, his absence would be so obvious it would kill me. So I decided we would start a new tradition that year and have the day just the three of us, our own family in our own home. We needed to start some new memories or the old ones would drown us. I explained to the family and they totally understood – they were still walking on eggshells with us and were happy to go along with whatever made it all more bearable. So I set about making a special day for us, even if it was a quieter version of the one we were used to.

I wrapped presents and planned a proper lunch with all the trimmings and did my best to enter into the spirit of it all. However, try as I might, I couldn't interest Ralph – he didn't react when I came home and showed him the presents that I had bought Michael and he didn't really join in when I tried to talk about how we would spend Christmas. Ralph stored his feelings away and was still drinking to block everything out. He also carried on spending as much time as possible out of the house and, in the end, that included Christmas Day as well. Michael and I spent it on our own, cuddled up quietly on the sofa, with me imagining James lying on his own. I had no idea where Ralph spent the day.

* * *

In a way it was a relief when Christmas was over – not least as it was another milestone we had survived. It was desperately painful to see in a New Year without James, the start of a year he would never see, another step further away from him. But it also gave me some time to reflect on what needed to be done and to re-engage with the fight to make sure that Thompson and Venables had their sentences increased. The minimum tariff felt like a joke and, now that Michael had arrived, I could switch my mind back to thinking about how to fight it.

I was also coming to terms with the practicality of my new life. Right up until the day of the verdict I was never alone – someone was by my side every minute of the day. But once the court case was over and everyone had gone back to their own lives, I knew I had to find a different focus. I had Michael and the fight for James – this was my new life and I had to get used to it. Sometimes the reality came crashing in on me to the point where I couldn't breathe, so I kept as busy as I could, hoping for any distraction at all.

Early in the new year, Sean came to the house and went through everything surrounding the sentencing one more time. I think the logistics made a bit more sense now my initial fury had died down a little – I knew that anger wouldn't get anything constructive done for James but I was determined this wasn't the end of the story.

When I talked to him for this book, Sean described the process, 'At the time, the way the system worked, the

Home Secretary would eventually make the decision on the final tariff, but he would always take into account the trial judge's recommendation, which was eight years. He would also take into account the opinion of the Lord Chief Justice and, for whatever reason, he had said ten years.

'That was it as far as you were concerned! The first battle was about to commence. You and Ralph decided you would start a petition, and I got it sheet typed up and printed off thousands of copies for you to give to family and friends. The petition demanded that Thompson and Venables should be detained for life. None of us believed that a whole life tariff would be set, but you and Ralph understandably felt that an eight-year tariff was an insult and needed to be substantially increased. You wanted Thompson and Venables to be punished for what they had done, rather than just spending a few years being looked after in a secure children's care home, which was what they got.'

Once I had decided the petition was the next step, it was full steam ahead. We organised tag teams, meaning that when I couldn't be out gathering names because I was at home looking after Michael, others would step in and stand on the streets getting as many names as possible. It was overwhelming to see how many people agreed that the sentence wasn't long enough for the crime – this was a community still traumatised by what had happened to James and they came out in their thousands to show it. I will be forever grateful for the support we were shown.

This push for justice also meant revisiting the complicated relationship that had developed with the press. As soon as the trial was over and Michael was born we were advised to give an interview to a magazine. The theory was that if people could see a picture of Michael and read an interview telling them how well Ralph and I were doing, the interest would quieten down. This would be our second big interview: early on, when we found out that I was pregnant, we were advised to do some press once Sean's statement about the pregnancy had gone out. It was a hell of a long day of interviewing and endless photos and it did me in. I remember getting back to my mum's house that night and being convinced that I was miscarrying.

That first interview didn't really make the interest in us go away either – the thirst for news obviously continued throughout the trial, something I understood and appreciated, and then continued throughout the rest of my pregnancy, which was a bit harder. The day after I came home from the hospital with Michael the press found out where we were living and stationed themselves outside our front door. I had not realised this until I opened the curtains that morning to find a bank of cameras pointing at the house. There were all these lenses poking through the trees in the garden, snapping away as I carried Michael down the stairs. I became a recluse really, living with the curtains shut day and night, existing in a house of darkness in order to protect the baby. I would phone Sean in tears regularly not sure how to make the interest go away. My brothers began to come round and sit with me during the day so that I had someone there, as Ralph was so often out. I felt safer with another person in the house with me.

We were told one more interview should make it all go away now that Michael was actually here and the trial was over, like the final piece of the puzzle. So we did a long day of shooting at a location house with Michael and in the end there was another big spread in *Hello!* magazine. But in reality it just seemed to fan the flames and they just wanted more. I had opened Pandora's box and it wasn't a pretty sight; it became a free for all.

But at the same time the support from the press was a huge boost to our campaign as they reported what we were doing and it actually led to a national newspaper backing us and printing coupons for their readers to support the petition. It was only three years after Hillsborough so I think they saw it as an opportunity to try and win back Liverpool's support. Nevertheless, they were one of many newspapers throwing their weight behind the drive to increase the sentence Thompson and Venables would serve. In a matter of weeks we managed to collect over 300,000 signatures supporting our quest to raise their tariff, and we made plans to go to London to present every single signed petition to the Home Secretary in person. We had some 4,400 letters of support agreeing that Venables and Thompson should remain in detention for life; a petition signed by nearly 6,000 members of the public, asking for a minimum period of detention of 25 years; and over 20,000 coupons cut out of a popular newspaper, together with 1,000 letters demanding a life tariff. There were only 33 letters agreeing with the judiciary, or asking for a lower tariff.

I felt proud to have achieved so much support and it gave me hope that we could get the result we wanted. The same couldn't be said of my marriage, which was hanging by a thread.

Chapter 17

Just Me and My Son Michael

Getting the justice James deserved became all consuming. Everything that he'd had ahead of him had been taken away, so going into battle was the only option. Once the signatures had been counted we all travelled to the Home Office in London to hand deliver them. We arrived with boxes and boxes of petitions – Sean, Ralph and me with Michael in my arms. It felt good to be doing something practical for James. I was convinced that Michael Howard would have to listen to so much noise and there was a real sense of achievement when we handed everything over. The press followed our trip down there and we made the front pages and the *News at Ten*, it felt like we had some real momentum but we had no idea if anyone would listen to us or how long these things took.

In the end, we didn't have to wait too long for a response

– less than two months later Michael Howard announced that, having taken everything into account, he would be raising the tariff from the original term of 8 years to a recommended minimum of 15 years. This meant rather than getting to start their new lives at 18, instead they would be 25 years old before they were released. This felt like a real victory – obviously my preference would have been a life sentence because I truly believed, and still do, that they present a real threat to any kind of civilised society. But the increase in the sentence brought a bit of peace, it felt like finally someone was listening to James' voice, finally he had a little piece of justice.

Now we had done something constructive for our boy. But, once that distraction had passed, and we had survived the first anniversary of James' death it became impossible to ignore the chaos of my marriage. As summer was on its way, it was suggested that Ralph and I get away from Kirkby – we needed some space, just the two of us, to talk through our problems and attempt to salvage what was left of our relationship. I was devastated at the thought of leaving Michael – he was still so small and we hadn't spent a moment apart. As Ray has said, 'Wherever Michael was, that's where we would find you, he never left your side.' It was going to be awful leaving him behind, but my sister Barbara offered to have him and I knew she wouldn't take her eyes off him. After what happened to James, the whole family had become as vigilant as me – in fact, people up and down the country had become so careful about child safety for toddlers that shops regularly sold out of toddler reins. Michael would be fine but I wasn't so sure the same could be said of Ralph and I – we both knew it was the last roll of the dice.

Ralph organised the trip and told me that we were going to stay with his uncle in Australia. A friend of ours, Ste Linder, had put on a series of events in order to raise money specifically to help us get away, so we used it to pay for flights. It was such a hideous thought, being so far away from my baby, but I told myself that I owed it to Michael to be able to look him in the eye and tell him I tried everything to keep our family together.

The day of our departure arrived and I was so distraught that, when the taxi arrived, I was curled up sobbing on the sofa. My brother had agreed to come to the house and watch Michael until my sister could arrive to collect him. Ralph was the first out of the door with the bags – I just couldn't bring myself to leave my baby boy. I stood by the door, clinging on to the doorframe and wept until my brother eventually coaxed me into the waiting taxi.

We were away for a fortnight – in all honesty I couldn't have managed any longer without Michael. The time away was much needed, it allowed us to focus on each other and talk a lot of things through. We were both lost and hurting, locked in our own version of grief, but I felt confident that we could try again. We had married because we loved each other and we had made three beautiful children, it would take work but it felt like we could come back from this very dark place if we both tried. I definitely boarded the plane home with hope for our future and this was reinforced as we took off and Ralph turned to me and said, 'I know what I want now, I want us to work as a family.'

I hoped the affair I suspected him of having was over and that we could really concentrate on our family. I was delighted but part of me did wonder if it was the drink talking, as he'd already had quite a few before the flight. Either way, it was what I wanted to hear and meant we were on the right path.

We landed and the first thing I did was rush to Barbara's to pick up Michael, my heart bursting with excitement at seeing him. I felt like I had been away forever even though it was only two weeks. Secretly, I was terrified that he might not recognise me – it was a long time to be separated and we have never been apart for that length of time since. I rushed through the door to scoop up my baby. Once we had thanked Barbara and had a cup of tea, we got a taxi home and Ralph brought the suitcases in from the car and put them in the hallway before disappearing. After a while, he came downstairs and shouted that he was popping out and would be back soon – and that was how my marriage ended. I shouted, 'Bye, see you in a bit,' and he left for good.

I fed and bathed Michael before putting him to bed, wondering where Ralph was and if he was okay. My brother

Gary came round so I made dinner and we watched some TV to distract me, but I couldn't settle. I was pacing around and eventually pulled back the curtains to look out of the window. The first thing I noticed was that the car wasn't on the drive – it had been there earlier after Ralph had gone out, and now it wasn't. I felt scared – the car couldn't have just disappeared, it must have been stolen, which made me feel very vulnerable in the house with Michael. I called the police to report it stolen, giving them all the details, explaining that I was with my brother but that I didn't know where Ralph was.

The police came to the house a few hours later to let me know that they had found the car with Ralph in the back seat – and he hadn't been alone. Something shut down in me right there and then, there was no going back. I had lost James and now my marriage was over too. Ralph was having an affair and I didn't have the energy to try and compete with her, I didn't feel like I should have to after all we had been through together.

I went upstairs to check on Michael and realised that it was just my boy and me now, and as long as I had him I would be fine. I got into bed and couldn't sleep but, in truth, I felt a bit relieved – I could stop fighting for something I knew deep down I couldn't save. I didn't have to go to bed anymore worrying about where my husband was, what he was thinking or who he was with. I was devastated that we hadn't made it, but there was also another reality: Ralph was also the only other person who could comprehend the utter devastation I felt about our son. We had made him together and we had buried him together and I thought that bond would see us through, but it wasn't enough to save us and I had to come to terms with that.

I remember lying there and thinking, *I don't know if I have the energy for this*, as I knew there was a rocky road ahead. In less than 18 months my simple and perfect life as a wife and mother had imploded. The day that Thompson and Venables stole my son from my side, they lit a match underneath everything I had and it all went up in flames. As time marched on it became clear there was nothing to be salvaged from the wreckage and the aftershocks just kept coming. But I had Michael to look after and James to fight for, so that's what I did.

One of the hardest things was the thought of telling people. Even though those close to us knew that things were tough, everyone expected us to pull it back together after Michael arrived. I also knew that the press would be all over the news as soon as it broke – it was perfect headline fodder: 'Heartbroken parents of murdered baby Jamie in shock split.' It would mean going back to those dark early days where every grisly detail surrounding the murder was endlessly raked over and my baby's face was on the front of every newspaper stand. My heart felt heavy at the thought and those old feelings of wanting to shut out the world descended dangerously again. Except this time I had no option – I couldn't just pull the curtains and climb under the duvet, I had a baby who needed me.

I was anxious about telling my family – they had finally stopped worrying so much about me and gone back to focusing on their own lives, which was a huge relief for me. We still saw each other all the time, but that raw anxiety for my state of mind had subsided and I know they all felt relieved that Ralph and I had Michael to focus on. They'd all done so much for us, pausing their own lives in order to hold up Ralph and I – the last thing I wanted was for them to feel responsible for me now that Ralph had gone. Initially, I decided to keep the news to myself as much as possible, so although I told my brothers and sisters, I didn't tell my mum. She had struggled so much over the last year – losing my dad and then watching me bury my baby had left her totally altered. Her world was still spinning and all the stress meant she was exhausted and so terribly sad, I couldn't face adding to that.

So I gathered my siblings to tell them and then banned them from telling Mum. They agreed to do it for me but I remember my brother saying, 'Fine, but she isn't stupid, Denise, you know what she's like – she knows immediately when something is up. You won't get away with it for long.' One person I did have to tell was Sean, because I knew that if the news got picked up by the press they would go straight to him for a comment, so I needed to make sure he knew what was going on.

Sean was surprised by the news. He told me recently, 'I thought you were good for each other – Ralph was never demonstrative but he was a quiet and steady guy. I remember getting the phone call from you to say you were splitting up and I was shocked. Ralph just never got over James and he never found a way through, whereas your way of coping was to throw yourself into the campaigning which took up all your energy.'

I tried my best to protect the family the way they had me but, in the end, I had no choice and the cat was out of the bag. Not long after Ralph went, my mum came round for the day to see Michael. We were catching up over a cup of tea when a black BMW suddenly pulled up outside the house. Ralph's brother, Jimmy, had recently bought a black BMW with a registration that began with an R, but Sean had a car with a similar registration. I peeked out of the window and saw what I thought was Sean's car and I panicked, thinking, *Oh God, Sean's here to talk about the divorce and Mum is here!*

I knew I was going to have to confess, I was sitting on the floor and thought, *I've just got to blurt it out.* So I said, 'Right Mum, Ralph's left me. Don't kick off, I'm fine, I've got Michael and it's for the best.' All the words came tumbling out while I still had the courage, and I tried as best I could to put a positive spin on it, but telling my mum the news opened up a real sense of devastation in me. Somehow telling her really brought home what I had lost. I had been on autopilot since he'd left and in total denial that he would cheat on me after all we had been through. Of course Mum had known that something was up, and she was so upset for me. The irony was that it wasn't even Sean's car in the end!

Once the shock had worn off, I decided that the priority was Michael – obviously I hadn't wanted him to grow up in a broken home, but he had two parents and he needed to know they were still fully invested in him. The problem was that Ralph didn't seem to agree with me. At first we worked out a system for weekend visits and they began well, but there wasn't the consistency that a small child needs and the contact was very sporadic. I found the uncertainty very hard to deal with – I would build myself up to handing Michael over, only for Ralph not to turn up. I also had to cope with being separated from my baby – after the way I had lost James, Michael wasn't out of my sight for a second, so imagine how I felt having to hand my baby son over to my soon-to-be ex-husband and goodness knows who else. Ralph was a good dad but I had no idea what was going to happen to Michael when I wasn't there – would they keep their eyes on him? Would they keep him safe? I hated every minute of it because I saw danger everywhere and, by the time Ralph left me, I hadn't even taken Michael to the shops. Never in my wildest dreams had I imagined a simple shopping trip with James would end the way it did and, as a result, I was terrified of everything.

Chapter 18

My Rock

Initially, I found it impossible to comprehend that life marched on despite the fact my boy wasn't here living it with me. It took me a long time to stop feeling guilty if I didn't think about James every minute of every day, but keeping busy with Michael was a godsend and helped push out the deep, dark thoughts. However, new challenges presented themselves as Michael grew from a tiny baby into a busy toddler, especially when it came to going out once he could walk. My anxieties came to a head when Michael celebrated his second birthday – the last one that James had seen. It was a bittersweet milestone.

I had been determined never to compare the boys or miss Michael's key moments by fixating on the fact that James had never reached them. But the deep-seated paranoia and worry never left me, and I can see now that it did get in the way of us enjoying some things that other children took for granted. It also meant that Michael was never out of my sight – he slept in my bed with me and we spent every minute together. There was no playgroup or nursery, no play dates without me, no staying over with his cousins, I had to have him with me all the time and that's just the way it was. I wasn't bothered about dating anyone new because I wasn't really interested in anything apart from Michael.

That meant I didn't have a social life to speak of. My brothers and sisters occasionally came round to babysit, forcing me to go out with my friends for a few drinks. They would say, 'Denise, you haven't let your hair down for months, we will sit with the baby while he sleeps, go out and have some fun.' Looking back it was strange to think that I was living such a secluded life when I was only 28 years old. I suppose it wouldn't have mattered if I had still been married, but I was a single mum with a murdered child and I didn't particularly feel like a catch with everything that I'd been through.

That all changed one night during the summer of 1996, when Michael was two and a half years old. I'd been going through a particularly hermit-like phase, during which I had barely left the house – sometimes everything overwhelmed me and I didn't want to see anyone at all. After a while, my brother Paul came round demanding that I went out for the night, so I arranged to meet some of the girls at the Cavern Club. Eventually I got ready and made my way into

James in Wales enjoying his first and last holiday.

My application for James' primary school place, which he didn't live to take up.

SACRED HEART PRIMARY SCHOOL
APPLICATION FOR ADMISSION TO NURSERY CLASS

NAME OF CHILD..JAMES PATRICK BULGER..

DATE OF BIRTH..16.3.90............ TEL: NO:.......

PRIMARY SCHOOL CHILD WILL ATTEND..SACRED HEART..........

HAS CHILD ATTENDED A PLAYGROUP..No..... WHERE.....

HOW LONG.........

POSITION IN FAMILY

Is he/she an only child. Ye.............

Ages of other children.......................

LIVING CONDITIONS

Do you live in a house, flat or maisonette (which floor).GROUND...

How many people are living in the house..3.................

How many bedrooms...ONE................

HEALTH

Is anyone in your home suffering from ill health...NO........

Is there anything about your child, you would like the staff to know,
before admission. For example - allergies (treated in confidence).
.....No...........
....
....
....

Signature of Parent..D.Bulger............ Date.................

Please fill in all parts and return the form personally.
When returning the form please bring Birth Certificate with you.

My beautiful boy's final resting place.

Loving Memory Of
OUR BELOVED SON
JAMES PATRICK BULGER
BORN 16TH MARCH 1990
DIED 12TH FEBRUARY 1993
HERE IS NOT A DAY THAT GOES BY
THAT WE THINK OF YOU AND CRY
YOU BROUGHT US
SO MANY HAPPY DAYS
WE WILL ALWAYS LOVE
AND REMEMBER YOU JAMES
MAY GOD KEEP YOU IN HIS CARE
TIL THE DAY THAT WE GET THERE
GOODNIGHT AND GOD BLESS
LITTLE INNOCENT BABE
LOVE HUGS AND KISSES MUM AND DAD

Just some of the flowers left by kind well-wishers.

The whole world was talking about my boy, and all I wanted was him home.

Above: My wedding to Stuart, along with the births of my children, were the happiest days of my life.

Right: My wedding invitation.

Denise Bulger and Stuart Fergus
request the pleasure of the company of

at their
Marriage
at St Chads Church, Kirkby
on Saturday, 12th September, 1998
at 12.30 p.m.
and afterwards at
The Pyramid Suite, Kirkby Sports Centre
R.S.V.P.

A family portrait, to mark the christening of Thomas and Leon.

Snowy fun with the boys – they are never out of my sight.

Above: My three handsome boys.

Below: I love this picture of my four boys together. I am so proud to be their mum.

Above: My wonderful family at the annual Black Tie and Tiara Ball that we host every year to raise money for the James Bulger Memorial Trust. I love this picture because we are celebrating James and his photo is in the background, so it feels like a family portrait.

Right: With the legendary Sir Trevor McDonald at the Black Tie and Tiara Ball — it was an honour to have him there, and to do the documentary, *A Mother's Story*, to mark 25 years since James died.

town, the girls were already there and we had a couple of drinks and a chat. We were queuing at the bar and I could feel myself relaxing when, all of a sudden, the bloke being served asked me if I wanted a drink.

According to Stuart, he glanced over his shoulder and spotted a petite girl in a red dress and he plucked up the courage to turn around as he was giving his order and ask what I would like to drink. He was out for a friend's 21st birthday in a big group, so it was quite brave to do it in front of his mates. I remember turning to my friend and saying, 'Oh go on then, it would be rude not to.'

We sat down for a while and Stuart asked if I was married and had kids, and it suddenly dawned on me that he didn't have a clue who I was. I was stunned, but I can't tell you how refreshing it was for a few minutes to be out and have someone talking to me like a normal person, not a victim, not 'poor Denise' or 'poor James' mum'. Suddenly one of Stuart's mates kicked him in the back of the ankle and called him back over to the bar. Stuart looked annoyed that we had been interrupted and went off to see what was wrong.

Stuart recalls, 'He told me who you were and I was mortified. I felt like such an idiot. I apologised, but you didn't mind at all, so I decided to try my luck and ask for your number. To me, despite the fact you were James' mum, you were just a gorgeous woman I wanted to have a drink with.

'I hadn't really paid much attention to the media

surrounding James' story and so I didn't know a lot of detail – had I known I would definitely have been too shy and anxious to make a move. In all honesty I probably would have thought, *Poor cow, I should leave her alone, last thing she wants on a night out is to talk to the likes of me.* But I got your number and we each went back to our mates, and I knew immediately that something was there. I left it a few days, so you didn't think I was too keen, and then called and asked you out.'

It felt very strange for me, the idea of going on a date. But Stuart seemed like a nice man, and the girls encouraged me, so I said yes. I didn't really think any more of it – having a small child at home takes up a lot of energy. Stuart still has a good memory of that evening, 'We arranged that I would pick you up on the Thursday, less than a week after we had met. I knocked on the door and your sister answered, inviting me in. We were chatting in the hallway when suddenly you came down the stairs in a knock-out dress. I thought to myself, *Blimey, she has really pulled out the stops here, she looks absolutely stunning.* I couldn't believe how amazing you looked. I was just about to tell you when you looked up at me and said, "Oh God, I had forgotten you were coming, I am just on my way out with my mates." I should have been insulted that you'd forgotten but it was genuinely hilarious. We ended up staying in for a takeaway and a few drinks, and I left knowing that I was smitten, but we took things really slowly.

'It was a long time before I was introduced to Michael and there was never any doubt he was your absolute priority. You were really straight down the line about the fact that you were a mother first and foremost. I also knew that you had been hurt by your first husband – it was clear that you needed time to learn how to trust again. That was fine by me, I knew from the first date that I wasn't going anywhere, I knew you were the one for me.'

It was a much slower process for me. I liked Stuart straight away but I needed to be sure I properly trusted him and that a new relationship wouldn't unsettle my son. For that reason, Stuart meeting Michael was low down on my list of priorities for a long time. But it soon became clear that, despite being younger than me – he was 20 years old and I was 28 – Stuart was really serious about us, baggage and all. There were no games, and he let me know immediately that he wasn't interested in anyone else. I was secure in his feelings for me and that felt great after the uncertainty at the end of my first marriage.

Finally, we decided that it was the right time for Stuart to meet Michael and it was hilarious. We arranged it so that Stuart would come round just before Michael's bedtime and so he arrived with some drinks, a box of chocolates and a bunch of flowers for me – something that continued every week for a long time, but mysteriously stopped once we were married!

Stuart also brought Michael a massive bag of sweets and

I warned him there were too many and that it wasn't a good idea to give him so many sweets before bedtime, but he ignored me and handed the whole bag over to Michael, who instantly set about demolishing the lot. After he'd finished, Michael started running around, no doubt experiencing a huge sugar rush. He warmed to Stuart immediately, cuddling up to him and chatting away. He was hanging on to Stuart's legs and said, 'I like you Stuart.' It was a really sweet moment and I felt myself relaxing, thinking, *Perhaps this wasn't such a bad idea after all.* Then, suddenly, Michael threw up right into Stuart's lap. It went everywhere and Stuart's face was a picture – he was horrified! I started to laugh and told Stuart in no uncertain terms that it would be his job to clean it all up as he'd been the one with the sweets, but it broke the ice perfectly. Michael liked Stuart, which allowed me to acknowledge that I liked him too. It all felt really strange, and another huge step away from James, but what could I do? I knew that standing still wasn't an option, all I could do was make sure that James was as much a part of my new life as possible, and Stuart has always been amazing about that.

Right from the start I told Stuart all about James, what had happened to him and the effect it had on me. I wanted him to know as much as possible about my lovely boy but I also didn't sugar-coat the devastation that Venables and Thompson had caused my family. I told him all that I could – Stuart knows exactly what I know – and more than once I offered him a way out, telling him that I would totally understand if it was all too much and he wanted to walk away. There were times I didn't even want to be me, so I had no issue imagining it might be impossible for anyone else to be with me. But Stuart has never been troubled by anything I have thrown at him – and there have been many times when he could have legitimately called it quits and I wouldn't have blamed him for a second. Right from the very beginning he was my rock and mainstay, he just stepped into that role with total ease.

We met in the June and had a few dates before Stuart went away on holiday. I thought that this would be a good time for us both to assess where things were. We missed each other a lot, and when Stuart came back we decided he should move in for a trial run. Michael adored him and everything just clicked into place, although it took my breath away when he first called Stuart 'Daddy'. We became a family and I felt an overwhelming sense of peace for the first time in a very, very long while.

Everything was different with Stuart. If he went out, he asked me to go with him. I knew when he was coming back and I knew that I was enough for him. I can't even begin to explain what a relief that was for me. But what made me completely fall in love with him was the way he was with Michael – he doted on him without reservation, he always called him 'our Michael' and treated him as preciously as I did.

It was a lot to take on his shoulders and in the early days

I was sure that our families would have something to say about the new relationship. Mine continued to be very protective, even more so after Ralph, but they welcomed Stuart with open arms once they got to know him. Ray says, 'If you were smiling that was good enough for us. The minute we saw you together we could see you adored each other and anyone who brought joy to your life was fine by me. It was so fantastic to see you *living* again and the way Stuart treated Michael was fantastic, like he was his own son right from day one.'

I think Stuart's mum struggled a bit more, and I could completely understand why. Stuart's parents split up when he was young and he had lived with his mum, so they were close. His mum had met and married her second husband and they left Formby and moved to Brighton where Stuart went to school. But as soon as he finished the sixth form, aged 18 years old, Stuart moved back to Liverpool to become an electrician and live with his dad in Crosby. Two years later he met me and, as a mother of lads the same age now, I can see that 20 was very young to settle down with a woman who already had a child – never mind everything else that came with me.

Stuart's dad lived in Liverpool and so, when they discussed me, obviously he knew who I was and all about James. He didn't really have an opinion, at least if he did he didn't voice it! But Stuart was too scared to tell his mum we were dating for quite a long time, so he ended up waiting until we moved in together. She wasn't impressed – her exact words were, 'She comes with a lot of baggage.'

I'm the first to admit that she was right and I often wonder what we would both say if our Michael moved in, at such a young age, with someone who had experienced so much deep trauma. I suppose you never know how you will react until it is your own child, maybe I would be the same. Either way, Stuart's mum and I didn't get off to the best start.

She came up one time early on in our relationship and met Michael, but the situation was strained. While I was understanding of her concerns as a mother, I won't lie and say that I looked forward to having her in the house – you could feel the disapproval coming off her in waves. In the end it was too much for her and, when we did eventually get married, she decided to stay away from the wedding – Stuart's dad came but she didn't. Stuart is just like his dad, laid back and relaxed, but his mum just couldn't get to a place where she was comfortable with us being together. Things did settle down over the years and, luckily, Stuart made up with her at the end before she died of cancer.

Things became serious quite quickly after he moved in, but it was still hard for Stuart to break through some of my defences – after all that had happened, my guard was well and truly up. He also had to get to grips with the fact that Michael was the most important thing in my life and that wasn't going to change.

Stuart and I laugh a lot about that now, he says, 'When

I met you, Michael was two and a half years old and still sleeping next to you. It took me months to ease him into his own bed and room – slowly but surely we agreed to do it a bit at a time. Whatever top you had been wearing that day, you would take it off and wrap around him so that he felt close to you in his own bed. Hilariously he was only next door, but it was a big adjustment for you both. It was a military operation and one I had to deal with sensitively and carefully for both of your sakes. I didn't want to come between you but we also needed to find a balanced way to be a family. It wasn't just the sleeping that we had to address, I also needed to find a way for you to let me in when it came to looking after Michael. When we had been together for a while, it was only natural I would want to shoulder some of the childcare, so I would ask to take him to the shops or the park and it was a straight no. You didn't even consider it, you would simply shut it down, and that was hard as you can't help but feel you aren't trusted.'

I can see now how difficult it was for Stuart but, in all honesty, that wasn't my priority. That sounds awful but I had been the one with James when he was abducted, he was my most precious thing and even I couldn't keep him safe. It was almost impossible for me to imagine anyone else doing a good enough job with Michael, even Stuart. Unfortunately for him, us meeting also coincided with Michael being the same age James had been when he was murdered.

Stuart has always understood my anxiety but he has

worked hard to normalise certain things – so rather than get annoyed when I said no to him taking Michael out, he would say, 'Come too.' I know it has been a hard process for him at times, but he did show me how life could be if I eased up and let things happen naturally. I spent a lot of our early relationship feeling terrified, but Stuart was there to reassure and support me. He came from a background with a dad and a stepdad who were really involved in his upbringing, so he was used to the idea of co-parenting. He never tried to be Michael's dad but he was there for me. I learnt how to have a partner when it came to the kids – and I would have been happy to share those duties with Ralph if he'd wanted to. As it was, Michael just didn't see much of Ralph so it was never an issue really. Without trying or any kind of conversation, Michael started treating Stuart like his dad and that was that.

* * *

I have always tried to see each of my children as their own person and not to compare them to James or to what he might have become – that's a truly unfair burden on any child – but in those early days I felt James everywhere. There have actually been a few instances where I genuinely thought James had come back to reassure me he was okay. One particular day stands out for me and I still think about it now.

Michael was playing with my niece and, as he was occupied, I took the opportunity to go upstairs and clean the bathroom. I was still wearing my nightie and doing the glamorous job of cleaning round the sink, so I had my back to the door, when I suddenly felt a hard tugging on the bottom of my nightdress. Michael was at the age where he could climb the stairs himself, so I turned around and said, 'What is it, lad?' but there was nobody there. I wasn't near anything else that could have caught the material. There was no explanation for that feeling of someone pulling really hard on my nightie, like they wanted my attention. I went downstairs and Michael and my niece were playing exactly where I had left them, neither one of them had come upstairs. Perhaps it was just wishful thinking, but I became convinced it was James, just letting me know he was there. Moments like that were both helpful and heartbreaking.

To this day it is often the small milestones or memories that still have the ability to floor me, but one that hit me particularly hard at the time was watching Michael turn three years old. I think we all felt it, though the family were too scared to say anything in case it upset me. We had a small party at the house with his little cousins and a few friends and I did my best, but I was on the verge of tears all day.

So much had changed – no James, no Ralph, there was nothing left from before 12th February 1993. It was like my old life didn't exist. James should have been bossing his little brother around, helping him open his presents and joining in the games – instead all that we had was his portrait smiling down from above the fireplace, frozen in time and destined never to grow up.

Chapter 19

Picking up the Fight

It was around this time that Ralph started to try and take an interest in his access visits. I am not sure what spurred him on to be in touch but all of a sudden he was insisting that one of his family picked Michael up, often taking him to his mum's. Things weren't good between us, I suppose there was still a lot of resentment on my part about his affair and, quite simply, we were both still grieving for James. What had once united us didn't anymore – we both had had a devastating experience that we couldn't bring ourselves to share and he felt like a stranger to me.

This was all made doubly hard by the fact that Michael was going through a bit of a clingy stage and he would cry hysterically when he was collected. It broke my heart to see him go, knowing that he was upset – he would hold his hands out for me and I couldn't do anything about it.

I hated every minute he was away, but I also wanted him to know that he was loved by both of his parents and so I knew his time with Ralph was important. I found the best way of coping was to go out as soon as Michael left the house. I would do a food shop and then buy something to keep me busy – I ended up with loads of new dresses that I didn't ever wear! I counted down the hours he was away and felt such relief when he was delivered safely back home.

The trouble was that the inconsistency started to creep in quite quickly and it was confusing for Michael. He went from kicking and screaming when he was picked up to sitting on the stairs with his coat and shoes on, resigned to going but then sad when Ralph didn't show up. It got harder as he got older and became more aware that his father wasn't keeping his promises. Sometimes I would tell him to ring a friend and invite them round for tea, sometimes my methods were a bit more extreme, much to Stuart's dismay!

One Easter when Ralph didn't arrive, I turned to Michael and said, 'Do you know what this house doesn't have? A pet. As it is Easter, shall we get a rabbit?' Stuart's face was a picture! So off we all went to pick a rabbit – we fell in love with a gorgeous white cloud of a bunny with black patches of fur and big blue eyes. Michael called her Jesse after a character in *Toy Story* and his face lit up the minute he saw her, which made up for everything else. The rabbit became a happy fixture – she used to wander in and out of the house and Stuart was roped into building her a two-storey hutch!

I worried that Michael would think that what felt like Ralph not wanting to see him was his fault and I didn't want that guilt and anxiety for my son. I asked Michael about it all recently and he said, 'I was supposed to see Ralph every Saturday and, when he did show up, he would collect me at midday and take me down to my nan's. I would stay until about 5pm before someone would drop me home. But he didn't always arrive and I would just be sat there on the stairs, wondering what I'd done. There was never any explanation about why he didn't show up and I didn't ever ask – I was too young I suppose. But as I got older it got more hurtful and, one of the last times he left me waiting, I turned to you and said, "I've had enough, there's no point, I don't want to do this anymore." You have always been by my side and on my side. Despite how things ended up between you and Ralph, you never once got in the way of our relationship. You always said, "If you want to see him, you go and see him and if you don't it's up to you." But in the end, never knowing if he would want to see me got too much and so I decided to stop the visits.'

* * *

Despite being worried about Michael, during that summer of 1996 I also had to pick up the fight for James again. Even though Michael Howard had successfully raised the minimum sentence Venables and Thompson were serving from 10 to 15 years, it seemed their lawyers weren't letting go. They had applied to the High Court, contesting Michael Howard's decision and it was the start of a long battle. I remembered what Sean said to me at the start of my campaign, when I told him that I would leave no stone unturned in the fight for justice, 'Be prepared, it is going to be a long road.' I don't think either of us had any idea just how long and bumpy it would be.

Sean says, 'It felt like whatever you and Ralph did went wrong. The Home Secretary was perceived to have been influenced by public opinion when resetting the tariff, and so the lawyers looking after Thompson and Venables argued that his decision was nakedly political. Its legitimacy was challenged because his function was supposed to be judicial, not someone making a decision intended to satisfy public opinion.'

Edward Fitzgerald QC, acting for both Venables and Thompson, argued that instead of listening to the emotional public, Michael Howard should have concentrated on the behavioural and psychiatric reports that were available at the time. Mr Fitzgerald argued that the two boys who'd killed my baby had made real progress since beginning their sentences. Part of the case put forward was that the surrounding publicity meant that the boys had been made unfair examples. It was argued that the public fury and hysterical press coverage, focusing singularly on their

young ages when the offence was committed, wiped out
the so-called great progress they had made while in their
young offender institutions. Mr Fitzgerald also stated that
the petition signatures collected by the family, alongside the
coupons supplied by a national newspaper, should have no
bearing on the sentence. He went as far as to argue that
Michael Howard becoming involved was unlawful.

The purpose of the first hearing was to seek a judicial
review of the situation but primarily what Mr Fitzgerald
wanted was to overturn Michael Howard's increased 15-
year tariff. I was distraught. We had fought so hard for what
I saw as a small increase – I still believed that anything less
than life was a travesty. For me, they had to go to adult
prison in order to receive proper punishment for what they
had done. I felt like 15 years had been a small bone to throw
us and now they even wanted that back. So began the chess
game, except that it wasn't a game to me – it was a marker of
what the system thought my precious son's life was worth. I
felt buoyed up by the fact that Mr Howard seemed poised
to fight the application and keep the increased sentence, but
I was also aware that his authority was being challenged. At
the heart of the issue was the question of whether the Home
Secretary should even have the power to fix a minimum
sentence. After the first hearing at the High Court, a full
judicial review was put into motion and we had to sit tight
and wait for the outcome.

As ever, Sean was there to guide me through everything –

Ralph had his own legal representation and we were doing things separately since the divorce. I also started working with Chris Johnson, an ex-editor at Mercury Press agency. He has been by my side throughout everything and now works with us at the charity we went on to set up in James' name. He helped me to navigate the press and generally manage all the overwhelming interest that just kept coming the longer the sentence fight went on.

The big difference for me was that this time I had Stuart by my side – right from the start he campaigned as if James was his own flesh and blood. Having him standing next to me was the greatest thing and made a horrible situation a bit more bearable. But I was also very aware that he could be about to see a different side of me – he hadn't witnessed me in the very depth of despair when it came to James. I warned him that things could get tricky, but he didn't even blink.

In July, the brand new Lord Chief Justice ruled against the Home Office: the 15-year tariff set by Michael Howard had been wrongly influenced by public petitions and opinion. In my opinion, Lord Wolff, who had recently been appointed, wanted to make his own mark on the criminal justice system and it didn't get much bigger than this.

Sean agrees, 'Once the House of Lords ruled that the tariff was no longer to be set by the Home Secretary, it meant that all rulings of this nature were now made by the judiciary. The petition backfired spectacularly. As a lawyer

I fully understand why the legal teams acting for Venables and Thompson went down this route but it is upsetting that the first beneficiaries of it were James' killers. It also meant that a new tariff had to be set.'

It seemed that in attempting to get Venables and Thompson a longer sentence we had also inadvertently changed the law in favour of James' killers.

The very little faith I had in the system evaporated completely at that moment. Nothing could be worse than my son being murdered, but the way the law seemed to side with his murderers was incredibly hard to bear and brought all those old feelings of powerlessness and anger right to the surface. It was as if the fact that Thompson and Venables were ten years old when they had murdered James wiped out the fact that they had ended my son's life. Their well-being mattered more than the crime they had committed, it mattered more than my son lying in the ground when he should have been starting school. This feeling only intensified over the next few months when the press began reporting details of what, apparently, day-to-day life was like for Thompson and Venables inside their institutions.

I couldn't believe it when I heard what the newspapers were reporting: they were living lives of luxury, a hundred times better than the ones they had before they murdered my son. Tucked away in their secure units they had their own bedrooms and bathrooms, TVs, consoles, games and every toy imaginable. We were also told they had the pick of designer clothes and the latest trainers. Of course, no one ever confirmed this was the case, but Chris Johnson and I agreed that the stories had to be coming from some source with inside access to the truth. Given the way that their sentencing was being handled, it was definitely possible that they were indeed being rewarded for murdering my son.

The blows kept coming and none bigger than finding out an American lawyer, Tom Loflin, was pushing himself onto the scene in the most unhelpful way. He was a huge supporter of both Thompson and Venables and expressed disgust that two eleven-year-old boys had been tried and convicted in an adult court of law. He started stirring up all kinds of trouble, writing to everyone involved, including the judge who had overseen the case. But, most crucially, he started corresponding with the lawyers looking after Thompson and Venables, encouraging them to continue the fight against their original sentences. His argument was that their human rights had been breached – he called their detention 'barbarism' and 'a monstrous injustice' – something that made my blood boil. Who did this stranger think he was, involving himself in something he knew nothing about – he hadn't buried his two-year-old child. As far as I was concerned, he was just another person jumping on the bandwagon and taking advantage of my son.

He started visiting Venables in particular, which culminated in him getting friendly with both sets of lawyers and preparing a case to take to Strasbourg and the European Court of Human Rights. This felt like the biggest body blow of all and I vowed that I would fight it with every breath in my body. How had we got here? We started the fight in order to have the sentence raised and now there was some random American lawyer arguing my son's murderers should never have been detained in the first place. It was madness and the rage I felt was indescribable.

Just as I prepared to roll up my sleeves and fight for my second-born, I realised I was pregnant. We were absolutely thrilled but I realised that, yet again, I would spend a pregnancy fighting the system and trying to make sure Venables and Thompson got what they deserved. In the end it didn't matter – I miscarried the baby before my 12-week scan. I was devastated and remember thinking that now I had lost a baby in every possible way.

Chapter 20

New Beginnings

A s ever, I was split between parenting in the 'now' and making sure that I carried on fighting for James. Just as all this business with Loflin blew up and I lost the baby, I also had to contend with Michael's first day at school, which was a terrifying milestone for me.

I fully admit that I was really overprotective of him as a small boy – on the rare occasion that we did go out into a public place, I took no chances. He was on harnesses, a wrist strap and he had to hold my hand – the poor kid was tied up in multiple leads and going nowhere! I only took him to the park or playground with other members of the family so there were lots of eyes on him and I found open spaces awful with my boys when they were young, I was just terrified. Even when Michael was in the buggy, he would have the bottom straps around his lap and a harness on the top half clipped into the belt strap. My eyes weren't off him for a second and if they were, someone from the family would be watching and standing with him.

So sending my baby off to school was awful – I had to keep telling myself, *It's Michael and not James, it will be fine.* As I'd refused to put him into nursery, his first day at school was just that and I worried it would be a shock for Michael. People often ask me what that first day was like for me but it should be more a question of how it was for Stuart! When Michael first started it was only for half a day – from 9am until 12:30pm – but even though it was a short day I was dreading dropping him off. I knew that walking away and leaving him there would be too much for me, so Stuart came with me. He recalls, 'It was fine on the way there and we talked through what was going to happen. We went into the classroom and, after a few minutes, the teacher said, "Come on parents, off you go now. Say goodbye to your child and they will see you later." All I could do was look at you, you were in such a state, but I also fully expected Michael to kick off when he saw us leaving. I was so nervous as we said goodbye, but it was hilarious because Michael just looked at us both and ran off – he didn't even look back! It was like he was saying: "I am freeeeeee!"'

Michael absolutely loved school – he probably couldn't wait to get away from me! How did I cope? Let's just say that the house had never been so spotless that first year – I cleaned from 9am to 3pm non-stop as I needed something to take my mind off the fact I couldn't see or speak to him and didn't know what he was doing from one minute to the next.

But the anxiety crept back in and I couldn't go the whole day without seeing Michael, I worried too much, so we arranged with the school that Stuart would bring him home for lunch. Michael would put his order in before he went to school and it would be ready as soon as Stuart brought him through the door. It might have been beans on toast or a bowl of hot pasta and we would all eat lunch together. This was genuinely the only way I could cope with those first few years without him by my side, I was consumed with fear that something would happen to him and I wouldn't be there to protect or help him when he needed me – just like with James. Michael seemed fine with the arrangement, and he says now, 'For the first couple of years in primary school I went home for my lunch, which didn't seem weird to me because it was just what we'd always done. I don't remember anything in particular standing out – no one ever spoke to me about you or James and I was well protected by my teachers. I think it helped that my school name was Fergus, even though I hadn't officially changed it at that point. You and Dad explained that you were registering me under that name so that I could keep a low profile. I had loads of cousins around the school too, so there were lots of eyes to watch me!'

Michael was definitely ready for school, he thrived and

eventually the head teacher suggested that he stay and eat lunch with his friends. That was a big step for me, but I knew it was about doing what was best for Michael and I didn't want him to stand out. It also helped that one of my sisters had just become a dinner lady at the school and she could keep an eye on him for me. Once he stopped coming home, we had a special arrangement that I would send a hot lunch into school for him and he would stay there and eat it. So my sister, Rita, would arrive at the house on her way to start work, before the lunch hour began, to collect whatever I had made and she would take it to Michael. It often meant that Michael was tucking into a steaming bowl of chicken and bacon pasta, and the rest of the classmates were having school dinners! I am not sure how popular I was with the dinner ladies, but it helped make me feel a bit better knowing I was still looking after him.

I slowly got used to our new routine but little did I know that Stuart was planning a surprise of his own, he wanted us to formalise our family by getting married. It took two proposals before I finally said yes. The first time wasn't long after we met and I disappointed Stuart by saying no. Stuart and I regularly disagree about how it happened. He says, 'It was our first Christmas together and I decided to go for it, I knew I loved you and I wanted you to be my wife. I thought it would be mega-romantic to buy a packet of chalky love hearts and find the sweet that says "marry me" – I ended up having to buy four packets before I eventually found the one I wanted. But instead of throwing the rest of the sweets away and getting rid of the evidence, I fed them to Michael and he promptly threw up, I never seem to learn when it comes to that boy and sweets! I'd bought you a bracelet and put the love heart inside the box, wrapped it all up and put it under the tree. On Christmas morning, you unwrapped it and went silent, I couldn't work out if that was good or bad as you are rarely lost for words! Eventually you looked at me and said no – I couldn't believe it. You later explained that you thought it was too soon, as we had only been dating a few months and I had just moved in, and you didn't want to rush things. Though I seem to remember you kept the bracelet!'

I always joke that he kept following me round the kitchen, standing behind my shoulder as I was trying to do Christmas dinner, saying, 'Will you marry me?' over and over again. We laugh about it now but I know it must have taken a lot for him to ask, and it was very romantic. But I felt it was all a bit too soon, especially as Stuart had just become a part of Michael's life. I didn't want to rush into anything. Things had been great but I was always aware that something could spring up to do with James and send me hurtling back three steps – we hadn't been in that situation at the time Stuart proposed and I was very aware that could change things. I am amazed that he was prepared to ask me again, but he did a year later and the second time it involved going to see a Michael Jackson concert. Stuart remembers, 'I knew I wanted to do it so I got in touch with a friend of ours who helped me to find the perfect diamond ring. He told me that he would get me tickets to the Wembley concert and book us a nice hotel so that I could do it in style. So you, me and Michael went to London and Norman came to the hotel to hand over the ring. We were all in the hotel lobby and I said I needed the loo so that I could get a proper look at the ring without you seeing it, so I said to Michael, "Do you want to come with me?" So off we go and Norman shows us the ring – it's the perfect size and looks beautiful, Michael is there taking it all in and I don't think anything of it. We go to sleep and the next morning we wake up and discuss what we are going to do that day and Michael pipes up, "Show Mum the ring."

'I bluster away trying to throw you off the scent by distracting Michael and I make the mistake of saying, "What are you talking about?" So Michael answers, "That ring that the man gave you, the sparkling one, show Mum." I was cringing inside but luckily you were easily distracted when I came up with some nonsensical story about having spotted a ring in a shop window the day before that I'd pointed out to Michael. You were more excited about seeing Michael Jackson than talking about jewellery!

'We went to the zoo for the day and then had dinner in our hotel. Even though it was quite posh they cooked chicken nuggets for Michael and gave him balloons. He started blowing up the balloons and letting them go all over the restaurant – people began to complain and you were mortified. I could feel you getting more and more stressed and I knew I had to get on with it, so I took your hand and asked you to give me the onyx ring on your finger so that I could have a look at it. I will never forget your face. If looks could kill, I certainly wouldn't have survived that night. You looked like you wanted to swing for me. I remember you said through gritted teeth, "Our Michael is causing havoc and you want to look at my bloody ring, what's the matter with you?!"

'You gave me the ring and I deliberately dropped it on the floor. At this point you were about to combust and hissed, "What ARE you doing?!" I quickly slid down on one knee and, holding out the ring box I'd had in my pocket, said, "Would you do me the honour of being my wife?"

'You were totally shocked and looked at me as if I had lost my mind. It was like a comedy sketch, you staring, me stuck down on one knee and a waiter standing in the corner, unsure if he should pop open the champagne or not. Embarrassed, you soon begged me to get up, not realising you still hadn't given me an answer, so in the end I handed you the ring and told you to put it on if you wanted to marry me!'

Of course I said yes, and now, alongside my children, Stuart is the best thing that's ever happened to me and I am thankful every day to share my life with such a strong and loving man. Our family is everything to me and the thought of being his wife was wonderful. By the time he proposed again, I felt confident that he'd seen the best and the worst of me, and that he was fully aware of what he was taking on.

We decided to have a big white wedding. My first one had been a really small and quiet affair; this time, after everything that had happened, I wanted to celebrate how far we had all come.

I set about planning the big day and loved every minute. It was really important to me that we had a church wedding but, because I'd already been married and divorced, it was hard to get permission. In the end we had to go to the Bishop of Liverpool for special dispensation – he was brilliant. Because of everything that I had been through with James he could see that the religious aspect was important to me.

It was a hectic time and, right in the middle of it all and a few months after the miscarriage, I realised I was pregnant again. There was so much to juggle and my emotions were all over the place. I was delighted about the new baby but we had a wedding to plan and I was still coming to terms with Michael's new-found independence at school. I started to feel overwhelmed again and my emotions threatened to get the better of me. Instead of panicking, I had to remind myself that a lot had happened since James had died and I hadn't really given myself any clear space to grieve. Instead I lurched from one hectic situation to another, particularly as I carried on fighting to keep Thompson and Venables locked up where they belonged.

We decided to push the wedding back slightly as I didn't want to be a pregnant bride. We booked it for 12th September 1998, three months after the baby was due. It was ambitious but I made sure everything was sorted before the pregnancy advanced too much. I definitely picked my dress while I could still fit into it! I decided to go the whole way and have the big white gown and veil. We would have bridesmaids and ushers and I was particularly excited by the fact that Michael would wear a miniature version of Stuart's top and tails. I asked my brother Gary to give me away, we would arrive in a horse and carriage and our first dance would be to Michael Jackson's 'You Are Not Alone'.

My pregnancy progressed well – this time around I was too busy with Michael to spend lots of time worrying. I think now that I'd managed two good pregnancies and births, with James and Michael, the possibility of Kirsty's stillbirth happening again seemed less likely and further away from the front of my mind. This would be my fourth baby but I still felt all of that excitement, particularly as it was Stuart's first baby. Although he treated Michael like his son, I knew it would be different for him watching my pregnancy progress and then being there when I gave birth. Michael was fully formed when Stuart met him, he would be there for this baby from the very start. I felt more secure this time around knowing he was right by my side too.

But none of that stopped the deep-rooted anxiety. I worried about how Michael would adjust – he had always come first and was used to my undivided attention. Soon there would be a new baby who needed me and that would be a big change. As the pregnancy progressed I found myself thinking, *What if the new baby has colic like James and screams for hours on end, how will we cope? How will I make sure that Michael doesn't feel pushed out? How will I feel, seeing Michael becoming a big brother and knowing that James had been denied that chance? Will having another baby feel like one more step away from my old life and from James?* All these questions would swirl around in my head and I tried my best to shut them out and enjoy my family.

Because I'd had a caesarean with Michael, it was decided we would do the same again this time around. I was a bit concerned about the recovery time and managing the new baby and an energetic Michael, but it made sense, and knowing what was happening and when helped to manage my anxiety. Stuart and I made sure that Michael felt fully involved throughout the pregnancy and talked to him all the time about the baby. He was five years old, so at the age where he understood what was happening. He would put his hand on my tummy to feel the baby kick and howl with laughter when it did. He was genuinely so excited at the thought of having a baby brother or sister and would sit on my lap and chat to my bump. It was a lovely time but, as always, my thoughts would turn to James and what he was missing. I went to the cemetery to put flowers down and tell him all about the baby. It still shocked me that that was the only way to communicate with him but I was determined to make him a part of our growing family. I never wanted to feel I was leaving him behind.

As my due date arrived, we made the now familiar trek to the Fazakerley Hospital. Thomas Stuart Fergus was born on 8th July 1998 at 7:47am, weighing 5lb 7oz. He was handed straight to Stuart for those precious first minutes and I couldn't stop looking at them – it was such a wonderful moment. I know Stuart was overwhelmed seeing his son come into the world, he was so emotional as they pulled Thomas out, and also concerned that everything had gone well. I was impatient to get back to my room and wait for Michael to arrive so he could meet his little brother for the first time. I made sure we did everything properly – we had bought Michael a present from the baby and I put Thomas in his cot next to my bed so I had my arms free to hug Michael. Suddenly I heard him thundering down the corridor, impatient to meet the baby we had spent months telling him about. His little head popped round the door and he came straight over to the cot and stroked Thomas' hand and hugged me, and that was it – Thomas was welcomed into the family and settled right in. We were a family of four and that felt bittersweet and completely wonderful all at the same time; because, of course, James should have been there with us and we should have been a family of five.

Life at home settled down very quickly and Michael became my perfect little helper, there wasn't a bit of jealousy at all. I would ask him to fetch me a nappy if I was changing Thomas or get me a clean bib if he'd been sick. Michael was so protective – he loved being involved and grinned as soon as he was given an instruction. One of the first things we did was tell him that he was grown up enough to give Thomas his bottle. We sat them on the sofa, Thomas all propped up with cushions and Stuart around the back supporting his head, and Michael proudly fed him. He was so pleased with himself, although he soon grew bored with the back rubbing when he had to wind Thomas – that was the end of that!

All my babies have been different, James was the only one to suffer from terrible colic, Michael was calm and Thomas was even more relaxed. We used to joke that we didn't even know we had him – he was such a good baby that even his crying was silent! One time he had earache and we gave him some Calpol, he slept on the sofa and I kept an eye on him but I later noticed that he had blood in his ear. We took him straight to the doctor and it turned out that he had a perforated eardrum and the doctor said he must have been in agony. He looked at me and said, 'Hasn't he been screaming the house down?' But he genuinely didn't make a sound so we had no idea anything was wrong.

We were in a sleep-deprived bubble for those first few exhausting weeks, and before I knew it our wedding day had arrived. It was magical to walk down the aisle and feel genuinely happy. I could see so many smiling faces, so many people who had been there in my hour of need. People were delighted that I had found my perfect husband and I felt on cloud nine. Michael stole the show with his cuteness as ring bearer during the ceremony, and then at the reception with his dance moves. Baby Thomas was there to share the day, even if he was too tiny to have a clue about what was going on. The one sadness, apart from James not being there, was that my mum missed the big day.

Her health had steadily declined since the deaths of my dad and James, I suppose life was never the same for her – it was too much loss and grief for her to handle. By the time our wedding day arrived, she'd had a stroke, was bedridden and had to be fed by a tube. We tried our best to get her to the church, even finding a big white taxi that could transport her wheelchair, but it was too much for her. I was devastated that she wasn't there to see my happy day. We had the ceremony and went on to the reception but I couldn't settle, I needed to see her. I persuaded Stuart to leave our wedding reception and drive me to the nursing home so she could see me in my dress and be part of the day, even from afar. So in we wandered, me in a full wedding gown, Stuart in the full top and tails, we must have looked insane! By that time she couldn't talk anymore but she still made sure she was heard – suddenly she pointed straight at Stuart and wagged her finger twice. I know that was her way of telling him that he'd better look after me and would have to answer to her if he didn't. He couldn't escape!

A month after the wedding Mum deteriorated and spent her final days in hospital. We would all go up and visit in tag teams, making sure she was never alone. I was distraught to see my mother dying, we had been through so much and I was also losing another link with James. Chatting to the nurses the day after she died, they told us that, as Mum was taking her last breaths, some of the patients were asking about the little boy who had been running up and down the corridor. The nurse was telling us that she kept explaining there was no little boy, that the ward was no place for small children. But two of the patients were adamant, they said, 'We definitely heard a little boy running along the corridor, he was hilarious and full of energy running up and down the ward, skipping and jumping.' I said to Stuart, 'That's the way James carried on, do you think it was him, that he was here to be with Mum as she died so they could go together?' It turned out that the two patients had heard the child running around at the exact time my mother passed away – it was as if James had come back for her. I like to think he was there as she breathed her last, so that she wasn't alone like he had been.

That wasn't the only occasion I felt James had come back to check up on us at this time. One night, Stuart and I were watching *Titanic* on the TV in bed and Michael and Thomas were asleep in their own rooms. We always left the landing light on just in case one of them woke in the night to use the bathroom. At the end of the film, I heard one of the kids shout, 'Muuuuummmmm.' I told Stuart to go as it was his turn, so he got up to do a check. We both heard someone call my name but the kids were out for the count, mouths open and in deep, deep sleep. In a way I wasn't surprised: the little voice sounded just like James, the way he used to drag out my name at the end and I was convinced it had been him. We also get lots of white feathers, which I am certain are a sign my boy has been to visit. I like to think he comes to check in and be part of everything.

Chapter 21

My Voice

Stuart has always been really hands on and loves everything about being a dad, which was just as well really as, a few months after Thomas' birth, I realised we were having another baby. We would have two children twelve months apart – I had no idea how we would cope but we were excited and a bit scared! The nine months passed in a flash and I had no time for the endless scans and worries that had occupied my previous pregnancies. Before I knew it, and almost a year after we had welcomed Thomas into the world, we were back at the same hospital having Leon Gary Fergus. He came into the world on 5th July 1999 at 12:30pm, weighing 4lb 14oz, and our family was complete.

My overprotectiveness remained just as intense, despite the fact there were more children to worry about. At night I used to keep both babies downstairs with me until I was ready for bed, and now and again Stuart would say, 'Take them up to their beds, it's not fair on them they are so tired.' So I would carry them up but then I'd be up and down all night checking on them every five minutes – I found it so stressful. We had baby alarms, pressure pads, you name it we had it. They were so close in age it felt like having twins really, and when I put them both in our bed they would sleep in the exact same way, holding their toys in the same hand, fingers curled over the top.

The two younger boys primarily slept in with us until they were two years old – going from Moses baskets (the same one I had bought for Kirsty and that James and Michael had slept in) to cots at the end of the bed before eventually moving into their own room.

My anxiety surrounding the kids got worse if there was something legal happening with Thompson and Venables – it would bring all the feelings of powerlessness flooding back, and I would end up clinging on to the boys even more so than usual. It was particularly tricky around the time that I was expecting Leon as the legal business with Tom Loflin refused to go away. He had been working behind the scenes with Venables and Thompson's legal teams to take their case to the very top – the European Court of Human Rights at Strasbourg.

Just before Leon was born, the European Commission of Human Rights concluded that the publicity and 'highly charged' emotion surrounding the trial meant that Thompson and Venables had been denied a fair trial and fair sentencing – meaning their human rights had been breached.

In September 1999, I was invited by the European Court of Human Rights to make representations to them concerning what exactly the rights of victims should be in criminal trials.

I felt so strongly about it that I left Stuart at home with the boys and flew to Strasbourg to be there in person. The Strasbourg hearing would decide whether Michael Howard's tariff was lawful or would have to be reconsidered. This was the final step of the sentence fight and I had to know I'd done all that I could. I was very emotional and all of that came to the surface when I bumped into Thompson's barristers at the airport. One came over and offered to buy me a drink, and my reply wasn't particularly polite, 'Are you taking the piss? You are about to defend one of my son's killers. Are you insane?'

He looked embarrassed and walked away, but I couldn't leave it at that and so I marched over and shouted, 'How could you?'

I carried on, 'How could you defend a killer? Do you have kids?'

He sat there with his hands behind his back and said, 'Yes I do, thanks.'

Well that was it, I spun round and addressed the other barrister, who was also standing there, 'Do you have kids too?' He replied that his wife had suffered a stillbirth and I shouted, 'So did I and, on top of that, I have had to cope with a murdered child. I hope you are both proud of yourselves.'

I couldn't help myself and the rage just overtook me. As a result we all kept our distance for the rest of the hearing. Sean spoke on my behalf, and we were invited to put across our views on how victims rights should be represented. We had been clearly told that we weren't allowed to address the court on the direct issue of the tariff or the Home Secretary's involvement, but we could talk about the impact of the crime on our family and how things could be changed to support other victims and their families.

Sean made two submissions. The first was that victims should be allowed to tell the court, after conviction but before the sentence is passed down, the impact of the offence upon them. This could influence how long the perpetrator should serve. This suggestion was accepted by parliament and led to the introduction of victim impact statements in England and Wales.

The second recommendation we made was that when prosecutors decide if they will accept a guilty plea to a lesser offence, they should consult the victim's family before they accept the plea. What this means in reality is that if the charge is murder, and the criminal offers a manslaughter plea instead, then the prosecution should liaise with the family first. The family obviously wouldn't have the right to veto anything, but we argued that they should be listened to and given fair warning about which way things might go. Both our recommendations were accepted and implemented.

Three months later, in December 1999, the European Court of Human Rights echoed the Commission's conclusion and ruled that Thompson and Venables had been denied a fair trial and fair sentencing. They pointed out that the age of criminal responsibility for children in England and Wales at ten – as stated in the Children and Young Person's Act of 1933 – is lower than most European countries, where the common age is fourteen (but not Scotland, where the age was eight until 2016). Given that the hearing was taking place in Europe, it was perhaps no surprise to see how they were ruling and that they were using the 1933 act as ammunition against us.

It had been explained to me in great detail that a large part of the trial was focused on proving Venables and Thompson understood their actions, but now it was being argued that Venables and Thompson were traumatised throughout the proceedings and therefore didn't have a chance to fully grasp what was being asked of them. The argument was that, because of the trial's public nature, it meant that they didn't get a fair hearing – apparently it was distressing for them to be near the family of their victim and to be put on trial in adult surroundings.

I found this especially upsetting as I was well aware of all the special measures that had been taken to ensure their comfort. I also remembered very clearly how they had been in the courtroom on that final day and it certainly wasn't distressed or traumatised. They had been laughing and joking, which didn't give me the impression they were remotely upset or troubled by the proceedings or the reality of being confronted by their actions. Yet again, it was all about their needs and feelings without a thought spared for James or us. In fact, it felt like we couldn't get anything right and even the concessions that had been made went against us. Apparently, the raised chair and dock, so that they could see over the rail, actually made them feel more uncomfortable and as if everyone was staring at them. Even though they had been close enough to their families and lawyers to share a laugh and joke as they were tried for the murder of my son, according to this latest report they weren't close enough to seek any comfort from their defence teams.

At this point, given how badly my son had been let down, I truly feared that the ruling would mean Thompson and Venables would be retried, or worse, let go immediately. They had already served six years – what was to stop a system clearly fixated on the comfort of these two murderers from deciding they had done their time? Although we had been reassured by Jack Straw, the new Home Secretary, that the killers wouldn't be released early, nothing would have surprised me. I repeatedly asked to meet Jack Straw once he took over as Home Secretary and he refused – he did eventually offer me a phone call but I have to admit to telling him what he could do with that offer. The idea he couldn't spare me half an hour of his time was baffling and summed up our situation – it felt as if the government didn't care about us. It didn't help that just before the European Court of Human Rights came back with their ruling, the Chief Inspector of Prisons David Ramsbotham prompted an outcry by saying Thompson and Venables should be released soon after their 18th birthdays. He later apologised to Jack Straw, but as far as I was concerned the damage had been done.

I felt happy that we had put our case across to the European Court in the strongest terms, but the ruling that really concerned me now, was the one that dealt with how long Thompson and Venables should serve.

This whole nightmare was rumbling on and we seemed to be bound up in much wider political and legal issues that we simply didn't understand. I had genuinely hoped that when Venables and Thompson went away it would be for a long time and it would bring us some peace. Instead it seemed that the fight just kept getting harder and more unfair. The tariff issue was all I could think about. Michael Howard's increased sentence had been overturned but a new one hadn't yet been set, as the Home Office had been waiting for the outcome of the European rulings. Now those rulings had come in and a new tariff needed to be fixed, but the Home Office was removed from the decision-making process. The tariff decision would now be made by a judge, rather than a politician – in this case by the brand new Lord Chief Justice, Lord Woolf.

Chris Johnson says: 'Once Thompson and Venables were sentenced, the whole system was geared towards healing them with no thought for James' family at all in my view. The phrase: "they were only ten" should be said with emphasis on the depravity of their actions rather than sympathy for their punishment. It should have been about what they really needed to be helped, rather than glossing over their true evil in order to make the system look good. The fact they needed real intervention was ignored. Because they were young perhaps some nimble and professional "parenting" to get them out of the criminal mindset they were in could have helped them become valuable members of society. They needed to be treated like children who were perverse and needed the tightest possible boundaries. It felt doubly tragic that the system seemingly made them worse and not better.'

A new year arrived and we were coping with the chaos of three lively boys, which was a brilliant distraction. We were trying our best to put the legal issues to one side and enjoy family life, but it didn't ever really leave me and I struggled to compartmentalise everything. Eventually there was a public statement from Lord Woolf that surprised us all: he was going to take into account our feelings about the sentence. Finally someone was going to ask me how long I thought my son's killers should be detained for. They were going to put us in touch with the Director of Public Prosecutions, who was there to listen to the views of victims of crime; in the case where those victims had been killed, they would talk to the remaining family. The director would then be the mediator between the family and the court, making sure that all views were communicated back to the judge and relevant legal teams.

It didn't take me very long to communicate my thoughts as I'd had them since the day James' body had been found. The children who committed the premeditated murder of my baby should never go free. They should be locked up for the good of everyone and to prevent the further crimes I was convinced they would commit if they were released. No other baby, family or human being should suffer the way we had and the only way to ensure that didn't happen was to detain them. Venables and Thompson were nearly 18 – the age they had been told they would be able to start again – and I didn't believe for one minute they had changed. It was also a pivotal age because, if they were detained after their 18th birthdays, they would have to be transferred to young offenders' institutions and be confronted with adult jail conditions, rather than the safe houses they were used to.

I prayed that Lord Woolf would increase the sentence, even by a few years. I felt sick to my stomach and I think it was the first real time Stuart saw the impact on me at home. Of course, I kept it away from the kids, but once they were in bed, everything swamped me and I started to slip off to our bedroom just to lie on the bed quietly and imagine what would happen if my son's killers were walking the streets. I clung to every last scrap of hope that a sense of justice would prevail, that those deciding our fates would remember the only real fate that mattered – my baby lying in his coffin, covered by soil.

Chapter 22

Release

I suppose it shouldn't have been a surprise when Lord Woolf's ruling came back in October 2000. Despite the pretence that our opinion as James' voice mattered, regardless of the fact that my son had been let down at every turn, the system always seemed to put the feelings of two child murderers before James. Even when the signs are obvious, the human state is to always hope against hope that the right thing will happen. In this case it didn't and my worst nightmare presented itself when Lord Woolf set the tariff at seven years and eight months. As if this wasn't bad enough, when you stripped back all the legal speak, what that meant was that the tariff expired immediately and their release would be imminent.

We had effected two major changes in the legal process, but they were the only successes we had from James' case – what we spectacularly failed to do was keep his killers locked up. We had changed a small section of the law, but I couldn't keep the promise I made to my baby as I buried him: that his killers would be punished for what they did to him – because they haven't been, have they?

Thompson and Venables had served just over seven years and, once the ruling came back from Lord Woolf, the case was sent straight to the Parole Board for their decision as to whether it was safe for them to be released.

For my family, the discussion had flipped in an instant from 'How can we keep them inside?' to 'How soon will they be roaming the streets again?' No one in authority seemed to understand how devastating this ruling was – even if it would take another three to six months, it looked like they would be free around the eighth anniversary of the murder they'd committed. It was argued that the time they had spent inside their institutions was the same as an adult being handed a 16-year jail sentence, with parole granted halfway through. Lord Woolf's final word on the matter was, 'The one mitigating feature of the offence is the age of the two boys when the crime was committed.'

Lord Woolf argued that transferring them to young offenders' institutions would 'undo much of the good work that had been carried out to rehabilitate them'. This marked another change in the law too as it was the first time that a judge had set the tariff for any child detained at Her Majesty's pleasure.

My devastation was all-consuming and I spent hours

talking to Sean and Stuart about it, to see if there was anything more I could do. Sean explains, '[Thompson and Venables] were ten-and-a-half when they committed the offence so reinstating the eight-year tariff actually meant that they would have to go into youth custody once they reached their 18th birthday. Lord Woolf therefore set the tariff at seven years and eight months, basically so they didn't have to go into custody. He was satisfied that the rehabilitation efforts lavished upon them had been successful and didn't want those expensive efforts to be undone by the prison system. Putting them into a young offenders institution would have meant time in a prison environment, instead of the secure children's home where you felt they had been mollycoddled. This wasn't a witch-hunt on your part, but we wanted them to hear the clang of the prison gates and feel some of the fear that James felt. It was a crushing blow to you and the family.'

Not knowing what else to do, I organised a rally to galvanise the support the public had shown us so far – anything to make noise. The government would have loved me to disappear but I was extremely happy to be a thorn in their side for as long as I needed to be. I was even more ready for battle when I heard that their lawyers were planning to go to the High Court and win Thompson and Venables lifelong anonymity. Not only were those boys getting out, but when they did there was a chance no one would know who they were or what they were capable of. Suddenly, the newspapers were full of James and the crime again, and various groups of people enjoyed having their say on whether my son's killers deserved lifelong sentences. There was also much debate surrounding the question of anonymity and if their lives would be in danger once they were released.

I will never believe that they were transformed by their time inside, in fact, we know that is completely untrue given Venables has re-offended twice, that we know of. I have been told of allegations of violent behaviour from both of them, assaults on other inmates and that Venables had had a long-standing sexual affair with his housemother. We weren't privy to any of the psychiatric and behavioural reports, but if even a tiny portion of the allegations were true, these were not reformed characters. I vowed not to let this go.

Chris comments, 'It was like a conspiracy of the establishment to self-heal. If they had seriously addressed the issue of those two and what they did, the system would have fallen down. Why hasn't there been a public enquiry into the failings by Liverpool City Council? The boys had gone to school in Liverpool where their behaviour was witnessed and developed. Their truancy was not even addressed – it was unusual in primary schools for kids to be absent so heavily and their behaviour should have raised alarm bells.'

Nobody in authority could sit down and say, 'What is the best thing for everyone? How can we do something for everyone?' Lord Woolf had been told that Venables was a good kid and that just simply wasn't and isn't true – how can it be? He's been recalled to prison twice. It is a lie and so why was no one ever prosecuted for perjury? I feel like I wasn't embraced by the system because I was trying to show that the system hadn't worked in this instance, and that is not what people wanted to hear.

Nevertheless, lawyers acting for Thompson and Venables carried on right to the top in their pursuit of a new and trouble-free life for the boys once they were released. The Right Honourable Dame Elizabeth Butler-Sloss was the next person to protect my son's killers. In January 2001 legal teams acting for Thompson and Venables won an unprecedented court order from the High Court when Dame Elizabeth Butler-Sloss granted them anonymity for the rest of their lives – ostensibly to protect them from revenge attacks by the public and, insultingly, from James' family.

There is not one time I have ever done a thing to degrade the memory of my son – I wouldn't lower myself to their level – and for anyone to suggest that I would be involved in any kind of attacks against my son's killers made me even angrier with the system and its failure to protect James and our family. The ruling was watertight: the media were banned from reporting any information whatsoever about where they lived, their identities, clothes, accents, appearances – basically any tiny details that might remotely give away who they were and what they had done. The order also stated that even if any of that information made its way online it still couldn't be widely reported by the mainstream media. This also included any details about the time they had spent in their children's homes, although this ban would be lifted one year after their release. Whatever way you looked at it, every possible eventuality was covered.

There was an outcry from the media, who argued these stringent conditions rendered their jobs impossible, as well as making a mockery of the freedom of the press to report stories in the national interest. The story had also gained international interest, due to the ages of Thompson and Venables, which meant publications abroad would also be hindered by these constraints. Their obvious concern was to sell papers, but there were some corporations who were genuinely outraged that two lads who had committed the most shocking crime of recent times would be allowed to move freely alongside the unsuspecting public. But none of this carried as much weight as the concern voiced by Dame Butler-Sloss that Thompson and Venables would be in grave danger if they were uncovered. This was of paramount importance even, it seemed, if it left the public at risk and silenced the press.

I couldn't quite process it all – somehow all the campaigning, all the tears, all the sleepless nights, all the fighting, had led us to this disappointing moment. It also opened the gates for others, who had committed similar depraved acts, to be given lifelong protection if there was a reasonable chance that society might rebuke them once they were released. I didn't understand why it was different for Thompson and Venables when there were other examples of criminals serving their time and later making new lives for themselves without getting new identities. Did it also mean that other adult killers could apply for the same special treatment if they were ever released? How could society function if we were going to end up living alongside murderers with new names and no idea of the crimes they'd committed? We were categorically told there were no grounds to challenge the ruling of either the Secretary of State or the Lord Chief Justice. In short, they wanted us to disappear.

The identity battle continued and I tried to steel myself for the next blow. Try as I might, even I didn't have any idea how badly I would cope with that.

* * *

Friday, 24th June 2001, turned out to be one of the worst days of my life. Little over eight years after murdering James, Thompson and Venables were released on life license and my carefully compartmentalised box of emotions went up in flames.

For all these years I have worked hard to be two people: the public Denise who will fight any battle for James, however long it takes and however hard it seems, and Denise Fergus, wife to Stuart and mum to Michael, Thomas and Leon. The two worlds rarely crossed over and certainly, if I had been campaigning hard for James, once I stepped through our front door, I left it all behind. I would get in, shower, put my pyjamas on and start making tea for everyone or clean and tackle the huge ironing pile. I've always answered any questions the kids have as honestly as I can – they know what I know – and we have always talked about James, but the lads never saw me cry. Until that day, when it all just seeped into one big meltdown triggered by my deep ache for James and the very real feeling that I'd let him down. It was like stepping back in time and it was scary for us all.

We went to the Royal Court of Justice to see them released, but they'd been let go the night before, to protect them from the press. I had wanted to look them in the eye one last time, but that wasn't deemed a good idea. We got home and I could feel myself dissolving like an aspirin, I hadn't felt anger like that for a long time and I knew I had to take myself away. I went up to our bedroom, blocking the door, and got into bed. But before I did that I am not ashamed to say that I smashed up pretty much whatever was in that room. I could think of no other way to channel the deep anger and bitter disappointment I felt.

It was like going back in time and the whole family rallied round me again – seeing them all there, hovering and worried about me, transported me back eight years and I felt like it erased everything I had worked for. I felt useless. I looked at them all surrounding my bed and I was grateful, of course I was, but that familiar and desperate need to be on my own came over me in waves. That's the first and last time I have ever kicked off like that since I have been with Stuart. It felt like I was drowning again and it all came down to the fact I hadn't been able to deliver on my final promise to my son. I promised him I would keep his killers locked up, I vowed that to him, but I couldn't deliver and the guilt swamped me.

I shut everyone out, including Stuart, but I had an overwhelming need to see Michael. I asked Stuart to collect him from school and he brought him straight up to me. I remember Michael walking in and coming over to sit on my lap – he was nearly eight years old, so more than capable of asking tricky questions if he'd wanted to, but he didn't. He just sat there on the bed, put his arms around me and let me cuddle him. I think those early days, when it was just the two of us, means that we do have a special bond where we often don't need words – it used to be like that when he was a baby. He would rest his head on my shoulder and look at me. But on this day, he knew that things weren't right and his little hand started stroking my arm, we stayed like that for a long time and didn't say anything.

Eventually I calmed down and came back to earth. Michael went off to have his tea and I stayed in my bedroom, lying in the dark thinking things through. It dawned on me that Thompson and Venables would mess up this chance at freedom; that this wasn't the end of the fight because they would do something wrong and the process would start all over again. I vowed that, as far as possible given their anonymity, I would watch their every move and be ready to pick up the fight at any moment. I have said in every statement and government letter that I have ever written, if anything happens to another family, there will be blood on the hands of the system designed to protect us against criminals. Our legal system isn't supposed to enable the behaviour of criminals by letting them go unrehabilitated, which in my mind Thompson and Venables were when they were released. I stand by that completely. When I am feeling more rational, I know I have done my best.

But then, I picked up the photo of James by my bedside and looked at his little face; he would expect me to fix this but I couldn't. The emotions were exactly the same as when I left The Strand shopping centre that first night without him – the same sense of letting him down – and it was truly the worst, worst feeling in the world.

I knew that lots of people had a vested interest in presenting this rehabilitation and release as a success story, but my only concern was that I had no idea where Thompson and Venables would be living. I had been given all sorts of assurances but I didn't believe any of them.

We were given 24 hours' notice before the rest of the world heard the release news in a statement by David Blunkett, who had now replaced Jack Straw as Home

Secretary. Blunkett outlined that Thompson and Venables would be on license (with 'strict conditions') for the rest of their lives and would be 'liable to immediate recall if there is any concern at any time about their risk'. He went on to state that the parole board had been satisfied that the public weren't in danger and that there was no 'unacceptable risk' to anyone. It was supposed to make me feel better that, as the statement read, 'the life licences include conditions which prohibit Thompson and Venables, whether directly or indirectly, from contacting or attempting to contact the family of James Bulger or each other. They will also be prohibited from entering the Metropolitan County of Merseyside without the prior written consent of their supervising officers . . . I am assured that Thompson and Venables will be kept under very close scrutiny by the Probation Service, whose principle aim is to ensure the protection of the public.'

* * *

So they were free and I was terrified. I became fixated on the fact that, despite the hollow assurances from the government, they could be living down the road and who would know? But they had every opportunity to find out all about me. Did they know where I lived? Did they know what my kids looked like and where they went to school? Were they visiting James' grave? I felt invaded and powerless. How was it fair that they knew everything about my life but I was forbidden from knowing anything about theirs? The people around me could see the anxious cycle I was in danger of slipping back into. If it was possible, I became ever more anxious about the kids.

Supermarket shopping was a living hell. I wouldn't go on my own, in fact I haven't been shopping alone since James was taken. When I did go, if I took the kids, then Stuart had to come with me. This meant all five of us would be trawling round the supermarket, the kids piled in the trolley, barely leaving any space for the food we needed to buy. Thomas and Leon would be in a double-seated trolley and I would make sure that Michael was right in front of me, standing on the trolley. Either Stuart or I would have our arms either side of him as we pushed, people must have thought, What on earth is going on here?

If I stopped to actually pick up some food I would shout out every few paces, 'Where's Michael, I can't see him?' and Stuart would calmly say, 'He's right here at the end of the trolley,' or we would be packing up at the checkout and I might have lost sight of Leon and I would scream, 'Stuart, where's Leon?' and he would calmly point to where he was playing. If I ever did leave the kids with a family member – usually Barbara – we would go round the supermarket as fast as we could, so we didn't leave the kids for too long. It sounds like insane behaviour, but once you have experienced the very worst thing, your mind just can't stop imagining it happening again.

Chapter 23

Keeping Focussed

'Stay where I can see you.'

How many times since I became a mum have I uttered those words, I wonder? The answer is too many – except that, when they really mattered, there was evil at play to overpower me. I spent years replaying my last moments with James and those thoughts were particularly intense once his killers had been out for a while. I went through a phase where I thought about it all the time and I saw danger everywhere. I remember one winter day, the year of the release, watching from the kitchen window as my boys raced around the garden, desperate to build their snowman before everything melted. They were in their element and I couldn't take my eyes off them, but there was nothing new in that. I didn't ever let them out of my sight, even in our own garden, always counting heads to make sure they were all still there. I know that it must have been hard for the kids at times when they were growing up, despite what they say.

The boys knew they had to stay in my sightline at all times. I had a special chair that used to tuck under the worktop that was just the right height for me to see every corner of our garden. Our house was like a fortress, surrounded by high fences and locked gates operated by switches inside the house. I knew this made it impossible for anyone to get in or out, but the elaborate security didn't bring me any comfort, nothing did really, not even the boys being right in front of me. I knew better than anyone else that having them within touching distance was no guarantee they would stay safe. After all, James had been right by my side and then he was gone forever.

I'd watch for ages as Michael, Thomas and Leon played, only stepping away from the window if I needed to go to the bathroom, and even then I would make sure that Stuart took my place until I got back. I was never that mum who caught up on the cleaning as they played out, delighted they weren't under my feet. Instead I would stand and stare, hardly daring to blink, always so aware that one of them could disappear in an instant. Never forgetting that there should be four little boys holding out their hands to catch snowflakes . . .

As time has gone on I have stopped my mind from imagining what James would be like as he played with his brothers. I try and concentrate on the present. That day, as the snow came down, I remember saying to myself, *Sod it! Get out there Denise, enjoy the snow with the lads. It's not often we get properly freezing weather like this.*

So I put on my boots and coat and ran out through the front door, ready to join in the fun. The snow was tumbling down and settling immediately and the kids were mega-excited that I had come out to play. I watched them circle round the 'safe' bit of the garden. They knew the rules, even if Stuart and I were outside with them the cut-off point was the tree to the left of our house. From a young age we had explained to them all that by the trunk of that tree, there was an invisible line that could not and must not be crossed. They knew it was because it meant mummy wouldn't be able to see them and they knew that wasn't okay. That snowy day, I began to work on the snowman's head with Thomas, adding layers to a big ball of snow. As we were rolling it across the garden, we reached the cut-off point and I absentmindedly kept on going.

Suddenly, Thomas stopped in his tracks. Looking panicked he shouted up at me, 'Mummy, mummy, you must never go over the line, that's breaking the rules. Stop there!'

It took me a minute to realise what was happening. He clearly needed reassuring so I patted him on the head and said, 'That's right lad, well done.' In my head I felt instant guilt, what kind of mother was I? Making my kids terrified to cross a line in their own garden in case I couldn't see them for a few seconds? But that is the life we have been forced to live after what happened and, once Thompson and Venables were out, that sense of terror was right back, sitting on my shoulder like the devil.

We had a big back garden with huge fences – no one could get over and out and no one could get in. I made sure they had lots of toys to keep them entertained and my house was open to all. We set up a mini-crèche at our place and had everyone back to us. Parents knew their kids were safe once the gates were shut and secure, and it meant I could watch the lads at all times. As they got older Michael wanted to go and play in the woods with his mates and there was a spot from the house where I could just about see them. Eventually Stuart would gently say, 'Let him go, he will be fine,' and I had to learn to ease up a bit, but every little thing was a nightmare.

It was around this time that, when Michael was six years old, he started being bullied at school. He was coming home and not eating his tea, putting himself to bed ridiculously early and not saying a word. This went on for a few days and eventually I went up and sat on his bed to get it out of him. After a bit of coaxing, he told me that he was being bullied by two lads in his class – just the usual name calling and general mean behaviour, but it was upsetting seeing Michael so affected by it. I went completely mad and marched up to his school, St Marie's, the next day. I wanted to see the head during school time so I could get a look at the boys doing it. I was also going to insist that I saw their parents. Stuart and I were walking to the head's office and suddenly I saw Michael standing with two boys – I could tell by his body language that they were the ones bullying him. I had been poised to go into combat for my boy, but instead I just froze on the spot. They looked just like Thompson and Venables in their school uniforms. There had been video footage of them, bouncing around in their school hall, shown on one of the many documentaries made about James' murder. As I looked from afar, it was as if time had stopped and it took my breath away.

After talking to the teachers and asking them to have a stern word with the lads in question, we sorted out the bullying but I was also keen for the school security to be as up to date as possible if the boys were going to be safe there. We sat down with the council and explained the situation now that James' killers had been released and they arranged for St Marie's to receive a grant. They had new gates fitted, security swipe cards and new CCTV installed. In all honesty I would have home schooled them in a heartbeat, but Michael wanted to be around his mates. Deep down I knew I would be doing him more harm than good just for my own peace of mind. We briefed the school that they must never let anyone but us pick them up and I knew I would just have to handle it, but it was so hard.

Because of all the fighting I'd done to get Thompson

and Venables longer sentences, I thought they were bound to have a grudge. How did I know they weren't outside my house as I slept, that they weren't going to befriend members of my family to get at me? Kirkby is a small place and everyone knows where we live, it wouldn't be hard to find out. Part of rehabilitation can involve going back to the scene of the crime. How did I know that's not what they were doing, that they hadn't gone to James' graveside?

It was hard for the kids, especially Michael as he was that bit older than the other two. But he says now, 'The key for me has always been that Mum never kept anything from us – if ever anything was going to be in the paper or on the TV and she knew about it, she always told us there and then, so there were never any surprises. It's just the way it's always been. James isn't a shadowy figure looming over us, if I have ever asked a question she has told me straight and everything has always been out in the open between us. I can ask anything and I know she will answer me if she can.

'It does make me angry though. I look at the kind of older brother I am to Thomas and Leon and I know that James could have been that for me. He could have been here giving me advice and steering me and that would have been amazing to have – concerts, football games, I could have followed in his footsteps and that was taken away from Mum and taken away from me. I am angry for her too and all that she has been through, but we stick together – if she's fine then I'm fine.

'When I was young and if I went out I knew I couldn't go far, I was always in the back with a ball. Mum was either looking out the window, or standing in the doorway trying to hide! It didn't bother me and it didn't bother my mates either – it actually didn't affect me because I have always understood why. I've always been protective of Mum and whatever made her less anxious was fine by me. When I was younger the main issue was the school trips – I would often come home waving a piece of paper wanting her signature for a trip away and she would just say no. After a while, I would go to Dad and explain what the trip was and then he would work on her for me! Sometimes the only way to go on the trip was if Dad came, which happened a lot. My friends loved coming to mine – some of them spent most of the time here talking to Mum!'

Even to this day, with the lads over 18, if they want to go anywhere, they go to Stuart first and his advice is always to drip-feed me the information slowly – to plant the seed and then leave it. It usually works if they start by saying that their mates have been talking about it and everyone is going. The problem is that they are all quite like me, so the softly-softly approach doesn't really happen! Of course now they come and go much more freely, so watching them from the window like a night club bouncer isn't really possible anymore! But I don't sleep a wink until everyone is home and I expect texts to let me know when they are on their way and how far from home they are. Even now

Michael is in his 20s, if he goes to the cinema and texts to say he's on his way home, I time him. If he's even a few minutes late, I go into a blind panic. I truly don't think the chilly fear I felt when I realised James wasn't by my side will ever fully leave me.

* * *

One thing that kept me going in the early months after Thompson and Venables were freed was the public support. It very quickly became clear that the general public were as angry about the release of them as we were. The letters came in their sack loads and the outrage was clear. It was so bad at one point that David Blunkett had to step in, before they were actually released, and issue a call for calm. He said, 'I think we all need to take a deep breath and to view what is said and done as we would view it if it were taking place in any other country. We're not in the Midwest in the mid-19th century; we're in Britain in the 21st century and we will deal with things effectively and we'll deal with things in a civilised manner . . . If people continue to provide the emotional adrenaline for others who are sick of mind to go and [attack the boys] then there will be a great danger. The greatest safeguard we can offer to people in the community is to rehabilitate Thompson and Venables effectively.'

There were numerous threats made by those who were against the release, including vows from some to hunt down Thompson and Venables and kill them. As much as

I understood the mood, we haven't ever wanted violence in James' name – then or now. Emotions were swirling round unchecked and I think the public could see what the government couldn't – that by giving criminals like Thompson and Venables new identities and back stories, we were letting evil slip through our fingers to assimilate back into society. After all, you can't protect yourself against what you can't see.

Despite the fact that the blanket media ban was in full force, it didn't stop the stories coming thick and fast and there were all sorts of theories emerging. We were treated to in-depth accounts of how the parole board decided Thompson and Venables were ready for release, which included sending a team of people to interview them both for two days. This team had access to all the reports from inside the facilities where they had been kept. Yet again time was spent trying to determine if they felt guilty about what they had done to James. While Venables apparently fared better than Thompson, they both passed with flying colours.

There were two problems with this as far as I am concerned – the first is that they had both been prepared carefully ahead of their release to become consummate liars, but they had to be, of course, in order to gain their freedom. Their new identities and back stories had been painstakingly crafted by the authorities, and it was their job to stick to the new narratives they'd been given. That meant the very people judging their levels of cunning were the ones coaching them to be deceitful. It seemed utter madness to me. The second issue was that apparently all the psychological tests being done on them, the Hurst Test in particular, were being incorrectly administered. The problem was that they were using the adult version of the test on them, rather than the one geared towards children, which would have been more representative of their state of mind at the time of the killing.

The report also glossed over the fact that there was strong evidence Venables was having an affair with his house-mother and she was never disciplined for crossing such a fundamental line with someone so clearly in need of rehabilitation. There were no repercussions and the case was a ticking time bomb. That meant it all got put into a box labelled 'too difficult', because one thing couldn't explode without the whole thing going up.

This was hard for the whole family and, as the months turned into a couple of years, I tried to keep focused on the happy times. It became more and more important to make sure that James remained a positive part of our lives, particularly as the tenth anniversary loomed over us. Thomas starting school was a milestone and almost even more traumatic than Michael going – mainly because I knew those two were out and roaming the streets. I understood it was unlikely that they knew where my family were but I had no way of knowing for sure and I felt sick at the thought of it. Thomas also had the opposite reaction to Michael when it came to his first day at primary school, which was really hard.

On Thomas' first day I stayed at home with Leon, and, although I was worried about him being out of my sight, I didn't think he would get too upset because Michael had been fine. Stuart took Thomas and, like before, he saw him in, settled him and went to leave. As he was getting to the door, he heard someone shout, 'Don't leave me, Dad!' and realised it was Thomas. The teacher was holding him back and he was screaming, 'I want my dad!'

Stuart left and came home and made the big mistake of telling me. Well, that was it, I was screaming at Stuart, 'Go and get him! If you don't go and fetch him I will.' It was like a comedy sketch – there I was putting on my coat and shoes, and Stuart was standing by the door with his arms out saying, 'You've got to let them go to school, Denise!'

I knew I had to let the fear pass and be as normal a family as possible – we had to stick together. This became even more concrete once Michael officially changed his name to Fergus. It all came about out of the blue as we sat down to a Sunday roast. We were chatting away and talk turned to our upcoming family holiday to Spain – we never usually went abroad so everyone was really excited. Suddenly Michael turned around and said, 'But it's not a family holiday is it because you have all got the name Fergus and I am a Bulger?' Stuart reassured him that it didn't matter and we were all one big happy family, but he was adamant it was an issue and he asked if he could officially change his surname so he could have the same name as his brothers, especially as he doesn't have a relationship with Ralph.

This conversation was typical of the open chats I have always tried to have with my boys – they know they can ask me anything at all – and it was no different when it came to discussing the brother they never knew. People often ask how I told Michael in particular about James, but it wasn't really a matter of sitting him down and saying 'You had a brother and this is what happened to him'. James is just part of the family. I didn't ever turn off the TV when anything came on the news about the case, there are pictures of James in the house and I answer any questions that are asked with complete honesty. Right from when the boys were young I would include James in the conversation. Often when we were sitting round the dinner table and one of the boys would do or say something, I would say, 'James used to do that,' and then tell them a little story about him to cement the point. It helped to introduce James to them at a young age and in a natural way. Often when he was quite young Michael would wander in and say, 'You and James are on TV again.'

I was determined to always be the person they could ask, especially once they went to school and I knew they would have to contend with other kids talking in the playground and repeating what they had heard at home. I know everyone handles these things differently, but I wanted it all out in the open for us. I am friendly with one other mum whose young son was murdered – she went on to have two more children, but she didn't ever tell them about their older brother. The murderer was eventually released and one day, on the way back from the school run, the mother came home to hordes of press outside her house. It turned out that the murderer had moved nearby and the press wanted a reaction. She was with her two other children, but they had no idea what was going on, so she had to sit them down and tell them about their murdered brother. I didn't want that kind of conversation with my lads.

There aren't pictures of James everywhere as I didn't want the house to be a shrine – but there's a lovely one over the fireplace that has been there from when I first moved into the house with Ralph. Michael also has a picture of James in his bedroom as you walk in. I was going to put one in Leon and Thomas' room and Stuart said, 'Don't just assume, ask them first,' so I did and they weren't sure. But I feel very lucky that we can all have those open discussions and that James is easily mentioned every day in our house. He's part of the family he didn't live to meet.

Chapter 24

Caught

During the years that Venables and Thompson have been free, lots has changed in the way things are reported, and the traditional media has had to make way for the lightning speed of the Internet. The world of instant news also means there have been issues with upholding that original ban on the publication of any information regarding Thompson or Venables. The rise in social media meant that the floodgates opened, sometimes dangerously, with young men wrongly being identified as either one of the killers. This has meant innocent men having to go into hiding and fearing for their lives.

Over the years I have been inundated with tip-offs and tweeted pictures of random men by people who believe them to be my son's killers. People have claimed to have up-to-date photos of them and there were various sites opened and dedicated to tracking them down. Sometimes it is more random and I get sent pictures of trainers or hands and told that it is either Thompson or Venables in the photo. Although the police always move swiftly to act and shut everything down, the thirst for information has remained high over the years.

There were more reports of luxurious lifestyles: expensive holidays in the sun, security guards and all sorts of privilege. It has been hard to sort fact from fiction and, in a way, the worst has happened – they were out – what could be more devastating than that? Anniversaries came and went and life carried on because I had no choice. The anxiety I felt about the fact that my son's killers were loose never really went away. Obviously they weren't meant to enter Merseyside but we know one of them came to the city to watch an Everton game; we also know that Venables has been out drinking in Liverpool, which is terrifying. My nieces are at the age where they are going to bars – what if one of them is unwittingly chatted up by him?

Initially, I was fixated on knowing as much as I could about them and I make no apologies for that – sometimes it feels like I did the crime and they are the wronged party. But I have to remember that their whole lives, and those of the people they encounter, will be built on lies. Unfortunately, someone innocent will be sucked into the deception and get hurt, and that is so upsetting, but it's not how I live and I am grateful for that.

When they were first released I drove around and sat outside buildings I'd been tipped off about, waiting to see if I recognised them. That didn't last long though, as I realised it was now my job to protect what I had. I've been asked time and time again if I would want to come face to face with them and ask why they killed my son – my answer is always, 'No, it won't bring James back.' It wouldn't matter what they said as far as I am concerned because they are professional liars – I couldn't ever believe a word they said. There is also no way that I could be in a room with them long enough to ask the question.

There was a lot of nonsense written about me master-minding vigilante groups to go smashing around Liverpool, trying to find out where they were and to do them harm. But I have always said the same thing: I would never tarnish my son's memory like that. More importantly, why would I risk serving time for those two animals when I have three lads who need me?

I have always said I don't want them hanged, killed or harmed in any way – all I ever wanted was for them to serve time in an adult prison and for them to understand that my baby's life mattered. I wanted them to have a proper punishment, instead they were being handed Mars Bars in court. When James didn't get justice the only thing I could do was to let them know that I wasn't going away. I wanted them to know that I was watching, waiting for them slip up. In the end it didn't take very long.

In March 2010, nine years after his release, Jon Venables reoffended and was recalled back to jail for breaching the terms of his release in what Jack Straw called 'extremely serious allegations'. It was reported that he was accused of child pornography offences – which followed earlier reports linking him to a sex offence. He was given a two-year jail sentence and would be eligible for parole within a year.

We had asked that, if there was any kind of news like this, I be let known by the Home Office or the Parole Board before the press. This was so I could prepare the boys for the increased press attention and process it myself before answering any questions the media might have. It was always hard being put on the spot and discussing something so sensitive – I don't think that ever got any easier. Unfortunately, I heard the news after it was leaked to a national newspaper and eventually discussed by Phillip Schofield, live on *This Morning*. In what turned out to be a really embarrassing situation, I became adamant it wasn't true, arguing I would have been told in advance about something as serious as Venables reoffending and I contacted the show to tell them the information was incorrect. Poor Phillip was mortified to have caused upset with a rumour and apologised profusely. I told him not to worry, obviously it wasn't his fault and I knew he'd never do anything to upset me, and after I'd finished watching the show, Stuart and I went off to see Stuart's dad.

On the way, Stuart decided to pull over and call the

parole office, just to let them know about the rumour and double check something else wasn't going on – we were reassured it was all gossip. A little while later they called back and told Stuart word for word what Phillip had said on the show – it was true. Not only had my son's killer reoffended, as I had been certain he would, but nobody had the decency to tell me, demonstrating that I was the last to know anything when it came to my son. We were in the car and the phone was on loud speaker and all the anger and frustration boiled over. 'Why the hell didn't you tell me that when we called and asked?' I screamed. The woman on the end of the phone answered in a very matter of fact way, 'Ralph knew, we thought you did too.'

I called Sean immediately. He says now, 'When Venables was recalled it was obviously under his new identity, meaning all that hard work to give him a new life was immediately compromised. We found out that the recall was for child pornography offences and he was subsequently given a custodial sentence because of the gravity of the images found in his possession. When he became eligible for release on parole again, we were allowed to make representations to the Parole Board as they considered his possible release – we were effectively the beneficiaries of our own law change and were allowed to read those submissions to the Parole Board via video link.

'We always felt, however, that we were fighting with both hands tied behind our backs when dealing with the Parole hearings, as we weren't allowed to see any of the psychiatric reports or the documentation upon which the Parole Board relied. This meant that we couldn't challenge any of that evidence. As a lawyer I understand why confidential medical reports are not disclosed to third parties but it does make me wonder whether the invitation from the Parole Board to make those representations isn't just politically correct window dressing.

'On one occasion I was told that Thompson was in prison in Kilkenny, Ireland for a serious violent offence under his new identity. Apparently the Irish police didn't know who he really was, even though he was being held on remand for such a serious offence. This information came to me via a Sunday tabloid late on a Friday afternoon, so I phoned the Home Office (we have no hotline number by the way, so I had to go through the same channels as everyone else, which can take forever). I got the Home Office to confirm late that night that Thompson was still in the UK and not in Ireland, meaning the story was false, so I was able to tell the journalist and they didn't run the story. This saved you a bit of heartache but, in the end, it all comes down to trust and believing in the system. You don't trust it and I understand why – it doesn't seem to trust you.'

I spent a lot of time on the impact statement for Venables' Parole Board. It was the first time that I felt someone was listening to me, and I poured my heart and soul into it. I wanted to make the point that his original license back in

2001 was based on a false premise and deception. I outlined the questions I had been asking in the years following his release:

1. Has he entered Merseyside or Liverpool?
2. Has he been in trouble with the law since his release?
3. Has he visited James' grave as part of his rehabilitation?
4. Does he live anywhere near where I live?

I went on to add, 'The answers I have received over the years were simply "No" or "You cannot be told". Knowing Venables' recall under the terms of his parole in 2010, I learned that the true answer to these questions should have been "Yes" or, more worryingly, "We don't check". I urge you to recognise he remains a danger to society in general and to my family in particular, since he breached the terms of his original license which was designed for our protection. I have appeared in the media and he will know what I look like and, whilst I have always done my best to keep my children out of the spotlight, there is every chance he will know what they look like too.

'I have learnt that Venables has been going to Everton games, some of my family support this team and could have, unwittingly, been sitting next to him. The risk that my family are exposed to all stems from the protection of anonymity afforded to Venables, the criminal, which is not extended to me and my family as relatives of the murder victim. Unlike other prisoners on license only a few people know his true identity. Even ordinary police officers could encounter him committing an offence and let him off with a warning, not knowing his true identity.'

The fact that he had been caught with child pornography seemed the most obvious sign in the world that he hadn't been 'fixed' by the system – possessing indecent images of children isn't a mark of successful reassimilation into civilised society as far as I am concerned. What worried me most was the timing. Our lads were on the cusp of wanting to start venturing out and I was terrified. It was one thing that they didn't serve their time and had been released, but now Venables was reoffending and we had no idea how long he would be behind bars for this time. He could have been out any minute. All the 'what ifs' started flooding my thoughts. For example, what if he goes to a night club and starts talking to Michael – that means that Michael would unwittingly be talking to the lad who murdered his brother. All this was going through my head and I wrote it all down. It was probably the first time I had been strong enough to put my case across.

I handed in the impact statement only to be told, 'If there is anything you don't want Venables to read, we advise you take it out.' That's how I discovered he had the right to read the statement I'd prepared. My immediate response was, 'In that case, I should be able to read his,' but I was told I didn't have that right. It was such a blow – this murderer even had the right to know what was going on in my head, my innermost thoughts. He got to hear how the misery he caused my family affected me every day. How is that justice? How is that right? I don't get to know his name but he gets access to everything I do and feel. It rendered the statement worthless, as I had to take out lots of information about my lads to protect them. I also felt it would give him great satisfaction to know he continued to blight my life and I refused to give him the power to hurt me or my family anymore. I ended up submitting my statement, I had to as it was for James, but I think that might have wiped away my last shred of belief in the system.

I also decided to attend the Parole Board hearing (although we were only allowed to do so by video link) so that I could represent James. This meant that Venables could see me but I couldn't see him – nothing ever seems to change on that front. Some of my friends were concerned and couldn't understand why I wanted to go back there and revisit all that pain, but I have always said that as long as there is a fight to be had I will do it for James. I want Thompson and Venables to know I will never go away, let them forget what they did to my son or let them ruin another family.

Chapter 25

Gone, But Never Forgotten

Writing this book has been my first chance to tell my story in my own words. Over the years so many decisions were made for me and so many things have been written about me, that I wanted the chance to tell the world how special my son was and what really happened on the day he left our lives forever.

Somehow, the 25th anniversary of James's death felt like the right time to deal with the pain and trauma his death caused, but, most importantly, to celebrate my magical little boy. James was more than a child murdered by two ten-year-old boys and not just a grainy black and white image – he was my funny, cheeky, lively son and his short life mattered.

In truth, I hadn't ever felt strong enough to revisit the nightmare of the day that James went missing and everything else that happened afterwards. I have worked so hard over the years not to exist in a world of pain, that I was terrified to open the door again and worried that doing this book would bring all the suffering back to the surface. I have had to mentally box away so much that I was terrified to dust it all off and delve back into it. But, actually, it has made me feel so close to James and, in a way, it has brought him to life a bit for Stuart. As I talk about him I can see the smile on his face so clearly, and that is the nicest feeling in the world.

I know Michael was initially worried, 'The only time it's difficult is when Mum is upset. I am so proud my mum is doing this book because she can set the record straight, but I worried it would upset her like Ralph's book did. When that was published I saw the headline "I blame Denise" and lost it totally. I went storming into the kitchen as she was hanging out washing and I exploded. But she ended up being really calm about it and comforting me. We all look out for each other in our family and my mates do the same for me. Sometimes they will see something on TV and they might raise it, but not very often. I am lucky really, I have lots of loyal people around me. The book has been a great thing and has helped Mum finally have her say. It's really helped her.'

Because of all the campaigning I've done over the years, people assume I am used to being in public but, contrary to what some think, I hate the limelight with a passion and it took a long time to put my anxiety to one side. I used to approach the cameras and in my head I would be saying,

I'm doing this for James, I'm doing this for James. Even now I have to take a deep breath when I go into a room and there are lots of conversations going on, but speaking up for James is the only way I can be a mother to him. I am his only voice.

People often ask me if I've ever been tempted to find out exactly what Thompson and Venables did to James on the day they murdered him and the answer is still no. At the time it happened there was no way I wanted to know, or could have coped with being told. And then, as the years passed, it became impossible to imagine finding out. In hindsight perhaps it would have been better to find out at the time, the equivalent of being kicked while I was down. It was like the stronger I got, the less I would have been able to cope with the details. And now it is too late and I am glad if my boys ever question me, I can hand on heart say that I don't know.

There has only been one time I thought I was ready for the facts and that was just after Thomas was born. I remember saying to Stuart, 'I think I need to know what happened so I can protect our boys.' So we went to Albert Kirby and he refused to go into detail, saying that I knew the majority of what was true but that he wasn't prepared to blow up my life by telling me anything else. I am grateful for that now. The public are still amazing to me, and to the rest of the family too.

Michael says, 'I remember I'd just started work and it was

around the time the Venables child porn story broke. It came on the radio and I was in the work van at the time with the lads and they immediately turned off the radio without saying a word. I told them that I knew about it and it was fine, but they just came back and said, "Okay, but we don't want you to have to listen to that in work – it will mess with your head." That was only three months in and it has been the same since. People are lovely most places I go, I was once in a bar and a security guard came up and said, "I recognise you, you're Denise's lad, if you ever need anything or there's ever any issues, here is my card and you call me any time." It's good to know there are good people out there.'

Sometimes it is hard as I can get followed around the shops, to the extent that I have had to walk away from a trolley full of shopping as it is too much. There are some days I just can't cope with it all and I just want to get in, get what I need and get out.

There was a time where the attention became sinister and I had a stalker. It was a difficult period and, eventually, the case went to court. The whole experience brought back some tough emotions, not least as the trial was taking place in the court down the road from The Strand shopping centre and I hadn't set foot there since the day James went missing. Officials agreed to let us give evidence via video link and they offered us a room at Walton Lane Police Station, but that was where they had taken Thompson for questioning after he'd been arrested. We requested another station and they offered us Lower Lane Police Station, but that was where Venables had been taken for questioning after he'd been arrested. One exasperated policeman said, 'What do you want us to do?' I wasn't trying to be difficult, I simply couldn't go anywhere I knew those two had been, the thought of it made me feel sick.

After a slightly farcical scenario where the stalker kept trying to argue that he should be able to question Stuart and I directly, he was found guilty and spent a short time in prison where psychiatric care was recommended. When he was about to be released the police came round to offer us a panic alarm and assurances that he had been banned from Kirkby and given a strict curfew. It was a very odd experience and, although it had nothing to do with James, it reminded me that he was everywhere. Those memories of police stations and courts were still so raw all these years later.

Social media hasn't always been my friend either and I have had to get used to trolling. When you're in the public eye for whatever reason, even someone like me, the mum of a murdered child, it's inevitable. I am lucky to have much more support than hate and, unless it is particularly scary or really bad, I just ignore it. There was one particular incident where I had to involve the police as things turned a bit ugly. I started to screen grab what she was saying as evidence (before she deleted the tweets) and I went to the authorities who decided that what she was doing warranted three years in prison. I am lucky that, all these years later, most people are still so supportive, especially in Liverpool. It is like they have taken James and our family to their hearts. I see that clearly when it comes to the support we get for the projects we have set up in James' name.

As the years have gone on it has become really important to make sure that something good and positive comes from James' short life. He was a ray of sunshine, full to the brim with energy and he had so much love to give. He was never stroppy, always wanted a hug and always ready for a dance. He was always right in the thick of everything and I wanted to offer some of that energy to children who needed it.

Initially, we were contacted by Esther Rantzen – she was already partnered with a children's charity and wanted to expand by working with us and using James' name on a house for struggling children. We talked for a while and looked at various possibilities and, although it didn't work out, it did make me realise that I really wanted to create a lasting memorial in his name.

So with that in mind, I kept going with the idea and we set up the James Bulger Memorial Trust, known as For James. The idea was a charity that would benefit and support young people who are disadvantaged in some way – kids who have been damaged either by bereavement, bullying, hatred or having been a victim of crime. The trust provides cost-free travel and holiday accommodation for children and their families. This is alongside supporting other organisations benefitting children in similar difficult circumstances. We fundraise all year round and the money goes towards the upkeep of the accommodation and the travel expenses we donate to those families.

People actually stop me on the street and give me money for the charity. I have a special donation pocket and I let them see me put the money in there and then I will tweet doing a thank you, something along the lines of, 'A lovely lady just stopped me in the street and gave me £10, which has gone straight to the fund, so huge thanks.' The calendar is packed full of events such as free family festivals, black tie dinners and charity walks. I love that we have set something up ourselves and that James' name remains ours. The charity is a huge part of my life, and Stuart's too, and it is so wonderful to finally see something positive coming from years of pain and misery.

* * *

James is part of everything we do – especially when it comes to the special occasions. There is a Christmas tree planted next to his grave and before 25th December we all go to the cemetery to decorate it as a family. We put lights and baubles on it and hang his stocking on there, to make sure he is included in all the preparation. On Christmas Eve, as it is getting dark and before the cemetery closes, we all go back down and Michael will put the star on top of James' tree as we are leaving. It's the last touch for James once darkness falls. As I love Christmas, I spend just as much time and effort decorating James' tree as I do our one at home. I can be there for hours! Stuart came up with the idea of adding lights that are on a timer, so it's the same as ours at home.

I feel happy when we've been to the grave as I know we have done the best we can for him, and I can then try and make Christmas Day just about the boys. James also has a special area in our back garden with flowers and ornaments, so for Christmas I always put lots of lights up so they twinkle through the window as we eat our dinner and open our presents. I cook so much food and we have the day just the five of us, no one goes out and no one comes in. This is something I have done since the first Christmas without James, the first one with Michael. When James was alive we would trawl around everyone's houses, making sure we saw everyone, like you do at Christmas. If I'd known it was his last one, we would have stayed all cosy inside just us and I wouldn't have shared him with anyone. Once I had the boys I decided to change that and make it all about them. We have our Christmas dinner in the conservatory and we do talk about James round the table. People often ask if Christmas is the hardest, but there is always a face missing around that table every single day. Christmas isn't any harder than any other day of the week.

There are other special occasions we mark at the cemetery – for James' 18th birthday I had a cake made in the shape of a bottle of champagne and left it on his grave. It must have looked very realistic as someone stole it, but nevertheless it was a nod to the fact he should have been enjoying his first legal drink. We also had the marble on his grave redone for his 18th birthday too – even as I ordered it and arranged for the job to be done I remember feeling shock. All these years later it still takes me by surprise that James is in the ground and that my baby has gone. A new gravestone is not exactly the gift you imagine giving your child on such a special birthday.

I try very hard to live in the present – I can't live in a world of ifs, buts and if onlys – if only I hadn't gone shopping that day, if only we hadn't stopped at the butcher's, what if we had been half an hour later? Why didn't I take his buggy? Thinking like that is the path to madness, as is searching for answers about why this had to happen to us – only Venables and Thompson know why they did what they did and I realised I had to stop asking why a long time ago because the answers aren't ever coming. There is no forgiveness in my heart for my son's killers.

Nor is there any peace since his killers were released. I know there are some people out there who think I should 'let it go', especially given how long ago James was murdered. To them I simply say, *Would you ever give up on your child, especially if he wasn't here to defend himself?*

There is also a school of thought that everyone deserves a second chance to put right their wrongs. In normal circumstances, I am the first to agree with that: any decent person who makes a mistake should be given the chance to make amends. But there are two things that stop me applying this logic to my son's killers. The first is that they aren't decent people who live by the same morals we do – they are murderers who went out, at the age of ten, to abduct and kill. The second thing that stops me being able to walk away is the fact that the system continues to protect Thompson and Venables above all else, in my view, even if it means compromising the public and it seems to me wilfully ignoring what they did to my son.

In my opinion, the government will never be able to acknowledge the very real threat Thompson and Venables pose to the public, because to admit that would require them to face the fact that their rehabilitation has, in my mind, failed. All the money invested in my son's killers may as well have gone up in flames, because they have not been reformed. I think that they manipulated their way to freedom and, after the first time Venables reoffended, I knew it would only be a matter of time before he slipped up again. As I said in my statement to the Parole Board in 2010, 'I urge you to recognise he remains a danger to society in general.'

So it came as absolutely no surprise to me that, nearly eight years after he was first recalled to prison for breaching the terms of his release, I found out that Jon Venables was back in jail for a second time. He was re-arrested in November 2017, at the age of 35, after officials discovered more child abuse images on his computer during a routine home visit. The official response was: 'His recall is a huge blow to those who have championed the efforts to reform him over the past 25 years.' My response was: *Here we go again. When are the government going to listen to me?*

I do feel it has all been one big cover up over the years, with the government having to believe in their own system. That has been demonstrated by how they have treated me each time Venables has been recalled. The first time in 2010, someone did at least come round to the house to see me. The second time in 2017, we were told in a hurried phone call after the news was leaked to the press. Stuart was on the phone to his dad, when he had a missed call from our probation officer. Stuart called her back and she said, 'I am just calling to inform you that Jon Venables is in breach of his license and has been recalled back to prison. All I can say is that he has been arrested.' My blood ran cold and, instantly, I was back to those dark, early days. They wouldn't tell us when he had been arrested or how long he would be in prison for. As usual there was no information for me. I was in the dark and James, it seemed, was the last priority. Imagine how I felt and continue to feel, having spent 30 years publicly campaigning for my son's killers to have received longer prison sentences, and living life not knowing where they are or what kind of danger they pose to me or my family.

The media ended up giving me more information than the system supposedly there to protect me and my family. It turned out that Venables had yet again been arrested for child porn images on his computer. I couldn't take the chance that another child could be hurt, especially as Venables clearly, in my mind, has learnt nothing, so we rolled up our sleeves, picked up the fight and set about trying to finally get justice for my son. As my statement to the press said:

Venables has now proved beyond any doubt what a vile, perverted psychopath he has always been. But what hurts me most is the way the probation service has tried, in my view, to cover this up.

Venables was taken back into custody a week ago, yet I was only informed hours before it hit the press. But it's clear that they were trying to keep this quiet, until they got a call from the media. They then phoned me last night at 8.40pm, in a hurried call, with few details given – just that he had breached his terms of the license and returned to prison. That left me extremely upset, angry, feeling insulted. I will be taking advice from my lawyer before making a formal complaint to the probation service.

I hope finally I might get some justice for my son, James. I predicted Venables would re-offend unless they kept a very tight rein on him and I pray that now, please, someone from the UK government will finally listen to me. Justice for James.

Time and my husband and children have given me a sense of happiness and peace I could never have imagined after the day James left my side. But I think the time has come, now 30 years after my son's murder and in light of the recent offence by Venables, that there is a renewed national conversation around the appropriate length of sentencing for under-age criminals. We have also started a petition to ensure the probation service is compelled to alert victim's families immediately after any offence. I will continue to do all I can for James until there is no breath left in my body – he will always be my son and I will protect him and his memory forever. The fight continues, it just changes as the years go on.

Chapter 26

Fighting On

Twenty-five years sounds like an eternity but it also feels as if that time has passed in the blink of an eye. I can honestly say there are more good days than bad, more laughs than tears, more cherished memories than nightmares – Stuart and my three boys make sure of that, every single day. I know how loved and looked after I am and I couldn't wish for more, but it still only takes one press report to plunge me back into the nightmare of February 1993, instantly casting me adrift in the horror story of James' murder.

Sometimes I still feel on the edge of that dangerous and terrifying precipice. This is not helped by the fact that, over the years, Jon Venables has seemed determined to keep reopening my wounds by breaching the terms of his licence. It was therefore no surprise to me when he was rearrested in November 2017, and it was splashed all over the papers just as I prepared to spend my 25th Christmas without my darling boy.

It was a quarter of a century since I had seen James rip open his presents from under the tree, or since I had held my energetic and excitable blond bundle in my arms. All of those wonderful memories were so vivid again, as I'd just finished writing this book as a tribute to my little boy. For the first time since his death, I felt delighted that the world would finally get to know the real James Bulger, rather than just the child in the picture. I had started to remember the sheer joy he brought me every day of his short life, rather than the terrifying pain of those first few minutes as I realised he was missing and then the endless agony of knowing I would never get him back. We were also filming a documentary with the wonderful Sir Trevor McDonald to mark the 25th anniversary – James was wonderfully real for me again, and that made me feel lighter and brighter as a result.

Then a wave of grief knocked me off my feet as soon as I heard that Venables had been recalled to prison. It was doubly difficult as I'd always said it would happen, but this time my anger felt different. This time I was determined to prove that the initial release of my son's killers had been mishandled, and the reason Venables kept reoffending was simply because he had never been rehabilitated in the first place. I was kept completely in the dark concerning what Venables had done, and I was terrified he had hurt another child.

Eventually I received a letter telling me that there would be a trial, that Venables would be there in person, that I could attend, but that I was legally prevented from publicly sharing this information in advance of the hearing. I couldn't believe it – after 25 years, was I really about to face my son's killer? Deep down I knew it wouldn't happen – how could I ever be allowed in the same room as him? Whether he would be there or not, it didn't stop me being determined to prove that Venables was, and is, a danger to society.

I decided to launch a petition for an enquiry into the initial release of Thompson and Venables, and the public, who have been behind me every step of the way since James' death, once again stood with me by signing in their thousands. It seemed to me that the only priority had been keeping my son's killers out of jail after so much money had been spent on their so-called rehabilitation. Finally, the world would see that Thompson and Venables had, in my view, actually been rewarded for their crime, that they hadn't been 'fixed' by the system at all.

As 2017 came to a close the signatures came pouring in. We celebrated Christmas just the five of us, although, as usual, I set a place for James at the Christmas table. I knew that we needed to get 100,000 signatures in order for the government to debate the issue and I was overwhelmed as

I saw the numbers rising. However, to get the case properly reviewed, I had to prove Venables had always been sexually depraved, even at the age of ten years old when he tortured and murdered James. The key was showing that he kept reoffending with child porn because his perversions hadn't been addressed at the time of James' trial, or when he was released eight years later. I will protect James' name until the day I die, but I also believe that, because of what happened to my son, I have a duty to protect other vulnerable children from Jon Venables. It soon became clear that the only way to prove the exact nature of how twisted he was at the time he murdered James was to find out exactly what had been done to my precious boy.

What happened next was one of the hardest things I have ever faced: I asked Sean to list the questions we needed answering in order to force the government to react. I had been asking some of those questions since the day I found out that Thompson and Venables had been arrested, and certainly in the years after their release. But some of the questions on the list finally had to be posed, even though my closest friends and family had spent 25 years protecting me from the answers.

In truth, I simply felt I had no choice: to get the enquiry I so desperately wanted (and to prove how dangerous my son's killers still were) it felt as if the government were forcing me to find out exactly what Thompson and Venables had done to my baby during his last hours on this earth.

Sean pulled together all of the relevant information and sent the list of questions ahead to Stuart so he could have an initial look. He went to the office to go through the email, making notes, and then he came home to discuss it with me. We went up to our bedroom (my sanctuary whenever there are any issues to do with James), closed the door and sat on the bed, going through each painfully raw question, one by one:

1. What evidence did Merseyside Police gather indicating that Thompson and Venables sexually assaulted James prior to killing him?

2. Why was that evidence not presented at the trial in Preston Crown Court?

3. Whose decision was it to suppress it?

4. Why did the trial judge not allow the jury to retire overnight to consider the count of abduction of Diane Power's child earlier on the day James was murdered?

5. Why was the evidence of James being sexually assaulted not presented to the parole board when Venables was originally released in 2001, or again at the 2013 parole board hearing?

6. Was the evidence relating to the abduction of Diane Power's child ever presented to the parole board? (It goes to the issue of premeditation and planning.)

7. Was the newly appointed Lord Chief Justice, Lord Woolf, influenced in his decision to reduce the tariff to seven years, eight months by a desire to ensure that the expensive rehabilitation efforts made for Thompson and Venables were not affected by their entry into the youth custody system at the age of eighteen? If so, was that a proper consideration?

8. What representations did Lord Woolf make to the parole board?

9. Was there a rush on the part of the relevant authorities to pronounce Venables and Thompson rehabilitated in order to release them before they entered youth custody? Did the authorities turn a blind eye to any evidence that either of them posed a risk to children?

10. The conviction of Venables in 2010 for possession of extreme child pornography (images of penetrative sex involving children as young as seven or eight) proves that Venables had an interest in

child sexuality years before it was discovered by the authorities. How was that sexual interest in children missed by all the experts?

11. Was a psychopathy test specific to youth offenders applied by the psychiatrists who examined Thompson and Venables or did they rely upon a test devised for adult offenders?

12. Was relevant material withheld from the parole board?

13. Sir David Omand conducted a review of the preparations for the release of Venables for the Home Office in November 2010 after Venables had been convicted of the child pornography offences. Why did Omand make no mention of the fact that before his release, Venables had sex with a female member of staff at Redbank? When the media made this public in 2011, Omand said that he was aware of the allegations but denied they were relevant to his report. Were the parole board ever informed of this illicit sexual encounter when they made the decision to release Venables in 2013?

14. An investigation of that incident was conducted by Arthur de Frisching, a retired prison governor, on

behalf of the Ministry of Justice. Why has that report never been made public?

There aren't really the words to describe how it made me feel, seeing all of these questions listed in such brutal terms. All the things I had protected myself from, all my very worst thoughts and fears, were right in front of me. Now my heart was breaking all over again and I know how worried those closest to me were. But I kept going for the simple reason that I was desperate for the government to finally hear me and the 100,000 people who had shown our family so much love and support.

But then, on the anniversary of the day my son's severed body was found tossed on a railway track, I found out that my petition had been rejected. How? By someone tagging me into a tweet they had seen online from a government spokesperson. They had been supposed to respond after 10,000 signatures but didn't, then we had 200,000 signatures, and they chose to respond on the 25th anniversary of James' body being found just as we were getting ready to spend the day at the cemetery. They even got his name wrong, calling him Jamie Bulger.

* * *

I barely had time to rally before the date of Venables' trial was upon us – I truly felt as if I had stepped back in time. I'd been extremely ill with flu for weeks, too sick to get out of bed, get dressed or even eat anything. Nevertheless, staying away from the trial was never an option. By this time, I knew Venables wouldn't actually be in the same room as me, he was giving evidence via video link, but hearing this voice ringing out around the court made me feel sick to my stomach. In my opinion, it was yet another example of the system protecting him at all costs and putting his comfort first – of course he didn't want to face me; that didn't mean he shouldn't have to. However, that soon became insignificant once we started to hear what Venables had actually done.

He pleaded guilty and was charged with having more than 1,000 indecent images of children, pictures that the Hon. Mr Justice Edis went on to tell the court were 'heart-breaking for any ordinary person to see'. Out of the images found on Venables' laptop, 392 were category A, 148 were category B and 630 were category C images. My son's killer also admitted to having a paedophile manual, a document that gave tips for how to have sex with small children 'safely'. It was gut-wrenching to even hear those words said out loud and I could see that everyone in the courtroom felt the same.

As I sat and listened, it was impossible for me not to feel that my son's killers were taunting me. Who had ever decided that Jon Venables was safe to be let back into society? But the Hon. Mr Justice Edis made a point that really stuck with me: '[In the category A images] some of them were babies. Given your history, it is significant that a number of images and films were of serious crimes inflicted on male toddlers.' In a strange way, this gave me more strength to keep going and make sure Venables stayed behind bars.

I was also reminded of his conniving nature when the judge told the court that Venables downloaded these sickening images on a day when he was undergoing assessment in relation to his life licence. The judge remarked that this 'showed how manipulative and dishonest [you are]. Your offences went back some months and required some ingenuity to keep it hidden.'

It couldn't have been more different from the verdict we had waited for 25 years previously, but it felt equally vital to see Venables get the maximum punishment. This time Ralph was sitting across the other side of the court. We didn't exchange a single glance let alone talk. Instead, I had Stuart by my side and holding my hand as we heard the judge find Venables guilty on all counts. He was sentenced to 40 months, which didn't feel enough, even if I was delighted to see him back in prison. More importantly, the fight for the government to hear James' voice went on. My team continued to push, even though we had been knocked back, and eventually we found out that parliament would debate James' murder and why Venables had been free to commit more offences.

It felt like the most significant breakthrough since I began my long, frustrating and unbelievably emotional fight – all I have ever wanted was for my son to get the justice he deserves. As I look at Michael, Thomas and Leon growing into wonderful men, excitedly planning new experiences and adventures, I know they will have to do it for James too. I can't watch James succeed at anything – instead all I can do is make sure no child ever has their life taken the way James did. I am determined that this will be his legacy.

When I found out the government would finally listen to our request, I was standing in the kitchen looking out at the garden we have built in his memory. It is peaceful and beautiful and means I always feel I have him nearby. Sometimes the cemetery isn't the place I feel closest to him, it's the garden we have built with so much love.

As I was pondering how far we had come, and how far we still had to go, a robin flew down and settled on the garden wall. I couldn't help but smile to myself. Whenever I see a robin I immediately feel James and Kirsty are by my side and I always say to Stuart: 'Here's my James and Kirsty come to see me.' I drank my coffee and looked up at the sign we put up on the kitchen wall every Christmas: 'When robins appear, loved ones are near', and I felt that familiar sense of calm.

I know my James is always with me and he knows I will always keep fighting in his name. It's what any mother would do.

Chapter 27

Our Ray of Sunshine

Seeing my face and name splashed all over the media is still a shock, even after 30 years of practice. It still makes my heart lurch to see the grainy picture of James used by all the papers whenever they talk about the case, along with the infamous picture of Venables and Thompson leading my son away by the hand to his death.

Since the book was first published in 2017 and I did the accompanying press, I have had so much lovely feedback. I am still stopped when I am out and about – I can be food shopping, at the train station or at the hairdressers – and strangers will come up and thank me for writing the book and sharing James with the world as only his mother could. So many people have said that reading the book brought James to life for them and meant they understood there was a very real child behind the headlines. That means so much to me as it was my main motivation for saying yes to doing the book in the first place – for me to bring James's memory back in a positive way.

In truth, I was scared to write a book. The only way I have survived the years since James's murder is to ruthlessly compartmentalise. I always say if there is a fight to be had I will be there having it until I die, but the minute I step foot back inside the house I am a mum and a wife. Whilst James is a huge part of our family life, the campaigning (and the inevitable heartache it brings) has to stay firmly outside our front door. It is the only way any of us would survive. Don't get me wrong, there are still deeply dark days and I rely on Stuart and our three lads to help me through those times.

But not everyone understands the fight. Amongst the people who stop me and tell me they've been following my story over the years, and they think I am brave to carry on, there are always the people who think I should be quiet and go away to get on with my life. When you have been doing this for so long, people do get fed up with seeing you in the media. I've received many lovely messages from around the world (it used to be letters, but with online activity now such a huge part of our lives it's mainly via social media or emails). I still get the odd one saying, 'Why don't you just give up and let it go?' I suppose people get used to you saying the same thing and become immune to the cause but doing the book gave everyone the chance to really remember why I am here doing what I am doing. It is for my little boy who didn't get to grow up and live the life he had the right to enjoy. My little James was taken from me in the most awful way imaginable by two people who have never been properly held to account; what mother wouldn't fight for that?

What I realised when I started the book is that I had built endless walls around myself and James, some of them were deliberately high as there was so much pain to try and protect myself from. When your child is murdered or taken from you in such a public way it is easy for the world to claim them and their story. And if you are still campaigning for justice then you have to be pragmatic and give yourself to the media machine and endless strangers in order to keep the story in the headlines. It can be easy to blur the lines and the very real person at the heart of the fight can be lost.

You can also lose yourself. By the time I started the book I think that is what had happened. After twenty-five years James's story had become largely about the two people who murdered him and the way in which he died. It meant that his short life and all that he was had started to fade into the background, those precious memories suffocated by his killers and the fight to see them serve a proper sentence. I realised that his murder and the sense of injustice at how the system has protected his killers had blocked out all the light that James gave me and our family. It had stopped me celebrating him over the years.

My actual memories of James – his little laugh, the way

he danced, his love of chocolate, the smell of his head and the way his blond hair bounced everywhere it was that soft – they had all completely faded for me. I didn't realise how much the finer detail of James had blurred until I started talking about him in a focused way for the book. That helped me remember how to think about him as a person rather than just automatically letting my brain go straight to what happened to him. Doing such an intense thing was obviously hard but it was also amazing. People are always surprised when I say doing the book was fun at times too. By that I mean it brought my distant memories of James back to life and in life he made me laugh all the time. The process gave him back to me and in many ways allowed Stuart and the boys to really feel his presence in a powerful and positive way.

Sometimes I would leave the writing sessions having spoken about James for hours; rather than feeling drained and wanting to be silent, Stuart and I would have a drink with the writer after some sessions and then drive home and carry on speaking about it. It was a way of keeping James there, extending the moment by remembering every single detail. Now I know that he will always be close to me as, anytime I feel those memories start to fade again, I have the book to pick up and remind myself. The book changed me; I am not sure it brought me peace in the most literal sense as that will only come when I feel I have justice for James, but it did bring James back to me in a way I didn't think was possible. The real person, not just the mythical child who sold papers and whose murder made every parent hold their own child's hand a little tighter.

Being a mother is the most important thing in the world to me; I have had five children and a miscarriage, so it is obvious having a family was all I ever wanted to achieve in life. Motherhood has been a very unique experience for me, and I don't think (thankfully) one many women can relate to, but amongst the pain there has been immense joy too. My boys are obviously my proudest achievement, but nothing can prepare you for becoming a grandmother. Peyton Kirsty Fergus was born on 3rd November 2020 and that wave of love knocked me off my feet.

She was born during the pandemic and my son, Michael had already moved out with Leanne ahead of lockdown, so we waited anxiously for news once we knew the big day had arrived. I was obviously so relieved that everything had gone smoothly with the delivery, but to hear they had given her Kirsty as a middle name in honour of my firstborn was a beautiful surprise. It was such a loving gesture and one I will cherish forever.

When a grandchild arrives it really does feel like confirmation of the circle of life; those moments that come around in the right order and cement the joy you've had as a mother. It's the right way round; the literal reverse of how it feels as a mother to bury your baby. Instead, your baby has a baby, and you wonder where all the years have gone as it seems only a minute ago that they were the toddler running around trying to open cupboards and getting into everything. In the blink of an eye that little boy, Michael, has become a father and as I watch him with his own daughter, I remember that he was born after James and I can't help but let my mind wander to what might have been. Would James be married with children? Would he have had boys or girls? What would he do for a living? It is a slippery slope I try very hard not to go down because it is a road to nowhere, but a new life does make you reflect on everything.

Just like James and Michael, Peyton never sits still, and she loves the outside just like they both did. When I sit and look at Peyton, I can see she is the spit of our Michael but then there are times when she will give a look or do something funny and I can see Leanne in her, so she truly is the best of both worlds. A little while after she was born, we had Michael and Leanne round to watch our old wedding video – Stuart had them converted from VHS tapes into USB sticks as a surprise for me and we were all laughing at Michael and his antics on the dancefloor. Seeing him on the screen like that it was clear for all to see that Peyton was his image. Moments like that are wonderful and I celebrate them fully and feel like any other grandparent.

Michael and Leanne are lovely parents – the baby couldn't ask for better – and I feel such pride that from day one, our Michael has done it all alongside Leanne. He got stuck in right from the get-go and is always right in the thick of it –

nappies, feeding, bedtime (though he is the softer touch and typically, Peyton has him wrapped around her little finger. Just the way it should be with fathers and daughters!).

I feel lucky and grateful; there were honestly times after James was murdered that I didn't think I would survive until the end of any given day. But it's all bittersweet in many ways as I watch everyone grow because there is always someone missing. I haven't asked Michael if he's made that connection in his head, or if he feels that constant sense of danger as Peyton starts discovering the world. I am sure he is more overprotective than some fathers might be because of how I parented him. He came only nine months after James's death, and I was still in the throes of deep, dark grief – but he loves every second of being a dad and Peyton keeps us all on our toes. She loves being outside, running around, looking into our pond and pointing out the biggest fish so we can feed them together. I cherish every minute of being with her.

So, yes, I am a grandmother, but it is different for me. There are restrictions on how fully I can celebrate Peyton and the truth is, having spent all these years looking over my shoulder with the lads, I'm now doing the same with my granddaughter. I work very hard to keep my fears in check – when Peyton is at ours, she is never out of our sight. All eyes are on her all the time and those old habits will never die. It takes me straight back to feeling anxious about dropping the boys at school and all the times I said no to school trips – that icy fear I felt every time I took the kids out of the front door or if they were a few minutes late home. And I recognise it's more than just anxiety shifting from one generation to the next. I know that fear has existed just below the surface for thirty years because I have never had the solace of knowing James's killers were locked up or have served proper time for their crime. I don't know what they know about me and my family, what bits of my life they've had access to. The one thing that has always tormented me is the thought that they have visited James's grave, which is accessible to anyone. But these are all things I will never know. The knowledge that those two have been out there somewhere has tainted everything and has had a profound effect on me being a mother and now, as a grandmother, I have to behave differently from the rest because I am forever different.

Michael quite rightly doesn't want the baby in the public eye, especially knowing that the fight for James goes on and with that comes media interest. So having to still fight robs me of the seemingly small things like being able to put a picture of Peyton on my social media, no matter how private the settings, in case it gets lifted and turned into a news story or in case Venables or Thompson see it. I would never ever do anything to expose her to this other side of my life – I am her grandmother, but I am still a mother campaigning for justice for her murdered son. The truth is that the repercussions of what those two did to my family reverberate down through the decades and generations in more ways than anyone can even begin to fathom.

Chapter 29

New Government, Same Fight

Writing this update, I realise I have spent more than half of my life fighting for justice for James – it feels both an impossible amount of time and yet like yesterday that he was taken from me. The other way to look at it is, thirty years on, the system that has always been more preoccupied with protecting two child killers than protecting society still hasn't learned its lesson.

I always say the quest remains the same despite the inevitable passage of time: justice for my son from the system so intent upon rehabilitating his killers that they couldn't see that very system seemingly made Thompson and Venables worse. And to make sure neither one of my son's killers ever gets to hurt another family like they did ours. If I get one of James's killers locked up for life, I will feel justice has been done. In the beginning I was adamant

I didn't want that – to throw away the key on them. But Venables has proven again and again that rehabilitation has not worked on him and the things he has done since killing James tell me there is no going back. He needs locking up for life to save another family from the pain I know he is capable of causing. I am not fighting just for James; I am fighting for everyone who needs and deserves protection from people like Venables and Thompson. It has been hard over the years to feel the system is stacked against the very people it should be there to protect but I have learned the hard way that for the authorities, preservation of the myth is sometimes seen as more important than the greater good.

There have obviously been some amazing moments, especially the change in law surrounding victim impact statements in 1996 and also our appeal in Strasbourg in 1999, but the ultimate goal has eluded me for such a long time and that is brought home to me every time I hear that Venables has reoffended.

As the late, great Chris Johnson (the gentle giant who had been by my side every step of the way and was chairman of The James Bulger Memorial Trust who sadly died of cancer in June 2020) always said, Venables and Thompson needed to be treated like children who were perverse and therefore given the tightest possible boundaries, rather than glossing over their depravity to make the system look good. Of course, they needed real intervention, they just didn't get it from the system seemingly there to do that. Those expensive efforts lavished on them in the children's home were deemed a 'success' and so it was decided that putting them in custody and into the prison system would undo that. For me that has always been where it all went wrong.

I knew when they were released on 24th June 2001 that the fight hadn't even really begun. And years of living in this cycle of disappointment has left me ever vigilant. So, in a way, when the phone rang late one night in November 2017, I just knew it was bad news. We were in our house with my manager, Kym, and we were talking about the filming of the Trevor McDonald documentary that was happening the next day. Suddenly the phone started ringing and, being that late, I had a bad feeling about the call. Stuart left the room and came back in a few minutes later with a look I knew only too well. Venables had reoffended. Stuart said:

'Venables has been recalled'.
Quick as flash, I asked, 'What for?'.
Stuart said, 'I don't know, they won't tell me.'

Kym's eyes went wide, and my instinct was to say, 'I hope he hasn't hurt someone else', which truly is my worst nightmare.

It is hard to describe the immediate ice around my heart when I heard the word 'recall' – my mind went straight back to that moment thirty years ago. It makes you realise that time passes and things change, and there are long periods of time with grief where you feel further away from the immediate rawness of things, but scratch the surface, and you are right back there in that place, right in the heat of the moment. And the thing that always threatens to tip me over the edge is the lack of information. They say he has been recalled but not what for, it's like Groundhog Day – they call (sometimes they bother to come round) so the system can say it has 'dealt' with me. After all these years we are still merely a box to be ticked and an exercise in paperwork shuffling.

The truth is that I feel the parole service only ever tells me anything to do with James's killers when they have lost control of the narrative, i.e. when the press have found out and are about to print a story that they will ask me to comment on. Then reporters knock at my door looking for a reaction and the whole cycle begins. It's actually just another form of control, or lack of depending on how you look at it.

After the Trevor McDonald documentary in 2018, the petition Chris Johnson had started for a public enquiry into the case – and all the information I believe has been systematically swept under the carpet, including the so-called rehabilitation of Venables – gathered great pace. Signatures had been slow and steady until the programme aired and then they started to come in thick and fast. The rule is that you need 10,000 signatures to get a reply from the government and 100,000 to get it to parliament for discussion. Our 214,000 signature-strong petition calling for a discussion of the case was rejected by a committee of MPs in 2018 and we were informed of the decision on the 25th anniversary of the day James's body had been found. I refused to give up – we had over 200,000 signatures but there was endless political turmoil and a looming General Election that rendered the petition stuck and declined as the government entered an official state of political purdah, where specific restrictions on communication activity are in place. Basically, it was an official reason to do nothing. By this time, it was the end of November 2019 and then Covid hit and that was that.

One of the consequences of having been fighting the same cause for three decades is that you see politicians come and go and it is hard to stay positive and believe someone will move beyond the publicity-friendly words and actually change the system. I have seen the good, bad and indifferent over the years, having gone from being blanked by Jack Straw (who, having ignored my request for a face-to-face meeting, eventually offered me a phone call that I declined), to eventually meeting Dominic Raab (then Secretary of State) in 2022. I have always realised that the media is an ally when it comes to getting the Government to react. I am lucky that so many of the newspapers have stood by me and helped me campaign for politicians to listen.

Obviously the horror of the pandemic affected everyone and it was hard to focus on anything other than that. But early in 2022 it felt like there was some space to pick up the momentum again. Kym arranged an interview in the *Daily Mirror* about the petition and the fact that, despite a record-breaking number of signatures, it had been immediately rejected and everything yet again seemed stuck in the system that wanted to bury its head in the sand.

As ever, it wasn't just about my family. What I wanted to understand was, at what point do we as a society have to admit that rehabilitation doesn't always work. At what point is it safer for the public if those in charge hold up their hands and say: 'We tried our best, we failed and now it is time to put the public's safety first'. At what point will we perhaps think about prioritising the families who have been victims of crime and who will mourn murdered loved ones forever.

All the clichés are true – time does in many ways stand still. Thirty years does seem like yesterday, the wounds don't ever heal when you have buried a child, but they certainly can never do so when one of the murderers responsible persists in reoffending and then continues to bid for freedom. As we all know, Venables was released in 2001 with a new identity, a clean slate despite the misery he heaped upon my family, and he was deemed safe to the public. By 2010 he was back in custody after reoffending, having been found with child abuse images and then we were right back there in 2017. My question has always been, will it take another child being murdered and another mother losing a child for the parole system to wake up?

That was what I said in my interview in the paper and, as ever, I asked the Government to meet me and help finally find a way to keep dangerous people in prison when they have shown they cannot be rehabilitated. I got my wish when, seemingly out of the blue, one of Dominic Raab's team got in touch to ask me to come down to London to meet with them and discuss the case. As the day of my meeting approached, I felt similar to how I always felt before these kinds of meetings: cautious and wary of being fobbed off. But I couldn't have been more wrong. What Dominic Raab was suggesting was a whole new switch up of the Parole System and, under his new law, that there could be intervention from the Ministry of Justice on parole board decisions.

He seemed genuinely involved in particular cases that evoked strong public opinion and where the Parole Board was under scrutiny. In May 2022 he had launched a scathing attack on the Parole Board after it rejected his appeal against the decision to free the mother of Baby P, the poor baby who had died after months of abuse. He was adamant that the decision to release Tracey Connelly, who was jailed indefinitely with a minimum term of five years in May 2009, should be reconsidered on the grounds of irrationality, but a judge upheld the original decision. Raab was furious and demanded a 'fundamental overhaul' that would limit the board's independence. He tweeted:

'Tracey Connelly's cruelty towards her son, baby Peter, was pure evil. The decision to release her demonstrates why the Parole Board needs a fundamental overhaul – including a ministerial check for the most serious offenders – so that it serves and protects the public.'

Connelly was released from jail in 2013 but was returned to prison two years later for breaching her parole conditions. She was subsequently refused parole in 2015, in 2017 and again in 2019. Raab also claimed that there was a failure to take into account all of the evidence, 'excessive weight was given to the purported effectiveness of external controls and that insufficient reasons were given', but the judge rejected all of those arguments.

A power to seek reconsideration of a Parole Board decision if a party believes the decision was irrational or unfair was introduced in 2019 after the uproar surrounding the case of John Worboys, 'The Black Cap Rapist'. The Parole Board's decision to release Worboys was overturned by the high court in March 2018 after two of his victims challenged it in November of the same year.

At that time one judge said that the Parole Board should have 'undertaken further inquiry into the circumstance of Worboy's offending and in particular the extent to which the limited way in which he has described his offending may undermine his overall credibility.' The judge quashed the board's decision to release Worboys and ordered it to hold a fresh hearing before a 'differently constituted panel'. There was talk of Worboys' 'apparent deftness in impression management' and the doubts it should have raised in relation to how guilty he actually felt about his crimes. This is something I have always said about Venables – that his manipulation of authority has been crystal clear since he was ten years old, and it is a skill that would have only become more developed as he got older. In November 2018 the Parole Board, having originally accepted that Worboys no longer posed a threat to the public, overturned its own decision, deciding that he should remain in prison after noting his risk and 'sense of sexual entitlement'.

The legacy of this case was also behind the decision by the Parole Board in May 2022 to allow victims to attend parole hearings. So, in reality I knew that, although I had been repeatedly let down previously, Dominic Raab was probably the best shot I'd had so far. The result of that was, that for the first time heading to London for this type of meeting, I was nervous. I suppose that's what thirty years of being ignored will do to you.

The pressure of finally getting to that room and seeing the thick folders piled up on his desk, my son's case notes there in front of me with handwritten annotation alongside pictures of Raab's children, suddenly all got too much. The whole experience of going into Whitehall is daunting, you are practically strip searched! They go through everything, and there are armed police in every corner of the room. Once

we were in it was like a maze getting to Dominic's office –
a tiny lift to squeeze into and then a long walk along a
narrow corridor with wood panelling and carpet that made
it feel as if we were being summoned by the headmaster.
In fact, that's exactly what Stuart was joking (quite loudly!)
when the door opened, and we were ushered in!

Once we got inside Dominic was amazing, especially when
it became clear I was quite overwhelmed and not necessarily
being the most articulate version of myself. He immediately
put me at ease by taking the pressure off and telling me he
would run through what he could do for me, rather than
putting me on the spot to pitch to him. He had done his
research (or his excellent researchers had), either way he
knew all about James and the subsequent twists and turns
of my fight. He told me straightforwardly that under his
new legislation it would basically be a case of two strikes and
you were out and that would apply to the three most serious
types of criminals: paedophiles, child killers and terrorists.
There would not be endless chances at rehabilitating anyone
who had committed this type of crime. And that meant,
under Raab's new law, Venables would never see the light of
day. This wasn't just a change that would benefit my fight
for James, it was something that would potentially change
the lives of so many victims of crime.

There were six or seven of us in the room and I suddenly
felt overcome so I asked my manager, Kym to pick
things up. She began to explain how the Parole Board in

particular had let me down over the years, especially in relation to communication around Venables reoffending and being recalled. She explained that for thirty years any communication from them to me was always a knee-jerk reaction or an afterthought, often when the press was about to run a story and always at the last minute without any proper detail. She explained that in 2017 when we were phoned to say Venables had been recalled a second time, it was at 9pm the night before I was due to start filming the next day with Trevor McDonald and the press turned up on my doorstep less than an hour later. I was only ever told what was going on as a last resort and so they weren't accused of not getting to me before the papers. And often things only came to light when the press went to The Ministry of Justice for a right to reply.

It was at that point that one of the other people in the room stood up and introduced himself as Gordon Davidson, the new head of the Probation and Prison Service. This had the potential to be a little tricky given the tone of the conversation! To give him his due though, he didn't even flinch and, actually, at the end of the meeting he got up from his seat and came over to put his hand on mine and apologise for all I had endured and to commend me for carrying on the fight. Since this meeting I will say that we have in fact had more unsolicited communication from his probation team keeping us up to date than from anyone else the whole time, which makes me feel more heard.

Our Petition was also discussed, and we were reassured that although it had been publicly 'closed' online it would be in fact looked at again and the Ministry of Justice team would be in touch to progress with this. And even though Dominic Raab said this was out of his hands and he had no personal control, we have in fact had contact since regarding this – again, another positive step forward.

For the first time in decades, I left that room feeling hopeful of meaningful change for me and every other family who has suffered as we have. I got on the train back home and put a post on Twitter about the meeting, and was amazed and so pleased when Dominic himself replied:

'Thank you, Denise, for your courage. I can't begin to imagine what you've been through over so many years. I was very moved to meet you, and you strengthened my resolve to reform the Parole Board'.

Soon after our meeting Kym received an email from Dominic Raab's office saying that it had been agreed that James's case would be officially debated, and I would be notified when a date had been officially set. And then, on 6th September Boris Johnson was ousted, and as quickly as it had appeared the glimmer was gone.

When Liz Truss was elected as Prime Minister, everything was paused and it was hard not to spiral right back to where I started. Raab was sacked, Brandon Lewis was put in his place and everything Raab had put in motion was shelved. I knew it wasn't just my case and that was what I was fighting for – everyone in similar circumstances to me but who perhaps didn't have the same platform.

So, in October 2022 I wrote to Liz Truss and begged her to ensure that Venables stayed in prison ahead of his parole hearing. I wanted her to follow through on what had been discussed with Raab and strengthen legislation to help keep dangerous offenders in prison and off the streets as had been outlined in the recent Tories Bill of Rights. I reminded Truss that Venables had been jailed on two previous occasions following James's murder – first recalled in 2010, nine years after his release, and then recalled back to jail a second time in November 2017 for breaching terms of his release. He was also, I reiterated, accused of child pornography offences and was obviously sexually deviant. With his sentence of two years and the subsequent delays caused by Covid and a steady stream of changing Tory personnel, Venables would be eligible for parole in July 2022 – and I explained in my letter that, to my mind, he still posed a significant threat to society and families like ours. My big concern was that with the parole hearing imminent and all the Government unrest, Venables might just be released and it would go unnoticed.

Kym also sent emails to see where the change of Prime Minister left us and our conversation but correspondence was slow so yet again it took an interview with a Sunday newspaper and collective outrage from the public to get this new Government to respond. The dance is all too familiar now and never ceases to amaze me, even after all these years. We do an interview and then the paper has to go to the Ministry of Justice for a right to reply, that puts the interview on their radar and jolts them into dealing with me. They clearly weren't best pleased about this so early on after the reshuffle and they immediately offered me a meeting with Brandon Lewis, the new Minster of Justice (after claiming they hadn't received any of our emails), which would have been great had it not been scheduled for the week when it became clear that Liz Truss's days were numbered.

Political turmoil is of course totally destabilising for every part of the country and paying our bills, keeping our jobs and our homes are the big concerns that we all share. But for me, a change in leadership meant starting from scratch and picking up the conversation I had already been having for so long. Raab's new law would have allowed ministers to block the release of the most dangerous criminals for public safety reasons, and now I was meeting someone I wasn't even sure would be there in a week. It had been a dream come true when the House of Commons agreed to debate James's murder and why Venables has been free to commit more offences. And now here I was, starting again.

When we met Brandon, who was welcoming and again understanding of my concerns, he did say that although he had taken the seat it didn't mean that the original bill

Raab had been working on had been scrapped. It was still being worked on, but his aim was to progress with certain parts of the bill first. I just felt the familiar sense of unease, I couldn't really pinpoint it, especially as the civil servants on the case reassured us that they would keep us updated throughout. There was hope but yet again I was cautious. And then Liz Truss resigned the next day, Brandon Lewis was no longer Secretary of State and it was Groundhog Day all over again.

I cling to the hope that the bill is fully enough formed that we will continue to make the progress all families who have faced injustice deserve. The one thing that has changed is that we now have communication channels that go beyond journalists knocking on my door to ask if I have any comment in relation to my son's killers being recalled. It means I am cautiously optimistic.

Chapter 30

Some Kind of Peace

The search for answers and justice has taken so many different twists and turns over the years, as these things will do when they go on for such a long time. One of my coping mechanisms has always been to try and think about James's murderers as little as possible, to keep them out of my brain. I try never to say their names and only talk about them when they give me cause to. Obviously over the years, my contact with those who worked on James's case has dwindled and it has been many years since we have spoken to Albert Kirby. So this far down the line it has always felt unlikely that I would meet someone new who was associated with the case right at the start. But that all changed in October 2022 when my manager, Kym arranged a phone call with forensic psychologist Paul Britton who was a witness for the prosecution in Venables and Thomson's original trial. This felt like such a huge moment – to speak to someone who right from the start had been instrumental in proving James's murderers knew exactly what they were doing when they took his life.

Paul was brought in after James's body had been found but before they'd identified any potential suspects. He was the person who encouraged the police to concentrate the initial search locally. When I spoke to Paul, he stated that, although he didn't ever personally meet or question Venables and Thompson, he was fully involved in training and coaching the case officers in how to interview them once they'd been arrested. He was clear that once Venables and Thompson were named as possible suspects in the frame, he knew very quickly that they were guilty and whilst others were blind-sighted and distracted by the fact that they were such physically small children (which meant that some thought it impossible they could have committed such a crime), his brain very quickly defined them as murderers. Just hearing that fact alone, I felt something fundamental shift in me. That has been such a block over the years – the excuse that they were 'only children' themselves who didn't deserve the adult labels of 'murderers' has always been so hard for me to bear. Hearing it from someone trained and impartial was an important and healing moment.

We talked on the telephone for a while and he was so lovely to me. I know he is obviously trained and brilliant at his job, but his tone was both commanding and reassuring and, most importantly, he seemed to really understand that whilst for the world James was a story to be 'followed', for me it was my actual life. He asked me if over the years I'd had as many answers as was possible or if there were still any holes that I hadn't been able to fill with information.

I hadn't planned to bring it up but Paul's manner meant that I found him really easy to talk to, which, despite all the years of practice speaking to strangers isn't something I naturally feel easy doing. I explained to him that despite my family's best efforts to keep upsetting newspaper and press reports away from me, some years ago I had discovered there has always been a suspected sexual element to James's death. At the point of the trial, it was decided that not all the evidence would be submitted, which meant the police were able to keep some of the more gruesome details out of the press. It was always said that the decision was taken primarily to spare me (heavily pregnant with Michael) and the family any more heartache.

But it means there has always been a question mark hovering over whether James's murder was sexually motivated, and that was definitely something the press consistently hinted at in their reporting. Most crucially, given the way Venables has consistently reoffended – namely being jailed for possession of child abuse images (some included children as young as two being raped by adults) and posing online as a 35 year-old woman who had abused her eight year-old daughter – it hasn't been difficult for me to imagine the very worst.

The decision not to tell me any details right at the start meant that it got harder to ask as the years went by. But when Venables reoffended most recently in 2018 – after pleading guilty to having more than 1,000 indecent images of children, including Category A pictures, the most serious, and a paedophile manual – I knew it might help get him locked up for good if it could be proven that his sickening tendencies had been there right from the start of his first crime.

With that in mind, I had finally taken the decision to allow Stuart to tell me more details of what happened to James that day, something I didn't even do in preparation for starting to write this book. For the book, I knew the writer had done all her research and she was very careful not to ask me any specifics I didn't know. It felt strange to have gone through that whole process not having read any detail about James's injuries and to now be trying to find out more, but it was all part of the fight I've always said I will have no matter how difficult it is. It doesn't get any harder than reading exactly what had been done to your murdered baby, but it had to be done.

Stuart and Kym sat me down and talked me through the detail and although it was helpful in giving me some more clarity about certain things, it didn't fully eliminate the doubts I had. It still left me with those unanswered questions and gaps that Paul was now asking about on our call. As soon as I explained this to him, his tone shifted slightly, and he told me in no uncertain terms that Venables and Thompson had 'no proper [full] sexual involvement with him [James]'.

He went on to say that James was 'injured in all sorts of different ways and whilst he might have been injured in a way that would have included if you like, all of his body, there wasn't what you would call an adult sexual attack on him'.

Stuart said, 'To see your expression there as [Paul] was talking to you, the only way I can describe it is one of pure relief. You obviously have never openly spoken about the particular possible sexual element to James's murder or reacted to the press reports that hinted at the act you would have most dreaded. To hear Paul say that didn't happen felt like a massive relief.'

Without going into too much detail here, whilst the thing I dreaded most didn't happen, it was very clear from some of James's injuries that there was a sexual fascination to what they did, even if it was at a slight remove. I still firmly believe that Venables's voyeuristic sexual deviancy was cemented that day and that some of the specific injuries James suffered prove that. The crimes Venables has gone on to commit sit fully with someone who gets kicks out of perverted situations he shouldn't be witnessing.

On the call with Paul, we talked about resilience and how human beings get through times they think they won't survive. Life is so full of 'what ifs' and they are the cruellest form of torture when something bad happens; I have had thirty years of questioning every decision I made that day James was taken. But he said something to me that really made me stop and think:

'One of the things you personally should never lose track of is that you brought up, in James' short life, a little boy who was loving and trusting and loved people, and all of that is very much your parenting. What you can say is that for the short life that he had, you were a good mum. No one can pat you on the arm and say, "there, there, it will be alright", because it won't. The awful revolting truth is that you had that part of your life ripped away in the most appalling circumstances. In my life I have seen so many dreadful things and I know what happened and how it happened, but I know nothing can ever take away from you the pain and grief that came to you that day he was murdered. Everything you have done since has been to pull yourself back together as far as you can with your family, as a human being. Most folks in your circumstances don't manage that, so hats off to you in that sense.'

To have that said out loud to me was moving and to get any kind of truth at this thirty-year point feels so powerful and, importantly, it leaves me determined to continue pushing for justice for as long as I need to. I feel relief to have some answers about what happened to James from a source with nothing to gain and no agenda – his only purpose was to bring me relief and I haven't met a huge number of people like that along this journey. The conversation brought me more comfort than I expected it to, and I felt a real rush of relief.

I realise that even though the fight is the same after all this time, I am not.

Talking to Paul really brought home to me how much I have evolved. Twenty, even ten years ago, I would never have had the ability or confidence to think about having that kind of conversation with anyone. Back then I wouldn't even have let the topic be raised in my company – anything to do with James and what happened to him that I wasn't expecting was immediately shut down with a word or a glance – people knew not to go there and not to try to break that ring of steel around me.

Thirty years on, I have developed the ability to talk about my experience more openly. I have learned that in the search for answers I have to ask questions, some of them very uncomfortable ones. I took a gamble speaking to Paul as it was uncontrolled information coming at me – usually those situations are filtered first by Stuart or Kym – but this time I put myself forward to hear whatever would come my way and I had no idea what to expect. I see now that I am a million miles away from that young mother in front of the cameras at my very first police press conference asking for whoever had taken my baby to bring him back, unable to look anyone in the eye because, really, I wanted to die. As the fight evolves, I feel stronger and braver even, and I am determined to help people in similar situations with less knowledge than me.

I suppose that wish to use what I know for the wider good has pushed me out of my comfort zone, particularly over the last few years. It started when I decided to say yes to writing this book and from there came the honour of working with Sir Trevor McDonald on *James Bulger: A Mother's Story*. Both things were really driven by the need to turn something so negative, what happened to James, into something positive. What I didn't realise is that by being so open I would help others who have lost children in similar awful circumstances.

Grief of any kind never leaves you, really you just learn to live around it, but when you lose someone, especially a child, in such a brutal way, it is a whole different process. You want justice, and to be heard, more than anything. Trying to deal with losing a child is such a lonely place to be and not every family gets access to the knowledge I have gained over the last thirty years during my fight. When you leave no stone unturned you learn every bit of the process, the good and the bad. I know there are grieving families out there who haven't been as fortunate as me with their support network and their knowledge of the justice system.

Even when you know how it works it can still defeat you at times, and I remember so well that feeling of not knowing where to even start.

I decided now was the time to put all that I know to good use, and I am currently in the middle of filming something really special that focusses on me offering support to families who have lost a child to murder. I never imagined I would ever be in a place where I felt strong enough to talk to others about their own experiences in this way, but I feel driven to help others in any way I can. My loss of James will never go away, but this feels like another way for his legacy to live on and help me continue to do some good in his name. I know he would be proud of that.

Acknowledgements

There are so many people who have given me love and support over the years, including those involved in this book, which is a tribute to my beautiful James.

Firstly, special thanks to all the police officers who worked around the clock to find my son and resolve his murder. I know that everyone involved gave the case everything and I will always be so grateful to you for all you did for our family.

Sean Sexton and Chris Johnson who were both there from the very start – whatever the situation they have guided and protected me. Sean has seen me through some of the toughest legal battles, and continues to do so as we carry on our fight for James. Chris sadly passed away in 2020 but I'll never forget how he helped me to navigate the media and press throughout the years. I'll forever be grateful to him for his help with James' charity. We miss him every day.

To my manager, Kym Darby, who has been instrumental in helping me achieve new goals to keep James' name alive. She has brought me new opportunities, including the chance to do this book, and I am so grateful. She has been there throughout this process and we have become close, and she's now the chairwoman of James' charity too – I am looking forward to what is to come and working together for a long time.

To my writer, Carly Cook, who I trusted completely to write my story and tell the world about my precious son. I have opened up completely, which I didn't think was possible, and I trusted her from the word go. I think she has been amazing, very committed and totally under-standing of how I wanted this book to be. I wanted it to be a celebration of James and I am proud that we have achieved that.

To Amanda Preston, my literary agent – thank you so much for finding the right home for this book, so that I finally get to tell my story.

To everyone at Bonnier who has helped to bring this book to life – Natalie Jerome, who believed in it right from reading the proposal and made it difficult to pick anyone else! To Beth Eynon for keeping everything on schedule, to the design team for the cover and to Karen Stretch for looking after the book PR.

To everyone involved in the charity that we run in James'

name – I know they will keep on doing all they can to support us and all the work we do.

Huge and special thanks must go to my wonderful sons, Michael, Thomas and Leon, who have always been so understanding about everything I have ever done in my fight for James over the years. They are loving, supportive and I couldn't be prouder of the men they have become. Also a mention to our little ray of sunshine, Peyton who is our first granddaughter.

To my wonderful husband, Stuart, who has been my rock from the moment he came into my life. He has been there, by my side, at all times over the years as I have fought battle after battle in James' name and memory. Together with Michael, Thomas and Leon, they have given me so much strength to carry on and have always understood why I needed to fight.

Thanks also go to my brothers and sisters for their constant support and for being there whenever I have needed them over the years. And to my wonderful mum and dad, who are no longer with us.

Final thanks go to the public, who have supported me over the years and helped to keep the fight going in James' name. I will keep going until James gets the justice he deserves.